THREATS

A HUMOROUS COMMENTARY ON THE DANGERS
THAT FACED 20TH CENTURY AMERICA

GEORGE KARP

D1280141

Copyright © 2021 by George Karp

All rights reserved. No part of this publication maybe reproduced or transmitted in any form, or by any means, electronic or mechanical, including photocopy, recording, or any other information storage and retrieval system, without permission in writing from the author.

I am dedicating this book to my late wife,
Rita Bari Karp

Yesterday is history – tomorrow is a mystery –
today is a gift of God, which is why we call it the present.

CONTENTS

ACKNOWLEDGMENTS

I would like to acknowledge the many people who inspired me to write this, my second book. My daughter Heather created the front cover; my sister Arlene helped edit the book; and my son-in-law Mark gave me much needed literary assistance. My other children, Jennifer and Vanessa were totally supportive of their Dad. I know my five grandchildren, Stella, Jeremy, Elizabeth, Evan and Conrad, can hardly wait to read the book. My many friends helped me towards reaching my literary goal. I hope everyone enjoys the book.

Again, thank you.

INTRODUCTION

Many people have asked me recently, "Why the heck are you writing this book?"

A friend, a retired publishing executive, told me that if a person seriously wants to **lose** money, he should write a book! He also confided to me that the best way to have a first book succeed was simply to write a second book!

My first book, ***Funny Things Happened: From Brighton to Boca*** was published in 2018.

That book is selling like hotcakes, whatever hotcakes are—*and recently reached the top 100,000 on the Amazon Best Sellers in Books list.* The book is a humorous memoir covering 70 years of my life experiences. Honestly, the thrill that I got when I received the first printed copy was unbelievable!

Now the question was what do I do for a follow-up book? I racked my brain thinking of a topic that would be interesting for the book-reading public and, more important, interesting for me to write about. Some topics came to mind that I very quickly rejected:

1) *Memories of my third-grade class of P.S. 225 in Brooklyn New York. Nope.*

2) *Highlights of the 1905 baseball season of the last-place Brooklyn Dodgers. No way.*

3) *My grandmother's 50 favorite recipes for boiled chicken. Not a chance.*

While walking my dog one night (*most of my great thoughts come when I'm walking the dog*), I had an epiphany. I've always been interested in history, and one recurring thought has always popped up in my mind: how many times, both directly and indirectly, has the United States been **threatened** in the 20th century?

Just what is a **threat**? The dictionary definition is: "A statement of an intention to inflict pain, injury, damage, or other hostile action on someone in retribution for some action done or not done."

I know all about the wars, the epidemics, the Great Depression, Fascism, Communism, and now terrorism. I realized that threats over the last century could make for a very interesting topic to write about and that maybe someone other than my children and grandchildren might read and enjoy such a book.

But I know that to some people, reading about history might be boring and sleep-inducing. I've been told that I have a good sense of humor, and so what I'm trying to do in this epic book is to infuse a bit of humor into it. I've included quotes and trivia, along with a large amount of serious facts, decade by decade of the 20th century.

I have also included other "nonthreatening" information—such as presidential elections, births and deaths, sports, and innovations—all with a touch of humor. Each 10-year period has a section called **Important and Unimportant News of the Decade**. I think that you will enjoy reading these humorous sections, *some of which I have italicized.*

The book is meant to be informative and educational to the reader. On a personal level, while doing my research, for the book, I really learned a lot.

So now that you have started to read my book, I sincerely hope that you will you enjoy it—and tell your friends about it!

In terms of generations, I personally can relate to threats to my family and to myself.

My grandparents were threatened by anti-Semitism in Europe, by the pogroms in Russia, by the problems of immigration, and then by World War I.

My parents were threatened by the Spanish flu pandemic, by the Great Depression, by the rise of Communism and Fascism, by domestic anti-Semitism, and then by World War II.

I was threatened by the Cold War, by the Soviet missiles in Cuba, by the Vietnamese War (*by not having a Saturday-night date*), and by so many senseless assassinations.

My children were threatened by terrorism and the horrors of 9/11.

My grandchildren hopefully, will not endure the threats that their previous generations have endured. Global warming, pandemics, domestic terrorism—who knows?

I only hope that the world and its leaders would read this book (*happy to send them a free copy*), learn from the mistakes of the past, and, with this understanding, create a very bright future!

1

1900–1909

THE CALM BEFORE THE STORM

The 20th century started with a **bang**! That bang was the bullet that assassinated President William McKinley in 1901.

It's interesting that the 21st century also started with a bang! That bang was the attack on our country in New York, Virginia, and Pennsylvania. The destruction of the World Trade Center's Twin Towers in New York City, killed 3,000 people.

Coincidentally, both events took place exactly 100 years and five days apart. McKinley was shot on September 6, 1901, while the World Trade Center attack took place on September 11, 2001. What a way to start a new century!

The decade of the 1900s was probably the **least** threatening decade to the United States of the 20th century. The biggest threats were not direct threats, but rather minor, indirect ones.

Presidential Elections of the 1900s

In 1899, Garret Hobart died, leaving the country without a vice president. At the Republican convention in the summer of 1900, New York Governor Theodore Roosevelt was chosen to be McKinley's running mate for the upcoming election. McKinley, the 25th US president ("I am a tariff man, standing on a tariff platform." Does that quote sound familiar?) was reelected in November 1900. The Republicans defeated Democrats William Jennings Bryan and Adlai Stevenson I, a rematch of the 1896 election, which the Republicans also won.

At age 58, McKinley was shot and subsequently died eight days later in Buffalo, New York. He was the third American president to be assassinated, following Abraham Lincoln in 1865 and James Garfield in 1881.

Teddy Roosevelt was vice president for only six months before assuming the presidency. At age 42, he became the youngest US president in history. He once said, "Believe you can and you're halfway there."

The assassin, Leon Czolgosz, was an American anarchist. He was found guilty and given the death sentence, the electric chair, commonly referred to as *the hot seat.*

Just what is anarchy? "Anarchy is a state of disorder due to the absence or nonrecognition of government and forms the absolute freedom of the individual—a stateless society." Unfortunately, or rather fortunately, anarchy has never really worked on a large scale.

The 1904 presidential election was interesting. Republican President Teddy Roosevelt, No. 26, and his running mate, Senator Charles Fairbanks of Indiana, trounced the little-known New York Judge Alton Parker and Senator Henry Davis West of West Virginia. On election night, the president-elect made a statement that he totally regretted eight years later: "Under no circumstance will I be a candidate in 1908." He neglected to say that he would run again in 1912 as an independent by forming the Progressive Party, better known as the Bull Moose Party.

Teddy Roosevelt was a national hero and was regarded by some as America's greatest president. He led the Rough Riders to victory in the short-lived Spanish-American War of 1898. From Spain, the United States got the colonies of Cuba, Guam, and the Philippines. This was quite a haul, considering the fact that America was not a colonial power.

Roosevelt accomplished many things during his time as president, from 1901–1909. He settled a long coal miner's strike, was a strict conservationist, and was known as the Trust Buster because of his regulatory reforms and antitrust prosecutions. He believed that the United States was now a world power, and he increased the size of the US Navy. His motto was, **"Speak softly and carry a big stick."** Most importantly, the children's toy, the teddy bear, was named after our 26th president.

In 1908, Roosevelt heartily endorsed his good friend William Howard Taft, the secretary of war. Taft and New York Rep. James Sherman easily defeated the Democrats William Jennings Bryan and John Kern of Indiana. Bryan obviously felt that the third time was the charm, but he was wrong, and he lost for a record third time. He also said, "No one can earn $1 million honestly." *How about $1 billion, Mr. Bryan?*

Taft has the distinction of being the fattest US president, weighing in at **350 pounds**. No. 27 had a special, huge bathtub installed in the White House so that he could get out of it without having to summon the Secret Service to pull him out. *Actually, he once did get stuck in the old tub, and several senators had to rescue him. It made the first page of The Washington Post!*

Question: What was Taft's connection to baseball?

Answer: *No, he did not play third base for the Washington Senators.* In 1910, he was the first president to throw out the first ball at a season opener, a tradition that has carried on for over 100 years. At that game, his 350 pounds were stuck in a small seat, making him feel uncomfortable. *In the middle of the seventh inning, he stood up to stretch—and so began* **the seventh inning stretch!**

The Russo-Japanese War

So how was the United States threatened in the 1900s? The major threat was indirect and a result of the Russo-Japanese War. *Some historians have labeled this conflict the Borscht-Sushi War.* Russia and Japan were quarreling over Manchuria and Korea, with no solutions reached. In February 1904, Japan attacked the Russian fleet in a surprise move. Japan won several battles over the next 18 months, but Russia refused to surrender. Finally, the war ended in 1905, and both sides signed the Treaty of Portsmouth, mediated by Roosevelt. He received the Nobel Peace Prize of 1906 for his role in ending the conflict.

The significance of the outcome of the war to the world was that a tiny, Asian country (David) could defeat a huge, European country (Goliath). The Land of the Rising Sun now considered itself an imperialist world power and was emboldened. Its main goal was to control Asia, its land, and its mineral wealth, starting with the annexation and occupation of Korea in 1909 that lasted until 1945.

Realizing the importance and the ambitions of imperialistic Japan, in 1909, the United States completed the construction of the Pearl Harbor Naval Shipyard and Intermediate Maintenance Facility in Hawaii. This was to be the hub of the US Navy in the Pacific Ocean. We all know of the Japanese surprise attack on Pearl Harbor in 1941, which will be discussed later.

Russia

Another indirect threat to the United States was also a result of the Russo-Japanese war. Mother Russia was humiliated both globally and internally by its loss to Japan. In 1905, because of famine and poverty, as well as the disgraceful defeat, rioting broke out in Saint Petersburg, then the capital of imperial Russia. The army fired upon the unarmed peasants, and thousands died. Known as Bloody Sunday, this was the start of the 1905 Revolution. Conditions worsened, ultimately leading to the overthrow of Czar Nicholas II in 1917 and finally the Russian

Revolution. The Soviet Union was soon established, and although the United States was its ally during World Wars I and II, the USSR (the Union of Soviet Socialist Republics) became our biggest enemy and biggest Cold War threat for over 50 years. More to come later.

Tensions began to build in Europe in the 1900s (**the calm**) that boiled over into the 1910s and the outbreak of the Great War (**the storm**). This was the greatest threat to America, and the world, in the 1910s. And so, it will be seen that the small tensions and nonthreats of the 1900s grew into the huge threats of the 1930s and 1940s.

Wars and Treaties of the 1900s

Twenty-five other wars—including the aforementioned Russo-Japanese War, where 150,000 were killed—were fought in this very peaceful decade.

The Boxer Rebellion was fought in China between 1898–1901. (*No, this was not a war about underwear where the boxers fought the tighty-whities!*) *The* Chinese government, the Qing Dynasty, and the young rebel Chinese Boxers fought against an eight-nation European alliance (including the United States and Japan). The Europeans won and forced the Chinese to pay huge reparations.

The Boer War was fought in South Africa between 1899–1902, involving the United Kingdom and the Boers, also known as the Afrikaners. The Boers were farmers, descendants of the original Dutch settlers of South Africa, and were enormously outnumbered by the British. (*I always thought that the British were fighting **wild boars** or, better yet, **bores**.*) The Treaty of Vereeniging ended this bloody conflict, the United Kingdom being the victor and now able to control the gold mines that had been discovered in South Africa.

Another major conflict was the War of a Thousand Days, lasting between 1899–1903. This was a civil war fought in Colombia. *No, not a battle between Columbia University and Harvard University, but rather in the South American country.*

Trying to prevent future wars, many peace treaties were signed during this decade, most proving to be useless. In 1902, England and Japan signed a treaty that Russia hated. Czar Nicholas II said, "An Englishman is a Jew." *Was this a compliment or an insult?*

Other peace treaties signed in the 1900s were between France and Italy, Germany and Russia, Japan and Korea, the United Kingdom and Siam, and Austria-Hungary and Turkey. Strangely, in 1907, Russia and the United Kingdom signed a convention, similar to a treaty. The United Kingdom and France signed the Entente Cordiale to settle international differences.

The most important treaty was the Triple Entente, an informal agreement signed in 1907 among Russia, France, and the United Kingdom. This bonding of the three nations was to offset the Triple Alliance that was signed among Germany, Austria-Hungary, and Italy.

Important and Unimportant News of the 1900s

1900

1) A huge hurricane devastates Galveston, Texas, killing 12,000 people, the deadliest natural disaster in US history.

2) A revolution takes place in the Philippines. Arthur MacArthur becomes military governor.

3) Construction begins on the New York City subway system. *Be careful of the closing doors.*

4) Italian King Umberto I is assassinated at age 56 by an Italian-American anarchist.

5) Marie and Pierre Curie coin the phrase "radioactivity" after discovering radium and polonium.

6) The International Ladies Garment Workers Union (ILGWU) forms in New York City.

7) Army Maj. Walter Reed experiments with mosquitoes to determine if they are a cause of yellow fever. *"Quick, Henry, the Flit!"*

8) Thomas Edison introduces the storage battery. "Genius is 1% inspiration and 99% perspiration."

9) The major colonialist countries—Great Britain, France, Russia, Germany, Austria-Hungary, and Italy—controls **half** of the world's population.

10) The first zeppelin flight occurs in Germany.

11) France wins the most medals in the Summer Olympics, held in Paris. *Are the judges French?*

12) Eastman Kodak introduces the Brownie camera. *It definitely is not digital.*

13) Giacomo Puccini composes his great opera, *Tosca*. Four years later, *Madame Butterfly* is introduced.

14) *The Wonderful Wizard of Oz* by L. Frank Baum is published, *and Judy Garland is not even born yet.*

1901

1) Queen Victoria of the United Kingdom, who served as queen since 1837, dies at age 81.

2) Guglielmo Marconi of Italy sends the first wireless transmission from England to Canada—over 2,000 miles. *He supposedly orders pizza to go.*

3) Oil is discovered in Beaumont, Texas, creating the Texas oil boom.

4) The Commonwealth of Australia is created.

5) A severe famine in Russia causes major rioting. *But there is plenty of vodka.*

6) Several small steel companies join together to form US Steel. Assisted by J. P. Morgan, this is the first billion-dollar company. Mr. Morgan famously said, "If you have to ask how much it costs, you can't afford it."

7) The first Nobel Prizes are awarded in Sweden.

8) Born this year: future Japanese Emperor Hirohito, jazz musician

Louis "Satchmo" Armstrong, and Walt Disney, creator of Mickey Mouse and Donald Duck.

9) Emil Jellinek of Germany creates the first modern automobile and names it Mercedes, in honor of his daughter. *If he had a son named Benjamin, the car would be a Ben's Benz!*

1902

1) The United States grants Cuba its independence.

2) The Antikythera mechanism, an analogue computer that ancient Greek astronomers built 2,000 years ago, is recovered from a shipwreck off the Greek Islands. (*And you thought that Apple created the first computer!*)

3) Edward VII is crowned king of the United Kingdom, succeeding Queen Victoria.

4) The Aswan Low Dam in Egypt is completed. The Aswan High Dam is finished in 1960. *What about the middle dam?*

5) The first Rose Bowl Game is played in California. Michigan beats Stanford, 49–0. *Are the bookies happy?*

6) Opera legend Enrico Caruso makes the first gramophone record. *It was not "Heartbreak Hotel."*

7) A major crisis (because foreign debts are not paid), in Venezuela occurs, with a European naval blockade.

8) Charles Lindbergh, a great American hero (or, controversially, an antihero) is born.

9) Anti-Semitism is rampant in Eastern Europe, with many Jews emigrating to the United States.

10) The American Automobile Association (AAA) is founded. *There are not too many members because there are not too many cars.*

11) Jazz music in New Orleans gains in popularity. Musician Jelly Roll Morton claims to have invented it.

12) French sculptor Auguste Rodin creates *Le Penseur,* aka *The Thinker.* *Over 100 years later, the sculpture is still thinking.*

13) Willis Carrier invents the air conditioner. (*It is rumored that his*

three assistants deserve the credit. Their names appear on all current AC
units: Norm, Hi, and Max. Only kidding.)

1903

1) The United States establishes Naval Station Guantanamo Bay in Cuba, in perpetuity.

2) The Wright brothers, Orville and Wilbur, conduct the first airplane flight in Kitty Hawk, North Carolina. *The plane travels at the unbelievable speed of 10 mph.*

3) Pope Pius X succeeds Pope Leo XIII and heads the Catholic Church for 11 years.

4) Panama becomes independent from Colombia.

5) King Alexander of Serbia is assassinated at age 26 in Belgrade.

6) In German Southwest Africa (now named Namibia), Germans conduct a genocide against Herero natives, killing over 100,000 people.

7) Henry Ford founds the Ford Motor Company in Dearborn, Michigan. The first Ford car built is the Model A. It sells for $800.

8) Ivan Pavlov of Russia establishes the principles of classical conditioning, ringing bells for dogs and observing their reactions. *He teaches his dog to answer the telephone.*

9) A fire in the Iroquois Theater in Chicago kills 620 people, the most severe fire in US history.

10) The first World Series of Major League Baseball is played; the Boston Americans (aka the Red Sox) beat the Pittsburgh Pirates, five games to two.

1904

1) The United States starts construction of the Panama Canal. It is completed in 1914. The United States then acquires the Panama Canal Zone from Panama for $10 million (*a steal!*) and retains it until 1979.

2) The first bodybuilding competition takes place at Madison

Square Garden in New York City. *Arnold Schwarzenegger was not there.*

3) A fire on a steamboat on the East River in New York City kills over 1000 people.

4) Jack Chesbro, a pitcher for the New York Highlanders (which later become the New York Yankees), wins an unbelievable 41 games this season, a record probably never to be equaled.

5) A German sailor paddles his canoe on a round-the-world trip, going from Vancouver, Canada, to Australia to South Africa to Brazil to London. The excursion takes three years *and plenty of blisters.*

6) The first underground subway line opens in New York City. For 5 cents, a person can tour the entire city underground.

7) The ice cream cone makes its debut at the St. Louis World's Fair. *The most popular flavor is vanilla-banana-strawberry-mango-fudge crunch.*

1905

1) German scientist Albert Einstein, age 26, discovers the theory of relativity. "Learn from yesterday, live for today, and hope for tomorrow."

2) The Trans-Siberian Railroad opens, connecting Moscow and Vladivostok, 6,000 miles apart. *The cost of a ticket is unknown, but the peasants probably can't afford it unless they have a discount coupon.*

3) The First Moroccan Crisis worsens relations between Germany and future enemies France and England.

4) Irish playwright George Bernard Shaw writes *Major Barbara*, three years after writing *Man and Superman. Was Clark Kent in a starring role?*

5) Because of revolutionary activity in Poland, Russian Czar Nicholas II relents and allows the Polish people to speak Polish.

6) In society news, Franklin D. Roosevelt marries Eleanor Roosevelt. *No, they are not brother and sister, but rather fifth cousins.*

7) Very cold weather in the Midwest: minus 40 degrees Fahrenheit in Kansas. *Dorothy and Toto are planning a trip to Boca Raton, Florida.*

8) Author Upton Sinclair writes *The Jungle*, exposing a huge public health threat from the food industry. *Hotdog sales plummet!*

9) The world's largest diamond is found in South Africa: 3,106 carats. *A rich lady will need very large fingers to display this rock.*

1906

1) A massive San Francisco earthquake and fire kills 4,000 residents and destroys 75% of the city.

2) Norwegian explorer Roald Amundsen locates the North Magnetic Pole. (*Was it ever lost?*)

3) France reverses its decision on the anti-Semitic Dreyfus Affair, dealing with espionage. Maj. Alfred Dreyfus is reinstated in the army.

4) The United Kingdom launches a giant battleship, starting the arms race in Europe. Attempting to compete, Germany starts its own program of building giant battleships.

5) The Victor Talking Machine Company of New Jersey introduces the first phonograph record player, the Victrola.

6) French psychologists develop the intelligence quota test, the IQ Test.

7) In the art world, Pablo Picasso and Georges Braque invent cubism. The great Mr. Picasso once said, "Every child is an artist. The problem is how to remain an artist once we grow up."

1907

1) At the Hague **Peace** Conference in the Netherlands, conventions on the rules of war are proclaimed. *Why not call it the Hague* ***War*** *Conference?*

2) Oklahoma becomes the 46th state in the nation. *"Oh, what a beautiful morning."*

3) The Romanian Peasant Revolt kills thousands. Anti-Semitism is a factor.

4) The first photostat machine is unveiled in Oklahoma City.

5) Honduras and Nicaragua engage in a war. The United States intervenes to end the fighting. *Play nice.*

6) The first motorized taxicabs hit New York City's streets. *Uber debuts only 102 years later.*

7) Charles Curtis of Kansas becomes the first Native American elected to the US Senate.

8) Question: What is the first European country to give women the right to vote?

Answer: Finland

9) In one day, over 11,000 immigrants from Europe are processed at Ellis Island in New York Harbor.

10) *Ziegfeld Follies* makes its Broadway debut and plays for the next 24 years.

11) President Roosevelt sends **the Great White Fleet** on a round-the-world cruise.

1908

1) An earthquake and resulting tsunami in Italy kill 150,000 people.

2) The Anglo-Persian Oil Company starts petroleum production in the Middle East in Persia. *Fill 'er up!*

3) The Model T Ford is introduced to the country for a bargain price of $850.

4) The Federal Bureau of Investigation (FBI) is created, with 34 employees. That number has risen slightly, to 35,000 employees.

5) In the crumbling Ottoman Empire, there is a Young Turk Revolution. *Whatever happened to the Old Turks?*

6) Austria-Hungary annexes Bosnia and Herzegovina from the Ottoman Empire. This is called the First Balkan Crisis.

7) Born this year: Lyndon B. Johnson, 36th US president; Thur-

good Marshall, first African American justice on the US Supreme Court; great actress Bette Davis.

8) For the first time, the New Year's Ball is dropped at midnight at Times Square (formerly Longacre Square) in New York City. *What time is it for Boca midnight?*

9) The Chicago Cubs win the World Series. *Loyal Cubbie fans will have to wait 108 years for another championship.*

10) Also for the first time, an American family travels by automobile from Los Angeles to New York City. The trip takes only 32 days. *Their GPS does not work.*

11) A giant explosion occurs in a Siberian forest, the largest explosion in recorded history. The cause of this blast remains unknown, with many theories abounding. *If a tree falls in a forest and no one is around to hear it, does it make a sound?*

12) A New York City policeman arrests a woman for smoking in public. *What is she smoking?*

1909

1) American explorer Robert Peary reaches the North Pole. Supposedly, one of his associates was at the same spot one year earlier.

2) A diverse group of people, including Blacks, Whites, and Jews, found the National Association for the Advancement of Colored People (NAACP) in New York City.

3) Guglielmo Marconi wins the Nobel Prize in physics for his work on radio.

4) In a prelude to the 1920 genocide, Muslim Turks massacre thousands of Armenian Christians.

5) German scientist Paul Ehrlich announces a cure for syphilis with his "magic bullet." Edward G. Robinson stars in the 1940 movie.

6) The first copper Lincoln penny is issued. The **1909 S VDB** penny is a collector's item that may be worth over $2,000.

Deaths This Decade of Notable People

- Queen Victoria, 81. Ruled the United Kingdom for almost 64 years.
- William McKinley, 58. Twenty-fifth US president, 1897–1901. Assassinated.
- Benjamin Harrison, 67. Twenty-third US president, 1889–1893.
- Jules Verne, 77. French novelist who wrote *Twenty Thousand Leagues under the Sea*. He said, "We shall one day travel to the moon, the planets and the stars, with the same facility and certainty as we now make the voyage from Liverpool to New York."
- Susan B. Anthony, 86. American social reformer and leader of the women's suffrage movement.
- Grover Cleveland, 71. 22nd and 24th US president; the only one to serve two nonconsecutive terms: 1885–1889 and 1893–1897.
- Geronimo, 79. Native American Apache leader who led raids against American soldiers.
- Theodor Herzl, 44. Austro-Hungarian journalist and father of modern political Zionism. "It is true that we aspire to our ancient land. But what we want in that ancient land is a new blossoming of the Jewish spirit."

Advances in Science This Decade

Internal combustion engine – Blood typing – Geiger counter – Vitamins – SOS signal – Electrocardiogram – Radar – Plastic – Neon lamps – Escalator – Helicopter – Cellophane

Important Innovations of the 1900s

Typewriter – Phonograph – Brownie camera – Windshield wipers – Color photography – Tea bag – Gun silencer – Electric washing machine – Paper cup – Vacuum cleaner – Assembly line – Color movies – Crayons – Safety razor – Instant coffee

---

In 1900, the population of the world was 1.6 billion people. The United States's population was 76 million people. The average life expectancy of Americans was 48 years.

In summary, the 1900s was probably the **least** threatening to the United States of all of the coming decades of the 20th century. Yes, this was the 10-year period of the calm before the storm. America would have to put up their hurricane shutters because the giant storm that was now forming in Europe would wreak devastation for four miserable years over the rest of the world.

2

1910–1919
THE WAR TO END ALL WARS

To paraphrase Mr. Charles Dickens, "The 1900s were the best of times; the 1910s were the worst of times."

The teens were a bloody decade—24 wars were fought in this 10-year period, with tens of millions of casualties.

There were four enormous threats to the United States in this unruly decade. Two of them were direct; two were indirect.

The first direct threat was **the Great War**. (*I don't understand what's so **great** about a war.*) Obviously, this war could not be called World War I because at that time there had not yet been a World War II.

The second threat in 1917 was indirect but became a direct and terrifying one that lasted until 1991. This was **the Russian Revolution**. The czar was overthrown and replaced by a new world order: **Communism**. For 46 years after World War II, the United States and the Soviet Union engaged in the Cold War that often almost threatened to become a hot war.

Threat No. 3 was indirect but had huge, direct ramifications decades later. **The Sykes-Picot Agreement** geographically divided the Middle East after the war and caused countless problems for the next 100 years.

The fourth threat was a direct and very real threat to the United States and the rest of the world in 1918. This was the Spanish flu pandemic, which infected 500 million people worldwide and left an estimated 50 to 100 million people dead.

Now for the **bad** news!

Presidential Elections of the 1910s

The 1912 election was a special one. Former President Teddy Roosevelt decided to run again, this time as an independent candidate since current President William Howard Taft had received the Republican nomination. Roosevelt's Progressive Party, **the Bull Moose Party**, with California Governor Hiram Johnson as his running mate, actually outperformed Taft and Vice President James Sherman's Republican Party. This split of the GOP (the Grand Old Party) gave the election to the Democrats, for New Jersey Governor Woodrow Wilson and Thomas Marshall of Indiana won handily. Wilson, president No. 28, was the only US president to have earned a PhD; his was in political science. He was also rumored to be a racist and supporter of the KKK.

In 1916, Wilson and Marshall were reelected, defeating the Republican's choice, Chief Justice Charles Evans Hughes and Charles Fairbanks, in a very close race.

Wilson suffered a near-fatal stroke in October 1919, just months after participating in the signing of the Treaty of Versailles. His second wife, Edith, kept the extent of his illness away from his cabinet, US Congress, the press, and the American public. Wilson could barely speak or move, and his wife screened and signed all his paperwork. In actuality, Edith was **the first female** president of the country. She led (or misled) the United States for 17 months, not wanting Marshall to take control and actually firing the secretary of state, Robert Lansing. She went from *FLOTUS to POTUS*, and nobody knew!

The Great War

From 1914–1918, Europe was in disarray. The United States attempted to stay out of the conflict, but in 1917, Wilson was forced to declare war, and soon millions of American young men were fighting and dying in Europe in what many called the Senseless War.

An anonymous quote: "War does not determine who is right—only who is left."

Let's go back a few years. Queen Victoria ruled the British Empire from 1837–1901. She was known as the Grandmother of Europe because so many of her royal relatives ruled various countries in Europe through marriage. Czar Nicholas II of Russia, King George VI of the United Kingdom, and Kaiser Wilhelm II of Germany were all first cousins. King George I of Greece, King Frederick VIII of Denmark, Queen Victoria Eugenie of Spain, and Queen Marie of Romania were all part of Queen Victoria's *mishpucha* (family). *I wonder if this grand group of related royalty had family circle meetings like my relatives had in the good old days in Brooklyn, New York!*

There were many tensions in the world that finally led to the outbreak of the Great War. For 40 years, most European nations were preparing for a large-scale war. A military competition began among the great powers of Europe, especially between the United Kingdom and Germany. France distrusted Germany as a result of the Franco-Prussian War of 1870, which Germany had won and which had led to German unification. Countries wanted either unification or separation, or were concerned with state-building.

There were alliances and there were alliances! As you have already learned, **the Triple Entente** was a pact signed in 1907 among the United Kingdom, France, and Russia. This offset **the Triple Alliance** signed in 1882 among Germany, Austria-Hungary, and Italy. There were separate agreements signed between Russia and Serbia, the United Kingdom with France and Belgium, and Japan with the United Kingdom.

An old Quote, "The sun never sets on the British Empire." It was said that at least one part of their territory was always in daylight. This related to the colonial expansion of Britain in the 18th and 19th centuries, especially in Australia, Canada, India, and many other parts of the world.

"New Imperialism" in the early 20th century revealed the colonial expansion of the European powers and Japan into Africa and Asia. This of course created rivalries, as now Germany wanted a place in the British sunshine. Also, Nationalism became an important factor in the days preceding World War I, especially in the actions of Serbia.

The British author H.G. Wells coined the phrase **"the war to end all wars"** in reference to the Great War. Wilson took credit for the phrase, although he only used it once. It is estimated that almost 200 million people were killed in the many savage wars of the 20th century. The quote should have been **"The war that didn't end all wars."** I guess Mr. Wells and Mr. Wilson were wrong in their predictions, as this was the first evidence of *"fake news."*

The spark needed to ignite the dynamite in Europe occurred on June 28, 1914. A Bosnian-Serb Nationalist in Sarajevo, Bosnia, assassinated Archduke Franz Ferdinand, heir to the Austro-Hungarian Empire. The world would never be the same!

Within days, almost every European country mobilized and declared war on the next country. The two sides lined up for battle. The Triple Alliance, now called **the Central powers**, recruited the Ottoman Empire (*"the sick old man of Europe"*), which was crumbling, along with Bulgaria, to fight alongside Germany, the Austro-Hungarian Empire, and Italy. *It was even rumored that Austria had declared war on Hungary!*

The other team, the Triple Entente, now known as **the Allied powers**, prepared for war. Serbia and Japan joined the United Kingdom, France, and Russia. Eventually, so did Belgium, Brazil, Greece, Montenegro, Romania, Siam, Portugal, China, and Liberia. *As they say in baseball, you can't tell the players without a scorecard!*

Both sides thought that this war would be short-lived and would end by Christmas 1914. They were right about Christmas, but the year was actually 1918. **"The guns of August,"** as author Barbara Tuchman declared, **"were now blazing."**

The war was fought on the Western Front (Belgium and France) and the Eastern Front (Russia). Between 1915–1917 on the Western Front, both sides battled with no clear winner. On the Eastern Front, Germany seemed to have the upper hand over Russia. In 1918, the Russian Revolution and heavy military losses caused that country to withdraw from the war.

Both sides introduced many new military innovations and strategies. On the Western Front, each side dug long trenches, and trench warfare was prevalent during this deadly stalemate. Tanks were used for the first time, and air warfare, zeppelins, and biplanes were introduced. Hand grenades and flamethrowers made their debut, as well as other new artillery weapons. The radio and the telephone (*not the iPhone*) were used, as they were the new technology of the day. At sea, submarines and modern warships proved to be deadly and effective.

The Germans used many types of poison gas for the first time in warfare. The effect on the Allied powers was devastating. England was forced to develop its own poison gas and retaliated on the Germans. After the war, the Geneva Protocol of 1925 prohibited the use of lethal gas as a weapon. Unfortunately, rogue nations have used chemical and biological weapons many times in warfare and internally over the last 100 years.

The main strategy of the Allied powers was a blockade to starve the enemy of food and water. The Germans had a similar strategy of using their submarine fleet (U-boats) to blockade supplies coming to Great Britain from the United States.

Several major battles were fought during the course of the war. The Germans were defeated in 1914 at the Battle of the Marne. The Allies suffered a huge loss at Gallipoli, Turkey, in 1915. Winston Churchill, the first lord of the admiralty, took responsibility for this disastrous defeat. In 1916, the great naval Battle of Jutland occurred, with the British victorious. The Battle of Verdun in 1916 was the longest battle of the war, with huge casualties on both sides and the Germans defeating the French.

Another anonymous quote: "It doesn't matter what war we are talking about. You won't find winners there; both sides lose."

You might ask, just what was the United States doing over this period? Wilson kept America neutral and out of the European war. This isolationist stance worked until 1917, when the time came for the country to enter the Great War. German U-boats were sinking American merchant ships with supplies intended for the Allied powers—a great mistake for Germany.

Finally, the tipping point was the Zimmermann Telegram. (*Today, it would have been the Zimmerman email.*) Arthur Zimmerman, the German foreign minister, sent a telegram to Mexico urging our southern neighbors to enter the war on the side of Germany. When Germany was victorious, Mexico would be awarded the present-day states of California, Nevada, Utah, Arizona, and New Mexico. The telegram was intercepted, shown to the president, and then released to the press. This was not fake news! The American public was furious and demanded immediate action.

The United States declared war on the Central powers in April 1917, and millions of American fighting men were soon deployed to Europe. Tremendous American casualties occurred, but the Central powers were defeated, and Germany and friends surrendered on November 11, 1918.

In 1919, **the Treaty of Versailles** formally ended the Great War. The Allies imposed severe terms upon Germany, which would have huge ramifications in the years to come. As a result of the war, many old empires ceased to exist: Austro-Hungarian, Ottoman, German, and Russian. At the same time, new nations were created—Poland, Ukraine, Lithuania, Estonia, Latvia, Finland, and Czechoslovakia.

The war to end all wars was finally over, but unfortunately for the world, war was only hibernating for the next 20 years.

The Russian Revolution

The Romanov Dynasty ruled Russia for over 300 years, from 1613–1917. Peter the Great, Ivan the Terrible, *and possibly Boris the Mediocre (just kidding)*, ruled this enormous country with an iron hand. In 1894, Czar Alexander III died and was succeeded by his son, the last Russian emperor, Nicholas II.

By the start of the 20th century, economic and social conditions in Russia were deplorable, and many people were demanding change. The defeat in the Russo-Japanese War in 1904 sent morale plummeting, and World War I went very badly for the Russians, with Germany winning many battles on the Eastern Front. Strikes and food shortages made Russian peasants take to the streets to protest against the autocratic government. They declared that the land should belong to the workers who toiled on it and not to the upper class. In January 1905, Russian soldiers fired upon demonstrators in Saint Petersburg—*no, not the one in Florida*. Bloody Sunday was the start of the 1905 Revolution that ultimately led to the Revolution of 1917.

Grigori Rasputin was a mystic figure who held influence over the unpopular czarina, Alexandra. He was a self-proclaimed healer who was deemed unpatriotic, and those loyal to the government ultimately murdered him in 1916.

Finally, in February 1917, and again in October and November, workers, peasants, and soldiers revolted and overthrew the czarist government. The czar, who had just abdicated, and his family were arrested and soon executed. In 1918, with terrible morale in the army and no food for the citizenry, Russia withdrew from the war, signing the Treaty of Brest-Litovsk.

Vladimir Lenin, who founded the Russian Communist Party, took control of the government and established a Socialist Soviet democracy (*democracy?*). Another Bolshevik leader, Leon Trotsky, appealed for a world Socialist/Communist revolution. Subsequent Communist revolutions did occur internationally—in Vietnam in 1945, in China in

1949, and in Cuba in 1960. But with the demise of the Soviet Union in 1991, Communism was basically dead. ***Bring back the czar!***

The Middle East

The **Sykes-Picot Agreement** was a secret treaty between the United Kingdom and France, signed in 1916. **Spheres of influence** were defined in the soon-to-be-dismantled Ottoman Empire at the war's end. The agreement gave the United Kingdom control of today's Israel, Palestine, Jordan, and southern Iraq. France would now control Syria, Lebanon, southeastern Turkey, and northern Iraq. Russia and Italy would be given a smaller amount of Ottoman territory.

The agreement created artificial borders in the Middle East with no regard to religious, ethnic or sectarian characteristics and ignored local identities, as the Kurds were placed into three new countries—Iraq, Syria, and Turkey. Supposedly, Sir Mark Sykes and Georges Picot used a ruler to draw a straight line on the map, giving one side to France and the other to Britain. The violence plaguing the area can be attributed to this agreement: the Israeli-Palestinian conflicts, the war in Iraq, the creation of ISIS, and the destruction of Syria. Hindsight being 20/20, *the Middle East would be in a better place if Mr. Sykes and Mr. Picot had agreed to play tennis that day in 1916 instead of agreeing to draw up a treaty that proved to be a dud.*

The Flu Pandemic

One of the deadliest pandemics in human history wreaked havoc on the planet between 1918–1920. In the fourth grade, we used to say, *"I opened the window, and in flew Enza."* But this was no laughing matter.

The pandemic was called the Spanish flu because it was reported that the king of Spain was gravely ill. *If the sickness had first been discovered in Brooklyn, New York, it could have been called the Flat-bush flu.*

From remote islands of the South Pacific to Eskimo villages in the

Arctic, the whole world was affected. Several theories abound as to where the pandemic started. Some say it began in Kansas. China was another suspect. Some say it began at an army hospital camp somewhere in France. At any rate, it was thought that 500 million people were infected, and between 50 million and 100 million died from this disease. Unbelievably it is thought that between 3% and 5% of the world's population died from it. In the United States, approximately 675,000 were killed. Life expectancy dropped 12 years after the pandemic: to 36 years for males and 42 years for females.

Young adults had the highest mortality rate, and, surprisingly, the very young and the very old survived. October 1918 was the deadliest month, as soldiers in the trenches became the most vulnerable. Doctors recommended large doses of aspirin, and many people died of aspirin poisoning. The mortality rate in Germany and Austria was higher than in England and France, which affected the outcome of the Great War.

The world has seen many flu pandemics over the last 100 years, but none have been as deadly as the one of 1918. With modern medicine on our side, we can only hope that this invisible enemy will never return. *Wrong*—in 2020, there was **the coronavirus, (COVID-19)**!

Wars and Treaties of the 1910s

The casualty rate of World War I was astonishing: the Allied powers suffered casualties of 18 million people, while the Central powers lost 15 million.

There were 26 other horrific wars this decade. The two Balkan Wars claimed 140,000 lives. The Mexican Revolution claimed 125,000. The Polish-Soviet War killed 100,000. The Dervish State War against the United Kingdom, Italy, and Ethiopia lasted 11 years and killed 6,000.

An anonymous quote: "Only the dead have seen the end of war."

Besides the Sykes-Picot Treaty, 30 other treaties were signed. Of course, the most important one was the Treaty of Versailles, which formally ended the Great War. The Armistice, which stopped the fighting, was signed on November 11, 1918, at 11 o'clock—the 11th hour of the 11th day of the 11th month.

Important and Unimportant News of the 1910s

1910

1) Czar Nicholas II visits his cousin, German Kaiser Wilhelm II, and both agree on spheres of influence in the Middle East. *Large amounts of vodka and bratwurst are consumed.*

2) Japan and Russia sign a mutual defense agreement while Japan annexes Korea and renames it Chosen. *The Koreans are definitely not the "chosen" people.*

3) Jack Johnson becomes the first African American world heavyweight champion. Race riots begin after Johnson beats James J. Jeffries.

4) King Edward VII of the United Kingdom dies. Bertie's (the late king's nickname) son, George V, becomes king.

5) Union of South Africa is established.

6) The art world celebrates Pablo Picasso, Henri Matisse, and Wassily Kandinsky, along with cubism, expressionism, and surrealism.

7) The Mexican Revolution begins against dictator Porfirio Díaz.

8) Halley's Comet is photographed (*not Bill Haley & His Comets*). It will not appear again until 1987.

9) The worst fire in the nation's history occurs in Idaho, burning 3 million acres.

10) The Boy Scouts of America form. Not to be overshadowed, two years later, the Girl Scouts of the United States of America form.

11) Slavery is made illegal in China.

12) New immigrants and first-generation Americans constitute approximately 75% of New York City's population.

13) *Because of a national meat shortage, Louisiana wants to engage in hippopotamus ranching. Hippo burgers are delicious!*

1911

1) Italy and Turkey fight in North Africa in the Tripolitan War. Italy wins using aircraft for the first time in warfare and annexes Libya.

2) The first Indianapolis 500 race takes place. *The winner zooms along at 75 mph.*

3) Machu Picchu is discovered in the Andes Mountains in Peru.

4) The Triangle Shirt Factory fire in New York City kills 146 workers.

5) President William Howard Taft sends 20,000 troops to Mexico to protect American capital as Mexican dictator Porfirio Díaz, who had been in power for 35 years, is overthrown.

6) Dr. Sun Yat-sen becomes the first president of the Republic of China.

7) Our 40th president, Ronald Reagan, is born, as well as Vice President Hubert Humphrey. Playwright Tennessee Williams also makes his debut.

8) The US Supreme Court breaks up Standard Oil Co. into 34 smaller companies. *"Breaking up is hard to do,"* but not to the Supreme Court.

9) Cy Young, the winningest picture in MLB history with 511 wins, retires from the sport. *Strangely, with all those victories, he never won the Cy Young Award.* He also holds the record for the most losses: 315.

10) Roald Amundsen and his Norwegian team are the first people to stand at the South Pole. *It's much too cold to sit!*

11) The US Government sues the Coca-Cola Company, saying that added caffeine is a deadly poison. *The government loses the case and cannot sleep for a week.*

1912

1) The British ocean liner **RMS *Titanic***, the largest ship afloat, strikes an iceberg in the North Atlantic Ocean during its maiden

voyage and sinks. Fifteen hundred passengers perish. *Maybe a movie should be made—oh, they did that already.*

2) New Mexico and Arizona are admitted to the Union as states No. 47 and No. 48, respectively.

3) The last emperor of China, a 6-year-old, abdicates the throne, ending 2,000 years of imperial rule. *His kindergarten classmates warmly greet him.* Sun Yat-sen is now in total control of China.

4) President William Howard Taft sends US troops to Nicaragua, Honduras, and Cuba, to protect American economic interests.

5) *Tarzan of the Apes*, written by Edgar Rice Burroughs, *swings on the vines* to make his debut.

6) The First Balkan War begins. Eventually, Bulgaria, Serbia, Greece, and Montenegro defeat Turkey.

7) Alaska becomes a US territory. Prior to this, it was a US possession.

8) Baseball great Ty Cobb of the Detroit Tigers jumps into the stands and *beats up a disabled heckler who just happens to have one hand. The $50 fine was not fine.*

9) Native American Jim Thorpe has his gold medals from the 1912 Summer Olympics confiscated after it's discovered that he professionally played Minor League Baseball in 1909. The medals are reinstated in 1983, 30 years after his death.

10) As a gift, Japan sends 3,000 cherry trees to the United States, and they are planted around Washington, DC. Some are still standing today.

11) A Paris orphanage holds a raffle to raise money. *The first prize is **a baby**. What was the second prize—two babies?*

12) Question: Which future famous World War II general competed in this year's Olympic Games?

Answer: Gen. Dwight D. Eisenhower? No. Gen. Douglas MacArthur? No. Gen. George Patton participated in the pentathlon event in Stockholm.

1913

1) The Second Balkan War begins. *Turkey wants a rematch.*

2) Greek King George I is assassinated and succeeded by Constantine I.

3) Eighty percent of American children say that they would rather work in a sweatshop than go to school. *The other 20% go on to own sweatshops.*

4) Sigmund Freud, Joseph Stalin, Adolf Hitler, and Leon Trotsky often patronize the Café Central in Vienna. *Hopefully, not at the same table.*

5) The great *Mona Lisa* painting is recovered two years after it was stolen. *Smiles all around.*

6) An angry, anti-Semitic mob in Georgia lynches Leo Frank after he is wrongly convicted of murder.

7) The Federal Reserve System, the central banking system of the United States, is created.

8) The 16th Amendment, which enacts a federal income tax on income over $3,000, becomes the law of the land.

9) Richard Nixon, our 37th president, is born, as well as his successor, Gerald Ford. Olympic champion Jesse Owens makes his first appearance.

10) In Liverpool, the first crossword puzzle appears. *What is 22 down?*

1914

1) The Great War begins. Read *The Guns of August* by Barbara Tuchman.

2) Two large boats collide in the Saint Lawrence River, and over 1,000 people perish.

3) A British soldier wrote a love letter to his wife, put it in a bottle and threw it into the English Channel. The bottle was recovered in 1999 and delivered to his 86-year-old daughter.

4) Benedict XV becomes the new Pope, succeeding Pope Pius X.

5) The "deadball" era in baseball is here as Frank (Home Run) Baker of the Philadelphia Athletics leads the majors with nine home runs. *Today, the batboy of the New York Yankees could hit nine home runs.*

6) The Panama Canal opens after 10 years of construction that leaves 27,000 workers dead. *A palindrome (A phrase that reads the same backwards as forward): "A man a plan a canal Panama."*

7) Henry Ford announces a new, historic minimum wage for his workers—*five bucks a day.*

8) Three famous Js are born: New York Yankee great Joe DiMaggio, world heavyweight champion Joe Louis, and one of the most important men of the century, Dr. Jonas Salk, discoverer of the polio vaccine.

9) A Massachusetts high school football team goes 13–0 and outscores their opponents 600–0. *They should have joined the NFL.*

10) President Woodrow Wilson sends the US Marine Corps to Veracruz, Mexico, to protect American interests.

11) The immortal Babe Ruth of the Boston Red Sox makes his pitching debut and wins 89 games over six seasons. He later becomes a New York Yankee outfielder and hits *only* 714 home runs.

12) The Federal Trade Commission (FTC) is established to protect consumers. **Orson Swindle** *is appointed in 1997 as a commissioner.*

13) Germany, France, Russia, and the United Kingdom observe a Christmas truce. Gifts are exchanged, Christmas carols are sung, soccer is played, and Europe is merry for a few days.

1915

1) A German submarine sinks the British ocean liner RMS *Lusitania*, killing 1,200 people.

2) The US Coast Guard is established.

3) The head of German propaganda in the United States inadvertently loses his briefcase on the New York City subway. A Brooklyn

commuter recovers it and turns it over to the police. It contains details about German espionage and subversion across the United States, and the newspapers publish the information. The American public is not happy, *nor is the commuter who did not get a reward for finding the briefcase.*

4) Ford Motors produces car No. 1 million.

5) Everybody's favorite singer, Frank Sinatra, is born—*not in New York, New York, but in New Jersey, New Jersey.* Playwright Arthur Miller also makes his debut.

6) Controversial, silent-movie drama *The Birth of a Nation* actually promotes the KKK.

7) The Armenian Genocide begins in the Ottoman Empire with the Muslim Turks murdering Christian Armenians. The term "Crime against humanity" is first used.

8) *A British inventor documents his life by entering his doings in his diary every 15 minutes until his death—68 years later. This waste of time and paper is 14,000 pages long.*

9) The first transcontinental telephone call is made between Alexander Graham Bell in New York and Thomas Watson in San Francisco. *Mr. Bell left Mr. Watson a voice mail message.*

1916

1) Pancho Villa, along with 1,500 Mexican supporters, cross the border and attack New Mexico. In retaliation, Gen. John J. Pershing invades Mexico but can't catch the speedy Señor Villa.

2) Montana elects the first woman to US Congress, Jeannette Rankin.

3) The Easter Rebellion, an uprising in Dublin by Irish Republicans against the English, occurs. Not a very happy Easter Sunday.

4) President Woodrow Wilson sends the US Marine Corps to Santo Domingo to protect the US Consulate.

5) The first Jewish justice of the US Supreme Court, Louis Brandeis, is appointed.

6) In a college football game, Georgia Tech beats Cumberland College, 222–0. *The game is not as close as the score indicates.*

7) The world's first confirmed billionaire is John D. Rockefeller. "Don't be afraid to give up the good to go for the great."

8) American Gen. John Thompson invents the tommy gun. *Hypothetically, if Gen. Wallace Nutting had invented it, would it be called the nutty gun?*

9) The British develop the first drone, an unmanned aerial vehicle. The American model, the aerial torpedo, is an early version of today's cruise missile.

10) In 1814, Francis Scott Key writes a poem called "The Defense of Fort McHenry." It's put to music 102 years later and renamed "The Star-Spangled Banner."

11) *Planters's Mr. Peanut is introduced. Police are called in at the factory when a peanut is **assaulted**. Funny?*

1917

1) "Lafayette, we are here," as American soldiers enter France. President Woodrow Wilson says, "The world must be made safe for democracy."

2) King George V formally changes his German-sounding family name to the Royal House of Windsor, *which seems to be a lot better than Saxe-Coburg and Gotha. Sounds like a Berlin law firm.*

3) Citizens of Puerto Rico officially become US citizens.

4) The United States buys the Danish West Indies from Denmark for $25 million and changes the name to **the Virgin Islands**. *Currently, many baseball and basketball players earn more than that each year, and they are not virgins.*

5) UK Foreign Secretary Arthur Balfour issues the historic **Balfour Declaration**, which creates a future national homeland for Jewish people in Palestine.

6) The Halifax Explosion, a maritime disaster in Nova Scotia, Canada, kills 2,000 and injures 9,000.

7) The second Russian Revolution starts with the Bolsheviks (the Reds) fighting the Provisional Government. The Reds win. The United States is the first country to recognize the new Russian government.

8) The National Hockey League (NHL) is established, with five Canadian teams participating. Currently, there are 31 teams: seven are Canadian, and 24 are American.

9) The cost of the first-class postage stamp soars *from 2 cents to 3 cents, an increase of 50%. Talk about runaway inflation.*

10) The Espionage Act makes it a crime to share information about national defense with the enemy. At the same time, the French execute Mata Hari for spying for Germany.

11) The Chicago White Sox win the World Series but have to wait 88 years (2005) for their second title. The Boston Red Sox win the World Series in 1918 and have to wait 86 more years (2004) to win their next championship.

12) The first president born in the 20th century, John F. Kennedy (No. 35), is born, along with great singer Ella Fitzgerald.

13) The Red Cross receives the Nobel Peace Prize. *Many Band-Aids were used in the Great War.*

1918

1) In a speech to US Congress, President Woodrow Wilson outlines peace negotiations—***the 14 Points***. *Some sports lovers think that he's talking about football.*

2) Moscow becomes the new capital of the Soviet Union. Saint Petersburg had been the capital since 1712.

3) T.E. Lawrence, aka Lawrence of Arabia, leads British and Arab forces in capturing Damascus from the Turks. *Peter O'Toole, star of the 1962 movie, is triumphant.*

4) New York City's worst subway accident kills 92 commuters.

5) Women in the United Kingdom get voting rights. The Royal Air Force (RAF) is founded.

6) Kaiser Wilhelm II of Germany abdicates and flees to the Netherlands, where he hides out for 23 years.

7) Iceland gains its independence from Denmark.

8) The USS *Cyclops* disappears in the Bermuda Triangle—also known as the Devil's Triangle—with 306 people on board. Many planes and boats strangely disappear in this region over the years. *It must be the aliens, playing games.*

9) One million horses are killed in Europe during the Great War.

10) In the entertainment world, notables are Irving Berlin, Eddie Cantor, Enrico Caruso, W.C. Handy, and Charlie Chaplin as the Little Tramp.

11) Russia transitions from the Julian to the Gregorian calendar. *The day after January 31 is February 14, so a child born in Russia between February 1–February 13, 1918, never really exists.*

1919

1) A storage tank filled with 2 million gallons of molasses ruptures in Boston, and a tsunami races through the streets in **the Great Molasses Flood** that kills 21 and injures 150.

2) The 18th and 19th Amendments are ratified, prohibiting intoxicating liquor and giving women the right to vote, respectively.

3) The Grand Canyon National Park is created in Arizona, one of the new Seven Wonders of the World.

4) The White Russians battle the Red Russians (Bolsheviks), *then pause and drink Black Russians.*

5) Race riots occur in 26 American cities. The riot in Chicago is the most terrifying, stemming from social and economic changes resulting from WWI.

6) Romania officially annexes Transylvania. *Count Dracula and his vampire friends all wake up.*

7) The United States adopts Daylight Savings Time, with many opposing and many supporting the action.

8) A notorious gambler, Arnold Rothstein bribes eight Chicago

White Sox players to throw the World Series of 1919 in the infamous **Black Sox Scandal.**

9) Twenty-eight nations sign the Treaty of Versailles but the US Senate does not ratify the treaty, and the country does not join the League of Nations because of isolationists in Congress. Some say that the Treaty of Versailles is the real cause of World War II.

Deaths This Decade of Notable People

- Florence Nightingale, 90. English founder of modern nursing.
- Mark Twain, 74. American author of *Tom Sawyer* and *Huckleberry Finn*. He said, "It is better to keep your mouth closed and let people think you are a fool than to open it and remove all doubt," as well as, "Reports of my death have been greatly exaggerated."
- Harriet Tubman, 90. African American abolitionist who founded the underground Railroad.
- J. P. Morgan, 75. Financier—America's greatest banker.
- Theodore Roosevelt, 60. Twenty-sixth US president. 1901-1909.
- Pierre-Auguste Renoir, 78. French painter who developed impressionism.
- Booker T. Washington, 59. African American educator, author, and civil rights leader. "I have learned that success is to be measured not so much by the position that one has reached in life as by the obstacles which one has overcome while trying to succeed."
- Franz Joseph I, 86. Emperor of Austria and king of Hungary.
- Andrew Carnegie, 83. American industrialist and philanthropist.

- William Frederick "Buffalo Bill" Cody, 70. American soldier and showman.

Advances in Science This Decade

Alzheimer's disease is named — The supercontinent Pangaea is formulated — The ozone layer is discovered — The concept of cholesterol is revealed — Ernest Rutherford discovers the proton — Blood transfusions are used for the first time — Margaret Sanger opens the first birth control clinic in Brooklyn, New York — Albert Schweitzer sets up a hospital in Africa — The planet Pluto is photographed for the first time (*Mickey Mouse is so happy*) — And sadly, Martha, the last passenger pigeon, dies

Important Innovations of the 1910s

Assembly line – Stainless steel – Dial telephone from AT&T – Pop-up toaster – Jukebox – zipper – Life Savers candy – Sunglasses – Maybelline mascara – Backless bra (*the most important*)

In 1910, the population of the world was 1.7 billion people. The United States's population was 92 million people. The average life expectancy of Americans was 51 years.

The decade of the 1910s finally came to an end. With so many wars and so many deaths and so much illness, our country and the world now looked forward to the next decade, which hopefully would be peaceful. But who could know that the 1920s would be planting the seeds for the horrors that would lie ahead for the world?

3

1920–1929

THE PEACE BETWEEN THE WARS

T he decade of the 1920s was the decade of healing from World War I. The war was finally over, and *peace had broken out!*

Nicknamed **the Roaring Twenties**, **the Jazz Age** (named by F. Scott Fitzgerald) or **the Golden Age**, this 10-year period was one of the most benign decades of the 20th century. This was the era of art deco, flappers, radio, the telephone, movies, sports heroes, movie stars—all good things. But unfortunately, all good things come to an end, as the decades that followed proved this point all too well.

Regarding threats to the country, there were three direct ones during this decade. There was one indirect threat, and this was **the mother of all threats**.

The first direct threat appeared just as the decade was ending—in October 1929. This was the Wall Street crash that started the Great Depression.

The second threat was the rise of organized crime in the United States. This came about as a result of the 18th Amendment, aka Prohibition.

The third threat was the horrific race riot in Tulsa, Oklahoma.

The indirect threat was the birth of the Fascists, the Communists, and the Nazis—**the rise of dictatorships**. The world would never be the same!

Presidential Elections of the 1920s

In the 1920 US presidential election, Republican Warren Harding, the Ohio senator, and Massachusetts Governor Calvin Coolidge decisively defeated Ohio Democratic Governor James Cox and Assistant Secretary of the Navy Franklin D. Roosevelt. The Republican platform called for "a return to normalcy." Interestingly enough, *Eugene V. Debs, the Socialist Party candidate, received 900,000 votes—but he was in prison at the time. Was that normalcy?*

Mr. Harding, the 29th president, said, "I don't know much about Americanism, but it's a damn good word with which to carry an election."

Harding died in 1923, and Vice President Coolidge assumed the presidency. An unbelievable Coolidge quote: *"When a great many people are unable to find work, unemployment results."*

Coolidge refused to use the telephone. He was an introvert and dubbed with the nickname Silent Cal.

In the 1924 election, Coolidge and running mate Charles G. Dawes, a diplomat from Illinois, easily defeated the Democratic dark-horse candidates—unknown corporate lawyer John W. Davis and Charles W. Bryan of Nebraska, brother of William Jennings Bryan. This was a brokered convention that lasted only 16 days, and on the 103rd ballot, with the conventioneers tired and hungry, they unfortunately chose the compromise candidate, Mr. Davis. *The Bryan brothers (who were not the tennis players Mike and Bob)* had a penchant for losing national elections: four in total.

For trivia fans, Vice President Dawes was a pianist and composer. In 1912, he wrote the music for the song that ultimately became the No. 1 hit of 1958, "It's All in the Game," sung by Tommy Edwards. Bet you didn't know that.

In 1928, the secretary of commerce, Republican Herbert Hoover of

California, along with Charles Curtis of Kansas, defeated the Democratic governor of New York, Alfred E. Smith, and Arkansas senator Joseph T. Robinson in a landslide. Smith was the first Catholic to run for president, paving the way for two future Catholic presidents—John F. Kennedy and Joe Biden.

Mr. Hoover promised the country "a chicken in every pot and a car in every garage." By the end of his four-year term in 1932, most Americans did not even own a pot to put a chicken in!

Wall Street Crash

Black Tuesday, October 29, 1929, followed Black Monday, which followed Black Thursday. *The stock market fell off a cliff, as did many investors and their brokers.* In wild panic selling that fateful Monday and Tuesday, the market **dropped 23%**, creating the largest financial crisis of the 20th century.

What happened? There was a huge amount of speculation, and many investors, both sophisticated and unsophisticated, believed that the market would rise forever. They had never heard of Sir Isaac Newton and his theory that hat goes up must come down. A person could buy stock on margin, putting up only 10%, with the margin rate at 90%. Investors were inundated with margin calls that resulted in panic selling. There were runs on the banks, which ultimately caused many banks to fail. The Financial Press exasperated the market crash, panicking many investors.

On October 14, 1929, *The New York Times* reported, (two weeks before Black Tuesday):

"Secretary Lamont and officials of the Commerce Department today **denied rumors** that a severe depression in business and industrial activity was impending, which had been based on a mistaken interpretation of a review of industrial and credit conditions issued earlier in the day by the Federal Reserve Board." *I think Mr. Lamont should not have a career as a fortuneteller!* The show-business newspaper *Variety* got it right with their famous headline: **"Wall Street Lays An Egg."**

Black Tuesday became the beginning of the Great Depression that would last worldwide for 12 years. The Roaring Twenties were now officially over!

Organized Crime

Organized crime burst on the scene in the 1920s because of the 18th Amendment, which the US Congress ratified in 1919. The amendment called for the prohibition of intoxicating liquors—meaning the production, transportation, and sale of alcohol was banned. However, **drinking** alcohol was not forbidden, and speakeasies flourished throughout the nation. These intoxicating liquors were smuggled into the country from Canada, Mexico, and Europe, although *poor-quality homemade booze (aka bathtub gin)* resulted in severe alcohol poisoning of many people.

Gangsters realized the potential of the outlawed booze business, and they quickly became very much involved in bootlegging by supplying thirsty citizens with their cocktails. The mob made so much money that they hired staffs of lawyers and accountants to launder their ill-gotten gains. Supposedly, they made over $100 million each year, equivalent to about $1.4 billion in today's dollars.

Chicago's Al Capone was the No. 1 man in this illegal business. He uttered these famous words: *"You can get much farther with a kind word and a gun than you can with a kind word alone."*

Some of his infamous mob pals were Lucky Luciano, Bugsy Siegel, Meyer Lansky, and baseball's immortal fixer, Arnold Rothstein. Mob violence gunned down hundreds of people during the 1920s. The Chicago Saint Valentine's Day Massacre in 1929, supposedly organized by Mr. Capone, saw many of his rivals machine-gunned to death. *And without even a Valentine's Day card!*

In the 1920s, the dictatorship in Italy cracked down on the Mafia, and many Mafia gentlemen left Sicily for New York City to do their business. There were many power struggles and countless killings between the underworld families in the large cities of the United States. The FBI became very active in combating organized crime. J. Edgar Hoover became the director of the FBI in 1924 and remained in that position until 1972. Mr. Hoover once said, "The thousands of criminals I have seen in 40 years of law enforcement have had one thing in common: every single one was a liar."

Finally, in 1933, the 21st Amendment repealed the 18th Amendment, which ended Prohibition, but unfortunately did not end organized crime. Now after 14 dry years, thirsty citizens were entitled to legally imbibe. *Inebriated America was happy once again!*

The Tulsa Massacre

In Tulsa, Oklahoma, the Greenwood District, which was known as Black Wall Street, was the wealthiest Black community in the country. On May 31, 1921, mobs of Whites, many of them Ku Klux Klan members, went on a rampage, attacking Black residents and businesses. This single worst incident of racial violence in American history left 39 people dead and 800 hospitalized. The commercial section of Greenwood was totally destroyed, as were schools and churches. No one was convicted of a crime, and decades of silence surrounded this massacre. How sad!

Dictatorships

Now for the big one! The 1920s witnessed the birth of the **"Isms"**—Fascism, Nazism, and Communism. Each left an indelible, horrible stain on the 20th century.

Mussolini-Hitler-Stalin. *No, this was not the double-play combination of the New York Yankees,* but rather three dictators who brutally ruled their nations with an iron fist. They murdered millions of people, including their own citizens, and ultimately destroyed their countries.

ITALY

Born in 1883, Benito Mussolini was active in Italian Socialist politics as a young man and became the editor of a Socialist party newspaper. As a young Marxist, he served in the Italian army in the Great War, where he experienced a radical political transformation. He became enthralled with the new, right-wing National Fascist Party (whose symbol was the ax) and was expelled from the left-wing Socialist party. *He realized that he could not dance at two weddings at the same time!*

Mussolini quickly became the leader of the new party and was soon elected to the Chamber of Deputies. The frightened Italian king, Victor Emmanuel III, named him prime minister in 1922, and he built a police state using extensive propaganda. In 1925, Il Duce (which means "the Leader") was declared the dictator of Italy and cracked down on Italian Socialists and Communists who were once his old friends. He wanted to build a new Roman Empire and coined the phrase ***"Make Italy great again."*** *Does this sound familiar? It was rumored that his red helmets had* **MIGA** *painted on them.*

He shouted, "Fascism is a religion. The 20th century will be known in history as 'the century of Fascism.'" His view of freedom was, "What is freedom? There is no such thing as absolute freedom."

In 1929, Pope Pius XI decided to support the dictator, and both leaders signed the Lateran Treaty so that Vatican City could become a sovereign state.

Il Duce and his Blackshirts had a great influence on Der Führer, Adolf Hitler, and his Brownshirts in Germany. *The French and English wore white shirts and were not invited to the party.*

GERMANY

Adolf Hitler, *unfortunately*, was born in 1889, not in Germany, but in Austria-Hungary. As a homeless young man in Vienna, he joined the German Army to fight in the Great War and was wounded.

Can you imagine what the world would have been like had he been killed!

He was a German Nationalist, horribly anti-Semitic, and joined the German Workers Party, where he became the head of propaganda. He changed the name of the party to the National Socialist German Workers Party, or **Nazi**. He designed the Nazi symbol, **the swastika**, and in his vitriolic speeches, condemned the Marxists and the Jews. His speeches, which preached of a Jewish conspiracy to destroy Germany, drew very large crowds. Hitler said: "If you tell a big enough lie and tell it frequently enough, it will be believed."

Economically, Germany was in a very bad way in the early 1920s, stemming from the huge reparations it had to pay as a result of the Treaty of Versailles. In 1923, the Beer Hall Putsch, an attempted coup of the government, occurred. The coup failed, and Hitler was arrested for high treason, serving one year in prison. While behind bars, he wrote and published a book, *Mein Kampf* (My Struggle), which preached the extermination of the Jews. By 1929, the Nazi party had gained recognition and much credibility. Hitler stated, "It is not truth that matters, but victory."

By the end of the decade, Hitler had gained the confidence of the beleaguered German people and had given them hope for the future. Too bad for the rest of the world!

THE SOVIET UNION

Joseph Stalin, the Man of Steel, was born in 1878 in Georgia. *No, not near Atlanta, but closer to Moscow.* As a poor young man, he joined the Marxist Party and became the editor of *Pravda*, the party's newspaper. He raised money for Vladimir Lenin's Bolshevik party through robberies and kidnappings. He was arrested many times and exiled to Siberia. Once he returned, Stalin, along with Lenin and Leon Trotsky, helped organize the Russian Revolution of 1917.

As a military leader, Stalin fought in the Russian Civil War against the White Russians. Lenin, who died in 1924, greatly disliked Stalin, but by 1927, Uncle Joe was in control of the government. He said, "The only real power comes out of a long rifle."

In 1928, Stalin started an economical plan for his country—the Five-Year Plan. He wanted a modern, industrialized nation and started many construction projects, using forced labor. His collectivization, or farmland aggregation, caused massive famines, killing millions. By 1929, he was the dictator of the renamed Union of Soviet Socialist Republics—the USSR, or the Soviet Union. His famous quote was, "The death of one man is a tragedy, the death of millions is a statistic." Stalin was personally responsible for that statistic!

CHINA

Stalin's Asian Communist counterpart was Mao Zedong, known to his nearest and dearest as Mao Tse-tung. Mao, born in 1893 into a wealthy Chinese family, was married at age 13 to a 17-year-old. He was an intellectual who discovered Socialism in 1912 while teaching history. He joined the new Chinese Communist Party in 1921, soon becoming allied with Chiang Kai-shek. That alliance was short-lived, and in 1927, his Red Army began a long battle with Mr. Chiang, except from 1937–1945, when the two rivals joined forces and fought the invading Japanese. For so many years, Mao, as commander of the Red Army, lived and battled in the Chinese wilderness, until 1949, when China officially became a Communist country. Mao believed that the Chinese revolution was the key to world revolution that would overthrow Capitalism and Imperialism. A Mao quote is similar to Stalin's quote: "Political power grows out of the barrel of a gun."

Contrary to popular belief, Mao did not invent mayonnaise!

On a lighter note, there was a threat to the pitchers of the American League. That threat was Mr. George Herman Ruth.

In 1920, the Boston Red Sox made a trade that haunted them for only 86 years—*the Curse of the Bambino*—by trading Babe Ruth, then **the best pitcher** in baseball, to the New York Yankees. Baseball's first superstar, now as an outfielder, led the Yankees to seven American

League pennants and four World Series wins. Starting in 1920, the Babe hit 54 home runs, while his runner-up hit 19; in 1921, Ruth hit 59 home runs, while the runner-up managed to hit 24. In 1927, Ruth hit 60 home runs, which was the record for the next 34 years until Yankee Roger Maris hit 61. Some say the 1927 Yankees, nicknamed Murderers' Row, was baseball's greatest team.

Summing it up, Ruth hit **714** career home runs, along with a **.342** lifetime batting average, besides winning **94** games as a pitcher! No wonder he was nicknamed the Sultan of Swat. He said, "Yesterday's home runs don't win today's game."

A great Ruth story: In late 1929, while negotiating a new contract, it was pointed out that the Babe was making more money than President Herbert Hoover. Ruth is said to have bellowed, *"What the hell has Hoover got to do with this? Anyway, I had a better year than he did!"*

Wars and Treaties of the 1920s

There were no catastrophic wars this decade, only 37 minor wars. *However, a bullet to the butt in a nonmajor war can be just as painful or lethal as a bullet to the butt in a major war.* The Russian Civil War, uprisings in China, and the Caco Revolt were among the conflicts of the 1920s. *Anybody know what a caco is?*

Most of the treaties signed this decade dealt with the Great War. The treaties of Trianon, Sèvres, and Saint-Germain effectively ended the Ottoman Empire. The Treaty of Lausanne concerned Turkey, while the Treaty of Locarno discussed European borders. The Five-Power Naval-Limitation Treaty was related to the world's navies, while the Nine-Power Treaty covered the Chinese sovereignty situation.

Important and Unimportant News of the 1920s

1920

1) The Mexican Revolution finally ends after ten 10 years of battle. Pancho Villa's slogan was, "Land and liberty."

2) The British Mandate establishes **Palestine**, the area previously ruled by the Ottomans and now to be controlled by Great Britain.

3) Armenia joins the Soviet Union, which becomes the first country to legalize abortion.

4) The League of Nations is founded.

5) US Attorney General A. Mitchell Palmer targets Communists and radicals. There is a big overreaction, and thousands are arrested.

6) The first commercial radio stations in Detroit and Pittsburgh broadcast election results.

7) The 19th Amendment becomes law, giving women the right to vote. The League of Women Voters is established.

8) The housing boom that resulted from the Great War becomes a bubble, which pops in 1926.

9) George Polley, known as the Human Fly, attempts to climb the Woolworth Building in New York City, *but is arrested when he reaches the 30th floor of the skyscraper. Why didn't he use the elevator?*

10) The National Football League (NFL) is founded, with 14 teams. Only the Chicago Bears and the Cardinals remain as original teams. The Galloping Ghost, Red Grange, stars in college and is the first great professional in the NFL.

11) Thomas Edison claims that he has invented a phone that can contact the spirit world. Then, in a local cemetery, he says he was only joking.

12) Explosives on a horse-drawn wagon explode on Wall Street in Downtown New York City, killing/injuring hundreds. *But what about the horse?*

13) Ray Chapman of the Cleveland Indians dies after a New York

Yankee fastball hits him in the head. Batting helmets are not mandated until 1970.

14) Judge Kenesaw Mountain Landis, a supposed racist, becomes the first commissioner of baseball. The position is created because of the Black Sox Scandal of 1919.

15) Former President William Howard Taft is appointed chief justice of the United States. *He goes from POTUS to SCOTUS—a first!*

1921

1) Hyperinflation ravages the Weimar Republic in Germany. It takes several years to stabilize the currency.

2) The Teapot Dome Scandal damages President Warren Harding's reputation. *Secretary of Interior Albert Fall takes the fall and is sent to jail.*

3) Russia invades *Georgia (not the Peach State),* and both then ultimately join the Soviet Union.

4) Outer Mongolia becomes independent from China. Inner Mongolia is an autonomous region of China.

5) Frederick Banting of Canada isolates insulin to treat diabetes.

6) The Emergency Quota Act limits the number of immigrants coming to the United States.

7) The United States and Germany sign the Treaty of Berlin, which officially ends the Great War.

8) Soon-to-be President Franklin D. Roosevelt, at age 39, is diagnosed with infantile paralysis, aka polio. "Men are not prisoners of fate, but only prisoners of their own minds."

9) The Tomb of the Unknown Soldier is established in Arlington National Cemetery in Virginia.

10) The first Miss America beauty pageant is held in Atlantic City, and the most beautiful is . . . Margaret Gorman of Washington, DC.

11) The country of Northern Ireland is established. Mesopotamia is renamed Iraq.

12) Coco Chanel creates CHANEL N°5. Women are ecstatic, and

so are men. Chanel said, "A woman who doesn't wear perfume has no future."

13) The largest civil uprising since the Civil War takes place, in West Virginia, when 10,000 coal miners battle 3,000 police. US troops were called in.

14) Eight Chicago White Sox star players are banned for life from MLB for accepting cash and purposely losing the 1919 World Series to the Cincinnati Reds. *A young fan said to White Sox star "Shoeless" Joe Jackson, "Say it ain't so, Joe."*

15) During a thunderstorm in Gibraltar, thousands of frogs fall from the sky. *Frog rain is not as serious as fish rain.*

1922

1) The Irish Civil War begins between the provisional government and the anti-treaty IRA forces.

2) Egypt declares its independence from the United Kingdom. At the same time, the tomb of King Tut is discovered. *King Tut has no comment on the independence.*

3) The Union of Soviet Socialist Republics (USSR) is established, with four original members. It ultimately expands to 15 countries (and then to none in 1991).

4) Mahatma Gandhi preaches nonviolence in India while searching for independence from the United Kingdom and is then imprisoned. "The weak can never forgive. Forgiveness is the attribute of the strong."

5) The United States establishes the World War Foreign Debt Commission to settle problems of allied war loans due from Germany.

6) If you are Australian, you may love Vegemite, which is created this year. If you are not Australian, you may hate Vegemite.

7) Rebecca Latimer Felton of Georgia, at age 87, is the first woman to serve in the US Senate, but only for one day. She is a White supremacist, favors lynching, and once owned slaves. *The KKK loves her.*

8) The hottest temperature ever recorded on Earth is 136 degrees Fahrenheit, in Libya. *The air-conditioner repair man is very busy that day.*

9) Pope Pius XI succeeds Pope Benedict XV.

10) The British Broadcasting Company (BBC) goes on the air in London.

11) America's first aircraft carrier, the USS *Langley*, launches; the Lincoln Memorial is dedicated in Washington, DC.

12) King George V officially opens Wimbledon's new tennis facility in London *and displays his powerful serve and awesome backhand.*

1923

1) An earthquake in Japan kills over 100,000 people. As a result of the massive earthquake, a "Firenado" was formed and kills 38,000 Japanese in 15 minutes.

2) Mickey Mouse and Minnie Mouse found the Walt Disney Company. Mr. Disney said, "If you can dream it, you can do it."

3) The Republic of Turkey is established, with Kemal Atatürk as its first president. Between martinis, he said, *"I have a reputation for drinking a lot. Indeed, I drink quite much."*

4) *TIME* magazine publishes its first issue. Its first Man of the Year Award, in 1927, goes to Charles Lindbergh.

5) Brooklyn, New York, biologist *Clarence Birdseye invents frozen food. Is that really his name?*

6) France and Belgium occupy the German Ruhr Valley. *Germany is not too happy with their visit.*

7) The distress signal Mayday is used for the first time. It comes from the French word *m'aider*—"help me."

8) Yankee Stadium, the House That Ruth Built, opens in the Bronx, New York. The Babe wins the first game, hitting a three-run home run.

9) The Ku Klux Klan conducts a racial massacre in Rosewood, Florida.

10) The tobacco companies encourage women to smoke by saying cigarettes are "the torches of freedom." *What nonsense!*

11) Warren Harding is the first US president to visit Canada. He plays golf in Vancouver, contracts pneumonia, and dies one week later. *He took the sudden death playoff in golf too seriously.*

12) The first electric refrigerator is sold in Sweden. *Its first sale should have been in Florida.*

1924

1) Native Americans become US citizens. Sadly, it only takes 300 years.

2) George Gershwin composes "Rhapsody in Blue," my personally favorite Gershwin piece.

3) The Immigration Act of 1924 restricts immigration from China, the Middle East, and southern Europe.

4) The first Macy's Thanksgiving Day Parade is held in New York City. *The Santa Claus balloon makes its debut. It is blown away and spotted flying over New Jersey.*

5) The Wrigley Building opens in Chicago, *constructed of bricks and chewing gum.*

6) Rogers Hornsby of the St. Louis Cardinals has a .424 batting average, the highest season average of the 20th century. He hits .400 three times and has a lifetime batting average of .358, second only to Ty Cobb's .366. *Not too shabby!*

7) Who was entertaining America? Buster Keaton, the Barrymores, Clara Bow, Tom Mix, Will Rogers, and Mary Pickford.

8) The Greek king, George II is deposed, and Greece becomes a republic.

9) Johnny Weissmuller wins three Olympic gold medals in swimming, jumps out of the pool, and stars in six *Tarzan* movies. *"Me Tarzan, you Jane."*

10) With the advent of the radio and Babe Ruth, baseball becomes the national pastime.

11) Two future presidents are born: George H.W. Bush and Jimmy Carter. Actor Marlon Brando makes his debut.

12) The Caesar salad is invented—*not by Julius Caesar*, but by Mexican chef Caesar Cardini.

13) Adolf Hitler is arrested for high treason, which is usually punished by execution. *The judge, a fan of Mr. Hitler, gives him clemency and says Hitler has "good intentions." The judge should be jailed.*

14) A Labrador retriever kills the Pennsylvania governor's cat. *The dog is given a life sentence—better than the electric chair.*

1925

1) In Tennessee, the Scopes Monkey Trial regarding evolution captures the public's fancy, but who won?

2) Chiang Kai-shek becomes Chinese leader upon the death of Sun Yat-sen.

3) *The New Yorker* magazine, containing funny cartoons, begins publication.

4) Forty thousand members of the Ku Klux Klan march in Washington, DC. *Laundromats in DC have a big day washing white sheets.*

5) The Soviet Union's secret police execute a British secret agent called the Ace of Spies.

6) Norway's capital, Christiania, changes its name to Oslo.

7) Sears, Roebuck—the catalog king—open their first store in Chicago.

8) Germany and the USSR sign trade agreements. The USSR has been secretly training German military. *A big mistake.*

9) New York City is the world's largest city. London had held the title since 1831.

10) Nellie Tayloe Ross of Wyoming takes office as the first female US governor.

11) F. Scott Fitzgerald publishes *The Great Gatsby*, five years after writing *This Side of Paradise*.

12) The Grand Ole Opry begins broadcasting in Nashville, *starring the Binkley Brothers' Dixie Clodhoppers—my favorite group.*

13) The world's first motel opens in San Luis Obispo, California. *The room rate is $1.25 per night. Is breakfast included?*

1926

1) Hirohito becomes the new emperor of Japan at age 25 and rules until 1989.

2) Dictatorships arise in Greece, Poland, and Portugal.

3) President Calvin Coolidge sends the US Marine Corps to Nicaragua to protect US interests.

4) Route 66 opens, from Chicago to Los Angeles. Nat "King" Cole sang "(Get Your kicks) On Route 66."

5) The first liquid fuel rocket is introduced, and the SAT, the college entrance exam is established.

6) The Great Miami Hurricane is the costliest American storm ever, killing hundreds and leaving thousands homeless.

7) The Slavery Convention in Geneva suppresses slavery and the slave trade. Currently, 99 countries have signed on.

8) Author Ernest Hemingway publishes *The Sun Also Rises*. Three years later, he writes *A Farewell to Arms*.

9) A busy year for famous births: Queen Elizabeth II, actress Marilyn Monroe, singer Tony Bennett, and Cuban leader Fidel Castro.

10) Millions of workers protest against poor working conditions and low pay during a nine-day General Strike in the United Kingdom.

11) American swimmer Gertrude Ederle, at age 20, becomes the first woman to swim across the English Channel, covering 21 miles in 14 hours. *When she dries off, she's given a ticker-tape parade.*

12) Swedish superstar Greta Garbo makes her American film debut. Her memorable quote was, "I want to be alone."

13) In boxing, Gene Tunney defeats Jack Dempsey, the world

heavyweight champion for seven years. *Dempsey said to his wife after the fight, "Honey, I forgot to duck."*

1927

1) Charles Lindbergh flies from New York to Paris, the first solo flight across the Atlantic Ocean. "I owned the world that hour as I rode over it, free of the earth, free of the mountains, free of the clouds."

2) An earthquake in China kills 200,000 people.

3) The first sound movie, the talkie, is released. Al Jolson stars in the epic film *The Jazz Singer*. The first Academy Award winner for best picture is *Wings*.

4) The Holland Tunnel opens, connecting New York and New Jersey. *Traffic update in five minutes.*

5) The Great Mississippi River Flood, the largest in US history, covers 27,000 square miles. It leaves 500 dead and 700,000 homeless.

6) The United Kingdom gives King Ibn Saud sovereignty over two kingdoms that are soon to become Saudi Arabia.

7) Italian immigrants Nicola Sacco and Bartolomeo Vanzetti are executed for murder. It's believed that because they are anarchists, they are not given a fair trial.

8) The worst school massacre in US history occurs in Michigan. A bomb hidden in a truck kills 44 people, mostly children.

9) Ford Motor Company discontinues **the Model T** auto. Now it is **the Model A**.

10) *Show Boat*, the first great, serious Broadway musical is produced. *"Ol' Man River" keeps on rolling along.*

11) Columbia Broadcasting System (CBS) is inaugurated, following the National Broadcasting Company (NBC), which launched the previous year.

12) The Peking Man is discovered in China. *The fossils estimated to be 400,000 years old. Some dispute this age and claim it to be only 390,000 years old.*

1928

1) Amelia Earhart, jealous of Charles Lindbergh, becomes **the first woman pilot** to cross the Atlantic Ocean.

2) The first transpacific flight takes place, from California to Australia, in only 83 hours. *How much is a coach ticket?*

3) The Kellogg-Briand Pact outlaws war. Fifteen nations sign it, including Germany, Japan, and Italy. *I guess it doesn't really work. People think it's a cereal commercial.*

4) Japan ends diplomatic relations with China. Trouble is brewing in Asia.

5) *Speaking of relations, the first home pregnancy test is introduced.*

6) George Gershwin does it again and composes "An American in Paris." Other important musicians of the decade include Louis Armstrong, Irving Berlin, Duke Ellington, Cole Porter, and Rudy Vallee.

7) A German dirigible flies across the Atlantic Ocean, from Germany to New Jersey. *It can't get through the Holland Tunnel.*

8) Sir Alexander Fleming of Scotland discovers the miracle drug penicillin.

9) The iron lung is developed for polio patients.

10) The St. Francis Dam in California bursts, causing a giant wave that kills 500.

11) The Muslim Brotherhood is established in Egypt. Several countries currently regard it as a terrorist organization.

12) *Buck Rogers* appears for the first time in the comic strips. Who knows what his first name is? If you said, "Anthony," you are right! Other comic strip successes this decade are *Little Orphan Annie, Winnie Winkle,* and *Gasoline Alley.*

13) *The best quote of the decade: Before being executed by the electric chair, George Appel's last words are, "Well folks, you'll soon see a baked Appel."*

1929

1) Yugoslavia is created, and its name is changed from **the Kingdom of Serbs, Croats, and Slovenes**. *New stationery is ordered.*

2) Communist leader Leon Trotsky is exiled from the Soviet Union and goes to Turkey.

3) Arabs attack and massacre hundreds of Jews in Jerusalem and other parts of Palestine.

4) The first public phone booth is introduced, in London. *Young people may ask, "What is a phone booth?"*

5) Many nations sign the Second Geneva Convention, which concerns the treatment of prisoners of war.

6) *Popeye the Sailor Man* makes his debut. *Now cans of spinach, his favorite food, are flying off the supermarket shelves.*

7) By the end of the decade, sadly, the infamous Ku Klux Klan has 5 million members.

8) Bill Tilden wins nine major tennis championships this decade, while Helen Wills Moody is victorious 10 times. In golf, Bobby Jones wins nine majors.

9) Civil rights leader Dr. Martin Luther King Jr. is born. So is memorable First Lady Jacqueline Kennedy Onassis, actress Audrey Hepburn, and Anne Frank, writer of the famous diary.

10) The soft drink 7UP is introduced. One of its ingredients is lithium citrate, which is used to treat mania and bipolar disorder.

11) The Museum of Modern Art (MoMA) opens in New York City. *Surrealism and art deco are the cat's meow.*

12) *In the first Academy Awards presentation, who has the most votes for best actor? Everybody's favorite dog—Rin Tin Tin.* But the academy says that a human has to be the winner. Emil Jannings gets the Oscar *and doesn't bark.*

13) Lambert Field in St. Louis is the first airport to have air traffic control. *The first controller sits in a beach chair, holding an umbrella and waving flags at the pilots.*

14) Leading scientific figures included Albert Einstein, Sigmund Freud, Niels Bohr, and Edwin Powell Hubble.

15) Trends of this decade included marathon dancing, mahjong, crossword puzzles, the Harlem Renaissance, and the Charleston.

Question: In what decade did the United States have the most presidents in office?

Answer: If you said, "The 1920s, with four presidents holding office," you are wrong! It is the 1840s and the 1880s, with five different presidents.

Deaths This Decade of Notable People

- Warren Harding, 57. Twenty-ninth US president. 1921-1923.
- Woodrow Wilson, 67. Twenty-eighth US president. 1913-1921
- Alexander Graham Bell, 75. Inventor of the telephone.
- Rudolph Valentino, 31. American silent-movie star.
- Claude Monet, 86. French impressionist painter.
- Enrico Caruso, 46. Most famous Italian opera singer.
- Vladimir Lenin, 53. First Soviet leader. "Liberty is precious —so precious that it must be rationed."
- Antonio Gaudí, 73. Spanish architect was the master of Catalan modernism.
- Pope Benedict XV, 67. Head of the Catholic Church from 1914–1922.
- Lothar Von Richthofen, 27. German World War I pilot known as the Red Baron.
- Pancho Villa, 45. Mexican revolutionary.
- Isadora Duncan, 50. American dancer and choreographer.
- Christy Mathewson, 45. New York Giants Hall of Fame pitcher.

- Annie Oakley, 66. American sharpshooter. *"You can't get a man with a gun."*

Advances in Science This Decade

Lie detector – Tuberculosis, diphtheria, and tetanus vaccines – Short-wave radio – Self-winding watch

Important Innovations of the 1920s

Hearing aid – Band-Aid – Magnetic tape – Foam rubber – Aerosol spray – Traffic light – Yo-yo – Short skirt – *Reader's Digest* – Portable radio – Bubble gum – Cordless telephone – Talking movies – Hair dryer – Air mail – Wheaties, the Breakfast of Champions

---

IN 1920, the population of the world was 1.8 billion people. The United States's population was 106 million people. The average life expectancy of Americans was 53 years.

The Roaring Twenties were finished! "Happy days are here again" now segues into "Brother, can you spare a dime?" The **good** times of the 1920s will morph into the **bad** times of the 1930s!

4

1930–1939
"PEACE IN OUR TIME": YOU GOTTA BE KIDDING!

To the world, the decade of the 1930s was probably the most threatening 10-year period of the 20th century!

There were threats galore! The worst economic depression, with historic unemployment, ravaged our nation, along with the rest of the world. A madman dictator terrorized his own country as well as the rest of Europe. An Asian empire was on the warpath and about to violently conquer Southeast Asia. Il Duce was aggressively leading his followers into a catastrophe. Fascist rebels won a civil war over a Republican democracy. The leader of the Soviet Union was purging and killing everyone in sight. Anti-Semitism in the United States reared its very ugly head when a luxury ship with 900 Jewish refugees was denied entry into our nonwelcoming country. Small wars and assassinations were occurring worldwide. Finally, in the closing days of the decade, **the big one**—World War II began. *Now for the bad news!*

Presidential Elections of the 1930s

In 1932, Franklin D. Roosevelt, Democratic governor of New York State, along with Senator John Nance Garner of Texas, defeated incumbent Republican President Herbert Hoover and Vice President Charles Curtis (the only Native American elected to the White House) in a landslide. *Evidently, Hoover's pot had run out of chicken!*

At his inauguration, Roosevelt famously said, "The only thing we have to fear is fear itself."

Another landslide victory occurred in 1936 when Roosevelt and Garner defeated Republican Kansas Governor Alf Landon and Frank Knox of Illinois. FDR received 523 (98.5%) electoral votes, the most one-sided election since 1820. *Mr. Garner wisely said, "The vice presidency isn't worth a warm bucket of spit."*

The Great Depression

As we now know, the stock market crash in 1929 was the catalyst for the Great Depression. *It has been said that there is a big difference between a recession and a depression. When your brother-in-law loses his job, that's a recession. When you lose your job, that's a depression!*

The numbers related to this awful period were staggering—US unemployment rose to **25%**, world trade fell by 33%, and world gross domestic product fell by 15%. In 1930, Hoover stated, "While the crash only took place six months ago, I am convinced we have now passed the worst."

Boy, was he ever wrong! Severe drought, extreme poverty, and the Dust Bowl ravaged the agricultural heartland of the country. There was a large-scale loss of confidence that was partially blamed on the Federal Reserve System, which sat idly by while many banks failed.

Our new President Roosevelt saw the recovery start in 1933. He introduced **the New Deal**, the Civilian Conservation Corps, and the Tennessee Valley Authority. All were meant to relieve unemployment and ultimately succeeded.

John D. Rockefeller shrewdly said, "These are days when many are discouraged. In the 93 years of my life, depressions have come and gone. Prosperity has always returned and will again."

Mr. Rockefeller was right on the money!

Hitler's Nazi Germany

If evil ever had a name, that name would be Adolf Hitler! No one in history was as malevolent as this tyrannical dictator.

In the early 1930s, Germany was struggling economically. The worldwide Great Depression created huge unemployment for the German people. The country was in dire need of a person or an organization to lift them from this morass. Unfortunately, it chose Hitler and his Nazi party to do the heavy lifting, and soon, this once cultured nation was transformed into a totalitarian state. Hitler proclaimed, "The very first essential for success is a perpetually constant and regular employment of violence."

The 1930 election resulted in the Nazis becoming the second-largest party in Germany; by 1932, it had become the No. 1 party. In 1933, President Paul von Hindenburg appointed Hitler chancellor of the country. Just weeks later, the Reichstag, Germany's Parliament building, was set on fire, probably by a Nazi arsonist. The government then passed a law that made Hitler the dictator of Germany, nullifying many civil liberties.

Very soon thereafter, Der Führer rolled up his brown shirtsleeves and got to work. He established the State Secret Police (SS), the Gestapo; trade unions were outlawed; and all non-Nazi parties were banned. Dachau, Germany's first concentration camp, was established and soon filled with certain Jews, the homeless, alcoholics, and other "undesirables." As a prelude to what was coming, Germans were told to boycott Jewish-owned businesses.

Within the Nazi party, Hitler eliminated his potential rivals in an event called the Night of the Long Knives. *This event was not held in a German steakhouse.*

Some quotes from Hitler's cronies, who all rose to the top of the Nazi hierarchy:Propaganda Minister Joseph Goebbels: "If we are attacked, we can only defend our selves with guns, not with butter."

Commander-in-chief of the Luftwaffe Hermann Göering: "Shoot first and ask questions later."

Head of the SS Heinrich Himmler: "Cruelty commands respect."

The Wehrmacht, Germany's army, swore a personal oath of loyalty to Hitler rather than to the German Constitution. Parliament passed the Nuremberg Laws, which allowed for the persecution of Jews. All German boys ages 10–18 were forced to join Hitler Youth, which was not like the Boy Scouts of America. Hitler said, "He alone, who owns the youth, gains the future."

Germany began a huge military buildup, disregarding the provisions of the hated Treaty of Versailles. In 1936, Germany invaded the Rhineland, which was occupied by France—and the world did nothing but watch. Germany and Japan signed a treaty that said that if the USSR attacked either country, the other country would go to war with the Soviets.

Hitler was humiliated in 1936 at the Summer Olympics held in Berlin. A Black American athlete, Jesse Owens, won four gold medals to the dismay of the dictator who preached the theory of Aryan racial superiority. Owens was definitely not an Aryan, nor a member of Hitler's "master race."

In 1938, Hitler's army marched into Austria and annexed that country in what was called the Anschluss. Austria then became part of the Third Reich. Another dark day for Europe also occurred that year with the signing of the Munich Pact. British Prime Minister Neville Chamberlain agreed to allow Germany to annex Czechoslovakia, saying, **"I believe it is peace in our time."** *I think that his cousin, basketball star* **Wilt Chamberlain***, could've done a better job and certainly would have scored more points.*

In November, German citizens went wild and destroyed Jewish shops and synagogues throughout the country. This horrific event was known as **Kristallnacht**, or the Night of the Broken Glass.

In late August 1939, Germany and the Soviet Union unbelievably signed a peace treaty that secretly allowed the Soviets to occupy Eastern Poland when and if Germany invaded from the west. A few days later, Germany did just that. World War II had started!

France and the United Kingdom, honoring their treaty obligations, soon declared war on Germany. The Soviet Union invaded Poland from the east, and Poland was no more. Soon most of Europe would be no more.

The Land of the Rising Sun

By 1930, the Empire of Japan had seen the military control the political structure of the country. Emperor Hirohito could not restrain his military government. Japan had few natural resources and had a great need for the resources of its Asian neighbors. They imported oil from the United States and rubber from British Malaya, and both resources were necessary for their military aspirations.

China, their huge neighbor, had abundant supplies of natural resources and became an easy target for Japan. In 1931, Japanese forces invaded Manchuria and quickly occupied the country. They set up a puppet government and changed the name to Manchukuo. Manchuria was strategically important for Japan in case of another war with the Soviet Union.

In southern China, Shanghai was attacked the following year. Japan, like several other countries, decided to leave the League of Nations. By 1936, the handwriting was on the wall about what was coming. Japan, along with Germany and Italy, signed an anti-Communist treaty.

The Second Sino-Japanese War began in 1937. (*The first war was fought in 1894, and some very old soldiers again put on their combat boots.*) Peking, the Chinese capital, was captured, along with Nanking. The ruthless Japanese murdered 200,000 civilians in a massacre that was called the Rape of Nanking. Mao Tse-tung and Chiang Kai-shek stopped their fighting and combined forces to battle the Japanese invaders.

When Hitler demanded that all Jews living in Japan, Manchuria, and China be expelled, Japan showed that they had a little bit of heart and said absolutely not. Their kindness disappeared on December 7, 1941.

Fascist Italy

By the early 1930s, worldwide depression had hit Italy very hard, with many bank failures. Dictator Benito Mussolini had other things on his mind, such as forming a new Roman Empire. The Italian strongman wanted to become the dominant power in the Mediterranean area and desired access to the Atlantic Ocean and the Indian Ocean.

In 1935, Italy invaded and conquered Ethiopia in the Second Italo-Abyssinian War. (War No. 1 was fought in 1895; the African team won.) The occupied territory was now called Italian East Africa, and King Victor Emmanuel III was proclaimed emperor. Il Duce wanted this colonial expansion for Italian prestige.

In violation of the Geneva Convention, Italy used poisonous mustard gas on the Ethiopians. For these actions, Italy was expelled from the League of Nations. At this time, Italy and Germany signed a treaty—the Rome-Berlin Axis.

Now with Il Duce buddy-buddy with Hitler, anti-Jewish laws were proclaimed in Italy, although Germany thought that they were too weak. Mussolini demanded the expulsion of all foreign Jews from Italy.

In 1939, Il Duce put on his marching boots and invaded and conquered the tiny country of Albania to add to his new Roman Empire.

The dictator said, "Democracy is beautiful in theory; in practice it is a fallacy."

The Italians loved Mussolini because he had done so much for the country in the 1920s and 1930s. But he made a tragic mistake for himself and for Italy—he allied himself with Nazi Germany. What a blunder!

The Spanish Civil War

Between 1936–1939, the Spanish Civil War took place. The Republicans (the Loyalists), who pledged their allegiance to the leftist Spanish government, fought against the rebel Nationalists. These insurgent, anti-Communist conservatives were led by Gen. Francisco Franco, who proclaimed, "We do not believe in government through the voting booth."

This was a war between Fascism and Communism, between dictatorship and democracy, and just a prelude to World War II. By 1939, the war was over. The Nationalists had won and remained in power for the next 36 years until Franco died.

This opening round of World War II was significant because European rivals aided both sides—the Nationalists by Nazi Germany and Fascist Italy, while the Loyalists were aided by the USSR and Mexico. (Mexico?) The United States, France, and the United Kingdom did not intervene in this conflict, but independent international brigades fought on the Republican side. Germany tested new weapons and also supplied munitions, soldiers, and air support. When the war was over, Franco executed thousands of his enemies.

Pablo Picasso painted *Guernica* in 1937, an anti-war piece that was probably his most famous. Ernest Hemingway wrote his classic novel *For Whom the Bell Tolls*, which was made into a great Gary Cooper movie.

Unfortunately, the world soon realized that the Spanish Civil War was just a dress rehearsal for the theatrics that were to come in Europe very, very soon.

The Great Purge of Russia

Joseph Stalin, dictator of the Soviet Union, was paranoid about counter-revolutionaries and enemies of his beloved country. Between 1936–1938, he decided to purge the Soviet Union of these people, and it is estimated that 1.2 million of his enemies were killed. Government officials, leaders of the Communist Party, affluent peasants, intellectuals, and leaders of the Red Army were targeted.

Anti-Semitism in America

Persecution of the Jews did not originate with Hitler. Anti-Semitism has been around since the Middle Ages in Europe, but in this country, it became more overt in the late 19th century. Over 2 million Jewish immigrants from Eastern Europe saw the Statue of Liberty for the first time. Many Americans felt that the newly arrived immigrants would deprive them of their jobs. Ultimately, the newspapers and magazines portrayed the Jews as money-grubbing Capitalists and/or Communists. *The publications just couldn't make up their minds about what they were.*

Henry Ford was not a lover of the Jews and proclaimed them responsible for World War I (*and the Penguin uprising in Antarctica*). He took the most despicable anti-Semitic book, *The Protocols of the Elders of Zion,* and placed this Russian book on the front seat of every Ford car that was purchased. Supposedly, he had 500,000 copies printed. *Jewish Americans were now driving Chevrolets.*

In the 1930s, anti-Semitism rose to a fevered pitch. American Jews were excluded from social, political, and economic life. They were blamed for the Great Depression and the threat of war in Europe. People called the New Deal policy by President "Rosenfeld" the "Jew Deal."

Father Charles Coughlin, a Catholic priest, had a weekly radio program that attracted 12 million listeners. He was virulently anti-Semitic and denounced the Jews, *blaming them for whatever was wrong in America, from bad weather to bad movies to the Red Sox losing.* Coughlin had nothing but glowing praise for Hitler and Mussolini. He actually said, "When we get through with the Jews in America, they'll think the treatment they received in Germany was nothing."

Certainly, not a nice guy and not a person to invite to a bar mitzvah!

The America First Committee, which included Charles Lindbergh, grew into a fanatic anti-Semitic organization. Lindbergh said, "Germany is undoubtedly the most powerful nation in the world in military aviation and her margin of leadership is increasing with each month that passes."

The German American Bund held parades in the late 1930s in New York City, where members actually wore Nazi uniforms and swastika armbands and carried Nazi flags. A 1939 rally at Madison Square Garden attracted 20,000 Jew-hating people.

By the late 1930s, hundreds of thousands of Jews attempted to leave Germany and emigrate to the United States. The quota of 21,000 immigrants had been established in 1924, and there was a great demand to increase this quota to allow these persecuted Jews entry into the country. Unfortunately, the opposition to increase the quota was greater, and nothing happened. Rumors of anti-Semitism within the US Congress, the US Department of State, and the Pentagon were quietly mentioned.

The low point of this situation occurred in 1939 regarding the SS *St. Louis*, a German cruise ship. The boat left Germany with 936 Jewish refugees aboard, all attempting to flee Nazi persecution by seeking asylum in the United States. The ship was denied entry into the United States and Cuba and waited for several days off the coast of Florida for Roosevelt's acceptance, but unfortunately, the needy passengers were not allowed to disembark. The *St. Louis* sailed back to Europe, and several countries agreed to take in some of the passengers. However, 255 of the original passengers perished in the Nazi death camps.

Mr. Hitler realized that since the United States would not take in the passengers, this gave him a green light for his plans for the Jewish Final Solution in the next decade.

Wars and Treaties of the 1930s

Besides the six horrific wars mentioned, there were 17 other wars fought during the decade, with casualties totaling hundreds of thousands.

There were many peace treaties, or war treaties, signed during the

1930s. Most of them were meaningless, such as the German-Soviet Union Nonaggression Pact and the German-Polish Nonaggression Pact.

Important and Unimportant News of the 1930s

1930

1) American Clyde Tombaugh discovers the planet Pluto. *Mickey Mouse is delighted to have a new friend.*

2) Haile Selassie becomes king of Abyssinia, which is soon to become Ethiopia.

3) Mahatma Gandhi starts a program of civil disobedience in India.

4) Constantinople has its name changed to Istanbul. (*"Why did Constantinople get the works, that's nobody's business but the Turks."*)

5) George Washington's sculptured head is unveiled at Mount Rushmore in Keystone, South Dakota.

6) A hurricane demolishes Santo Domingo, the capital of the Dominican Republic.

7) American tennis player Helen Wills Moody wins the first of eight major tournaments. British player Fred Perry also wins eight majors this decade.

Question: In tennis, what is the term **"love"** derived from?

Answer: The French word **"l' oeuf."** It means **"the egg,"** which looks like a zero. Everyone knows that.

8) Princess Margaret of the United Kingdom—who said, "My children are not royal; they just happen to have the queen for their aunt"— is born. So is financier Warren Buffett, who wisely said, "Rule No. 1: never lose money. Rule No. 2: never forget rule No. 1."

9) The US Government imposes new high tariffs on Canada. Does that sound familiar?

10) Two inventor brothers, the Galvins, create a car radio called a motorized victrola, shortened to Motorola.

11) Shantytowns, nicknamed Hoovervilles, spring up throughout the United States.

12) The German dirigible *Graf Zeppelin* sets up a transatlantic travel route from Germany to Brazil.

13) America's first supermarket, King Kullen, opens in Queens, New York. *Buy one, get one free?*

14) *An Iowa man sits on a flagpole for 51 straight days. Three questions: Why does he do it? How does he sleep? And how are the bathroom facilities?*

1931

1) "The Star-Spangled Banner" becomes the national anthem of the United States. *Play ball!*

2) Al Capone is sentenced to 11 years in prison for tax evasion. But before he goes, he sets up free soup kitchens, serving 120,000 meals. *What a nice man.*

3) Floods in China kill 2.5 million people.

4) New York has a big year with the opening of the Empire State Building and the George Washington Bridge.

5) Elijah Muhammad founds the Black Muslim Party.

6) *Dick Tracy* and his yellow raincoat appear for the first time in newspapers.

7) Nevada legalizes gambling. *There's a stampede at the blackjack table.*

8) It's a year of scary movies—*Frankenstein* and *Dracula* show their ugly faces. Two years later, *King Kong* swings from the top of the Empire State Building.

9) Great American poet Robert Frost wins the Pulitzer Prize for poetry. He does it again six years later. He once said, "By working faithfully eight hours a day, you may eventually get to be boss and work 12 hours a day."

10) A Swiss physicist ascends to 52,000 feet in a balloon. *Scientists at NASA think he is still circling the Earth.*

1932

1) A famine in the Soviet Union kills millions. *The government says they are just sick with flulike symptoms.*

2) Charles Lindbergh's baby is kidnapped in New Jersey and is soon found murdered.

3) Hattie W. Carraway of Arkansas becomes the first woman to serve a full term in the US Senate. *There's a rush to create a new bathroom.*

4) A British submarine sinks, killing 60 sailors.

5) A riot between Hindus and Muslims in Bombay (Mumbai) kills thousands.

6) Fifteen thousand World War I veterans—the Bonus Army—march on Washington, DC, demanding immediate bonus payments. *They get their money—four years later.*

7) The first federal gasoline tax is imposed: a penny a gallon!

8) Dust storms in the Midwest start the *Great Dust Bowl, which is not a football game.*

9) Iraq becomes an independent kingdom, as does Saudi Arabia.

10) The US Government seizes Al Capone's big Cadillac. President Franklin D. Roosevelt later uses it as a limousine. *Did the Secret Service ever look in the trunk?*

11) It was so cold this winter that Niagara Falls completely freezes. *Honeymooners have to stay indoors. They do not complain.*

12) Annual tuition at Yale University is $1,056. In 2020, it is $55,500.

13) Japanese insurgents plot to kill Charlie Chaplin to provoke a war with the United States, but he is not an American citizen. Why not choose Greta Garbo? Wrong again; she's a Swedish citizen.

14) Because of the Great Depression, attendance in at baseball games falls dramatically. The New York Yankees, led by Lou Gehrig, Babe Ruth, and, later, Joe DiMaggio, win the World Series five times this decade, while everyone listens to radio broadcasts of the games.

The lively ball is introduced, and everyone and their mother seem to bat over .300.

15) A German canoeist paddles his kayak from Germany to Australia between 1932–1939. He does not know that the war has begun, and he is sent to a prisoner of war camp in Australia without his kayak.

16) Radio City Music Hall opens in New York City. *Every Big Apple lady with shapely legs wants to be a Rockette.*

1933

1) An assassination attempt by Giuseppe Zangara is made on President Franklin D. Roosevelt in Miami. Chicago Mayor Anton Cermak is murdered instead.

2) Frances Perkins becomes *secretary of labor*, the first female in a US cabinet post. *Nothing to do with childbirth.*

3) "Gloomy Sunday," the Hungarian suicide song, is heard. Rumor has it that many people commit suicide after listening to this song.

4) Jewish protesters in New York City call for boycott of German goods in response to Nazi persecution of German Jews.

5) The 18th Amendment, Prohibition, is repealed. *Thirsty Americans can drink again.*

6) The Loch Ness Monster is allegedly seen. *This may have to do with Prohibition being abolished.*

7) Australia and Norway claim most of Antarctica. *Where can they buy earmuffs?*

8) The United States and the Soviet Union begin formal diplomatic relations.

9) US Supreme Court Justice Ruth Bader Ginsburg is born. She wisely said, "Fight for the things that you care about, but do it in a way that will lead others to join you."

10) Wiley Post, who is blind in one eye, becomes the first person to fly solo around the world—15,000 miles in seven days.

11) Lots of firsts: the first singing telegram, the first drive-in movie

(New Jersey), the first All-Star baseball game (Chicago), the first Krispy Kreme doughnut store (Tennessee), and the first radio broadcast of *The Lone Ranger*. "Hi-Yo, Silver! Away!"

12) President Franklin D. Roosevelt gives his first Fireside Chat on the radio, and the American public loves it.

13) Five-year-old Shirley Temple signs a seven-year movie contract, for $150 per week. *She signs with a red crayon.*

14) Albert Einstein moves from Germany to the United States to work at Princeton University. *He does not try out for the Princeton basketball team.*

1934

1) Winston Churchill warns British Parliament of the coming German air menace. He is so right.

2) The Dionne quintuplets, five identical girls, are born in Ontario. *Diaper service business is booming.*

3) President Franklin D. Roosevelt establishes the Export-Import Bank to encourage commerce. (*Or is it the Import-Export bank?*)

4) The Securities and Exchange Commission (SEC) and the Federal Deposit Insurance Corporation (FDIC) are established. No depositor has ever lost any insured funds as a result of a bank failure.

5) The largest pearl ever found weighs over 14 pounds. *The oyster has to be the largest oyster ever found.*

6) *Donald Duck makes his debut in a cartoon and does not wear pants. Actually, the word "duck" refers to the female of the species, so his real name should be Donald Drake. And Drake's Devil Dogs should be called Duck's Devil Dogs. Confused?*

7) Bank robbers Bonnie Parker and Clyde Barrow are shot to death in a police ambush. John Dillinger and "Baby Face" Nelson are also eliminated.

8) Dictatorships are established in Brazil and Bolivia.

9) The US Gold Reserve Act outlaws the private possession of

gold. Citizens must sell their gold to the US Department of the Treasury at $20 per ounce.

10) *Flash Gordon* appears for the first time in the comic strips, joining his pal *Buck Rogers.*

11) *The St. Louis Cardinals's Gashouse Gang pitcher "Dizzy" Dean wins 30 games, while his brother "Daffy" Dean wins 19 games. Another brother, "Dopey" Dean, doesn't like baseball but likes to play gin rummy.*

12) *The first laundromat opens in Texas. The owner is cleaning up!*

1935

1) President Franklin D. Roosevelt is busy: the Social Security Act becomes law, the Works Progress Administration (WPA) is created, and the National Labor Relations Act is formed.

2) Social Security sets the retirement age at 65; life expectancy is 61. In 2020, it is 79. That's why Social Security is in trouble.

3) Senator Huey Long of Louisiana makes the longest speech in US Senate history: 15 hours. He speaks 150,000 words. Three months later, he is assassinated. Any connection?

4) An earthquake in Pakistan kills 40,000, and one in India kills 60,000.

5) The Mayo Clinic establishes the first blood bank. Experiments begin on the artificial heart.

6) Jockey shorts are introduced. *Wedgies are invented.*

7) Persia officially changes its name to Iran. *Now there are Iranian cats and Iranian rugs.*

8) Alcoholics Anonymous is founded.

9) The Congress of Industrial Organizations (CIO) forms.

10) The youth loves swing music. The big bands of Benny Goodman, Count Basie, and Glenn Miller are big favorites.

11) Singer Elvis Presley is born, along with actress Julie Andrews, baseball great Sandy Koufax, and director Woody Allen, who famously said, *"Eighty percent of success in life is just showing up."*

12) An income tax of 79% is imposed on incomes exceeding $5 million. Only one person is affected—John D. Rockefeller.

13) The Moscow Metro opens. *Does Joseph Stalin get a free pass?*

1936

1) It's the year of three kings in Great Britain. George V dies and is succeeded by his son Edward VIII, who rules for 11 months. He abdicates the throne to marry "the woman I love," American divorcee Wallis Simpson. The new king is his brother George VI, who rules for 16 years.

2) *LIFE* magazine publishes its first issue.

3) The United States proclaims nonintervention in the Spanish Civil War.

4) The Arabs revolt in Palestine against the British in opposition to Jewish immigration.

5) A famine in West China kills 5 million people.

6) The National Baseball Hall of Fame opens in Cooperstown, New York. The first five players voted in are Walter Johnson, Christy Mathewson, Honus Wagner, Babe Ruth, and Ty Cobb.

7) The Hoover Dam opens in Nevada. *It has nothing to do with vacuum cleaners.*

8) King Farouk becomes ruler of Egypt at 16 years old. The 300-pound king is on the throne for 16 years. *It has to be a very sturdy throne.*

9) Bruno Richard Hauptmann, the kidnapper of Charles Lindbergh's baby is executed in New Jersey.

10) Margaret Mitchell publishes her only book, and it is a blockbuster—*Gone with the Wind.*

11) The Triborough Bridge in New York City opens. It is now called the Robert F. Kennedy Bridge *and only Democrats can use it.*

12) The Johnstown Flood in Pennsylvania is devastating, causing great damage and killing 25 people. Because of the flood, an 18% tax on alcohol is imposed in Pennsylvania that is still being paid today.

1 3) Senator John McCain is born, along with basketball superstar Wilt Chamberlain, who proclaimed, "Everybody pulls for David, nobody roots for Goliath."

1 4) The Great Stork Derby in Toronto ends. The event has women compete to see how many children they can have within a decade. *Four women win the prize for having nine children in* 1 0 *years. Do they have a contest for men?*

1937

1) The Irish Republican Army (IRA) unsuccessfully attempts to assassinate British King George VI.

2) Neville Chamberlain becomes prime minister of the United Kingdom. History shows that this is not a good choice.

3) The German zeppelin *Hindenburg* crashes in Lakehurst, New Jersey, killing 36. One guess whom Adolf Hitler blamed for the disaster.

4) Thanks to Joseph Stalin, because so many Soviet citizens have **disappeared** (*that's a funny word for it*), the 1 937 Moscow phonebook is canceled.

5) Amelia Earhart vanishes while attempting to be the first woman to fly around the world.

6) Joe Louis becomes the world heavyweight champion and holds the title for the next 1 2 years. He wins 29 consecutive fights, and his career record is 66–3.

7) British mathematician Alan Turing publishes a paper on computers. *Bill Gates and Steve Jobs must have read it.*

8) America gets to know Hollywood's biggest stars: Jean Harlow, Clark Gable, Katharine Hepburn, Bette Davis, Errol Flynn, and Shirley Temple.

9) The Soviet Union creates a research settlement on an ice drift in the Arctic Ocean. *It drifts away and is supposedly seen near Hawaii.*

1 0) The Golden Gate Bridge opens in California. Well across the

country, the Lincoln Tunnel opens, connecting New York and New Jersey.

11) John Steinbeck writes the great novel *Of Mice and Men*. Two years later, he publishes *The Grapes of Wrath*.

12) President Franklin D. Roosevelt has plans to enlarge (aka pack) the US Supreme Court but is met with disapproval. *The bathrooms would also have to be enlarged.*

13) The film *Snow White and the Seven Dwarfs* is a huge hit. *The original names for the Seven Dwarfs were Blick, Flick, Glick, Plick, Quee, Snick, and Whick. I'm sure you know that.*

14) Spam is introduced—not computer spam, but edible spam. *Computer spam tastes better!*

1938

1) At the Évian Conference in France, no European country will accept German Jewish refugees. Sadly, the United States will again take in only 27,000.

2) *Pilot Douglas "Wrong Way" Corrigan takes off from New York, flying to California. He makes a* **slight mistake** *and winds up in Ireland.*

3) Oil is discovered in Saudi Arabia. *The royal family becomes very, very rich.*

4) Benny Goodman & His Orchestra are the first jazz musicians to give concert at Carnegie Hall in New York City.

5) There's panic in the streets as Orson Welles broadcasts *War of the Worlds. People believe that the Martians are here, but aren't they?*

6) The Atomic Age begins, as nuclear fission is discovered in Germany. Thank goodness the Germans never used it.

7) Kate Smith, the First Lady of Radio, sings "God Bless America" for the first time. In later years, she sings it at NHL Philadelphia Flyers games.

8) A 450-ton meteorite explodes 12 miles above Earth. Small pieces land in Western Pennsylvania.

9) Cincinnati Reds pitcher Johnny Vander Meer sets a record that no one probably will ever surpass: he throws two consecutive no-hit games.

10) *Superman* makes his debut. His alter ego is Clark Kent, mild-mannered reporter for the *Daily Planet,* who changes his clothes in a phone booth. *What will he do now with no phone booths?*

11) The Great New England Hurricane devastates the Northeast, killing 700. Hurricanes aren't given names until 1950.

12) Byron "Whizzer" White of Pittsburgh leads the NFL in rushing in his rookie year. In later years, he rushes to Washington, DC, where he becomes a US Supreme Court justice.

13) American Don Budge wins the four tennis Grand Slams, all in one year.

14) In the Race of the Century, Seabiscuit defeats the favorite War Admiral in a two-horse race at Pimlico Race Course.

15) *TIME* magazine names Adolf Hitler Man of the Year. *Should have been Madman of the Year.*

1939

1) Albert Einstein tells President Franklin D. Roosevelt that an atomic bomb is feasible in the near future.

2) Pope Pius XII becomes the new pope. Many feel that in later years he is too silent regarding the Holocaust.

3) Amelia Earhart cannot be found and is declared officially dead.

4) Earthquakes kill 32,000 in Turkey and 30,000 in Chile.

5) Hollywood's Golden Year produces *Gone with the Wind, The Wizard of Oz, Wuthering Heights, Gunga Din,* and *Stagecoach.*

6) Faisal II becomes the king of Iraq at age 3. *Some feel he does not have enough experience and should have waited until age 4 to become king.*

7) The United Kingdom issues the White Paper restricting Jewish immigration to Palestine.

8) The first baseball game is televised. Not to be undone, football is also televised for the first time.

9) LaGuardia Airport opens in New York, named after its popular mayor, Fiorello La Guardia.

10) Swallowing live goldfish becomes a fad, especially at Ivy League schools. *It's called goldfish gulping, and business at local fish stores booms.*

11) African American singer Marian Anderson sings at Lincoln Memorial because the Daughters of the American Revolution refuse to let her perform, and sing to an integrated audience. As a result, First Lady Eleanor Roosevelt resigns from the DAR.

12) New York Yankee great Lou Gehrig gives his tearful farewell speech after his diagnosis of amyotrophic lateral sclerosis (ALS). "I might have had a tough break, but I have an awful lot to live for." Sadly, he dies two years later at age 37.

13) In the closing days of this horrific decade, Germany invades Poland and starts World War II.

Deaths This Decade of Notable People

- William Howard Taft, 72. Twenty-seventh US president. 1909-1913.
- Calvin Coolidge, 60. Thirtieth US president. 1923-1929.
- King George V, 70. British king from 1910–1936.
- Sigmund Freud, 83. Founder of psychoanalysis.
- Thomas Edison, 84. America's greatest inventor.
- John D. Rockefeller, 97. Wealthiest American of 20th century.
- Pope Pius XI, 81. Led the Catholic Church from 1922–1939.
- George Gershwin, 38. American composer of classical and popular music.

- Marie Curie, 66. First woman to win Nobel prize, winning in 1911 for chemistry.
- Rudyard Kipling, 70. English journalist and novelist.
- "Ma" Rainey, 53. American blues singer.
- James Naismith, 78. Invented the game of basketball.
- Clarence Darrow, 80. American lawyer who defended high-profile clients. *"When I was a boy I was told that anybody could become president. I'm beginning to believe it."*
- Oliver Wendell Holmes Jr., 93. US Supreme Court justice for 30 years.
- Will Rogers, 55. American humorist who famously said, "Don't squat with your spurs on."

Advances in Science This Decade

Jet engine – Richter scale – Electron microscope – High-speed photography – Synthetic rubber – Cyclotron – Blood bank – Yellow fever vaccine

Important Innovations of the 1930s

Scotch tape – Parking meter – Paperback book – Electric guitar – Sliced bread – Electric razor – Trampoline – Shopping cart – Zoom lens – Tape recorder – Canned beer – Teflon – Baby food – Cheeseburger – FM radio – Polarized sunglasses – Fiberglass – Chocolate chip cookie – Chair lift – Nighttime baseball – Stereophonic sound – Fluorescent light – Nylon – Zippo lighter – Photocopier – Monopoly – Tampon (*the most important to half the population*)

In 1930, the population of the world was 2 billion people. The United States's population was 122 million people. The average life expectancy of Americans was 60 years.

Just a thought: **what if**, in 1939, President Franklin D. Roosevelt had met with Hitler face to face? Would the future have changed? After all, in later years, President John F. Kennedy met with Soviet Premier Nikita Khrushchev, President Richard Nixon met with Mao Tse-tung, and President Ronald Reagan met with Soviet General Secretary Mikhail Gorbachev.

Hundreds of years ago, Chinese strategist Sun Tzu wrote *The Art of War*, which said, "Keep your friends close and your enemies closer." *I think that the world leaders in the late 1930s should have read his book instead of going to the movies to see The Wizard of Oz!*

5

1940–1949

ENEMIES BECOME FRIENDS; FRIENDS BECOME ENEMIES

"Whistle while you work, Hitler is a jerk, Mussolini is a meanie and blah, blah, blah."

This ditty, from the film *Snow White and the Seven Dwarfs,* was sung by every kid in Brooklyn, New York, in the early 1940s.

The six-year period from 1940–1945 was **the most violent period** of the 20th century. World War II was no longer a threat—it was **real**! Adolf Hitler had set the world on fire, but where were the planet's firemen to help extinguish the flames? The United States and the world fought a war on three continents, and six years later, 50 million people no longer existed. Amazingly, 3% of the planet's population was gone. And there were plenty of other threats!

The Holocaust, the most inhumane act ever conceived, ravaged Europe. The atomic bomb was created and dropped, devastating Japan. The most populated country in the world fought a civil war for 22 years, and the side ruled by a vicious dictator won the battle. The hot war finally ended, but the Cold War began and lasted for only 46 years.

In the early 1940s, Hitler's Nazi Germany and Japan's military government were America's supreme enemies. The Soviet Union and

China were our allies and good friends. But by the late 1940s, the tables had turned, and Germany and Japan were our new best friends, and the USSR and Communist China became the villains. *It sounds like the world was controlled by teenage girls!*

Presidential Elections of the 1940s

In 1940, Democratic President Franklin D. Roosevelt and Secretary of Agriculture Henry Wallace defeated in a landslide Republican Wendell Willkie, an unknown Midwestern businessman, along with Oregon senator Charles McNary. This was an unprecedented third term in office for Roosevelt.

Because of the war, the country did not want to make any political changes. In the 1944 election, Roosevelt and Missouri senator Harry S. Truman soundly defeated Republican New York Governor Thomas Dewey and Ohio Governor John Bricker. Roosevelt would now serve an unparalleled fourth term. The 22nd Amendment now limits the presidential term to two terms (eight years).

Sadly, in April 1945, Roosevelt suddenly passed away. The nation mourned. Vice President Truman barely knew FDR, having only met with him twice. Now he became the 33rd president of the United States.

After Roosevelt's death, there was no vice president for 3.5 years. There have been 18 times that the country has been without a vice president. The longest time the country didn't have a second-in-command was from 1841–1845. A little trivia—who was the president then? John Tyler. Everyone knows that.

In the 1948 election, Truman and Kentucky senator Alben Barkley (nicknamed the Veep) defeated Thomas Dewey (again) and California Governor Earl Warren. Mr. Warren later went on to become chief justice of the United States for 16 years. Truman, the last president without a college degree, famously said, "The buck stops here."

In one of the great goofs of all time, the *Chicago Tribune* published this headline in error: **"Dewey Defeats Truman."** *I don't think the editor-in-chief asked for a raise that week!*

World War II in Europe

The decade began quietly. The German-Soviet invasion and occupation of Poland went smoothly, although not for the Poles. For six months, the world waited apprehensively for more German aggression, but none came, and this period became known as the Phony War. But in the spring of 1940, all hell broke loose as Nazi Germany invaded and conquered Norway, Denmark, Belgium, the Netherlands, Luxembourg, and finally France. The blitzkrieg, or lightning war, destroyed the Maginot Line in France as the French were totally overrun in six weeks—*six weeks?* Monsieur Hitler laughed while visiting Paris for the first time as millions of Parisians cried. The British army assisted France, but the Germans quickly defeated them. Both armies retreated to Dunkirk in France and were about to be destroyed. An armada of British military and civilian boats rescued 400,000 soldiers in a crucial maneuver. Prime Minister Winston Churchill bravely said, "We shall never surrender."

For 57 consecutive nights, German planes bombed London, causing heavy English casualties and destruction of property. The Battle of Britain took place over this period in 1940, with the Royal Air Force unbelievably defeating the Luftwaffe. This was the first major turning point of the European war. Joseph Kennedy, the United States ambassador to Great Britain, infamously and **incorrectly** said, "Democracy is finished in England."

Other quick German conquests were Romania, Hungary, Bulgaria, Yugoslavia, and Greece. Other than Greece, the other four countries, along with Slovakia and Croatia, were induced by Germany to join the Axis powers.

In June 1941, Hitler suddenly broke his peace treaty with Joseph Stalin, and Operation Barbarossa—the invasion of the Soviet Union—

began, a huge and costly **mistake** for Germany. Germany's 3 million invaders were the largest army the world had ever seen.

At first, the war on the Eastern Front went very well for the Nazis. Then the Russian winter began. The Germans needed oil, *earmuffs,* and other supplies for the front lines, but were denied by the Russians on the outskirts of Moscow. Huge casualties occurred on both sides, and finally, the Germans retreated. The Soviets, now using young boys to fight, won the Battle of Stalingrad.

France was the largest country to be occupied by Nazi Germany. In 1940, the country was divided in two—Germany occupied Northern France, and Southern France was known as the Free Zone and governed by Marshal Pétain, a French World War I hero. He was a Nazi sympathizer, and his Vichy government was anti-Semitic, anti-Communist, and anti-British. The French militia, the Milice, swore allegiance to Hitler and were hated by the French. After the War, Pétain was found guilty of treason and sentenced to life imprisonment.

The Resistance started in 1940 and gained popularity, reaching its peak in 1944. The movement engaged in sabotage and helped the Allies liberate France. With the United States now actively fighting the war after the Pearl Harbor debacle, the Americans and British defeated the Germans and Italians in North Africa by 1943. Mr. Churchill prophetically said, "This is the end of the beginning."

In 1943, the Americans invaded the island of Sicily from North Africa and then invaded mainland Italy. With the tide now clearly turning in the war, 180,000 Allied forces crossed the English Channel and invaded Normandy in France on **D-Day, June 6, 1944**. The Battle of the Bulge was the last major German offensive of the war, with huge losses on both sides and neither really winning.

The Yalta Conference, held in the Soviet Union in February 1945, discussed the post-war division of Europe. The Big Three attended: FDR, Uncle Joe, and Mr. Churchill.

With the Soviets moving from the East and the Americans and English from the West, Germany was overtaken and surrendered in

May 1945. After almost six horrible years, it was **VE Day—the war in Europe was finally over**!

World War II in the Pacific

The quiet of a peaceful Sunday morning in Hawaii on December 7, 1941, was suddenly shattered when 360 Japanese planes attacked and destroyed the Pearl Harbor Naval Shipyard and Intermediate Maintenance Facility. This horrible raid by the Land of the Rising Sun killed 2,300 American servicemen. The United States declared war on Japan, and Roosevelt called the event **"a date that will live in infamy."**

However, a month before, the US ambassador to Japan warned Washington, DC, that an attack on Pearl Harbor was imminent. Unfortunately, this warning was ignored. Rumor had it that Roosevelt knew the attack was coming but did nothing because he wanted to go to war with Japan's ally, Germany. Bottom line, bringing America into the war proved to be a huge mistake for both of those countries.

Japan needed oil and other natural resources from Southeast Asia. Immediately, the Japanese invaded the Philippines, Guam, and Wake Island, territories of the United States and Malaya, Burma, Singapore, and Hong Kong belonging to the United Kingdom. The Dutch East Indies and their oil supply fell quickly to the Japanese. Gen. Douglas MacArthur retreated from the Philippines and famously said, "I shall return." He kept his promise and did so two and a half years later.

Question: What Asian country became an ally of Japan during the war?

Answer: Siam (Thailand)

For the first time in 128 years, a foreign power attacked North American soil when Japan bombed Alaska and invaded the Aleutian Islands. The turning point of the war in the Pacific took place in June 1942 when the United States won the Battle of Midway. Over the next three years, US forces, while incurring great casualties, retook Guadalcanal, the Philippines, Marshall Islands, Guam, Okinawa, Corregidor, and Iwo Jima. The conflict was almost over.

Truman, wanting to quickly end the war because of possible Soviet intervention, had a tough decision to make. He could order an American invasion onto mainland Japan, which would be very costly in terms of American lives. Or he could use a new, secret weapon that would devastate the enemy and lead to an immediate surrender. The weapon was used, and in September 1945, Japan formally surrendered. This was **VJ Day**, and after almost four years for America, **World War II was finally over**!

The Atomic Bomb

America's secret weapon was **the atomic bomb**. It is conceivably **the greatest threat** to mankind—ever!

In 1938, German scientists discovered the concept of nuclear fission, a new form of gigantic energy. The United States, fearing German development of this atomic energy for warfare, established the Manhattan Project in 1942 in Los Alamos, New Mexico, under the leadership of physicist J. Robert Oppenheimer.

By August 1945, the A-bomb was ready. Little Boy, bomb No. 1, exploded over Hiroshima, Japan, and killed 80,000, mostly civilians. Bomb No. 2, Fat Man, targeted Nagasaki, with 40,000 fatalities. Fortunately for Japan, there was **no** bomb No. 3, as they immediately surrendered to MacArthur.

By the late 1940s, the Soviet Union obtained blueprints for the bomb from a network of Russian spies. By 1949, the USSR successfully tested their first atomic weapon.

The A-bomb soon became obsolete, as the new weapon de jour was the **H-bomb** (the hydrogen bomb), *which made the A-bomb look like a mere firecracker*. Currently, besides the United States and Russia, seven other countries possess nuclear weapons—the United Kingdom, France, China, India, Pakistan, Israel, and North Korea. Hopefully, no one will ever press the button!

The Holocaust

The definition of Holocaust, or Shoah, is the destruction or slaughter of people on a mass scale. This was the manifestation of absolute evil. Hitler convinced the German people that they belonged to a master race, the Aryan race, that was superior to all others. He repeatedly stated that the Jews belonged to a race that was inferior to the Nazis. He said, "The great masses of the people will more easily fall victims to a big lie than to a small one."

Der Führer had two main goals: to conquer Europe and then spread Nazism to the rest of the world and to eliminate every Jewish person in Europe. Hitler's threat, sadly, was real and almost became reality. By the end of World War II, he had succeeded in killing 6 million Jews, two-thirds of the Jewish population of Europe. By Nazi definition, a Jew was a person with at least one Jewish grandparent. Mr. Hitler also was not particularly fond of Blacks, disabled people, homosexuals, Communists, and Gypsies. In 1942, the Wannsee Conference discussed the Final Solution, the mass murder of the entire European Jewish population.

In the large cities of Europe that the Nazis conquered, ghettos were established that the Jews now occupied under the harshest of conditions. The invading Nazis massacred thousands of Russian Jewish civilians. Resistance to the Nazi tyranny occurred in the Warsaw Ghetto Uprising in 1943. Almost 13,000 brave Polish Jews were killed in the four-month uprising that ended with the destruction of the ghetto in Warsaw, Poland.

Concentration camps—really, death camps—were established: Auschwitz, Majdanek, Treblinka. Jewish people of all ages from every conquered country were transported by train to the camps, where Zyklon B, a poison gas, was used to kill the prisoners, both young and old, and then the bodies were sent to ovens to be cremated. Nazi doctors carried out horrible medical experiments on the inmates. By 1944, even though the Germans knew that they would be defeated and the war would soon be over, stepped up their maniacal actions and killed 9,000 Jews **daily** at Auschwitz.

And what did the US Government do about these mass murders? **Nothing!** They did not attempt to rescue the prisoners or bomb the camps or the railways leading to the camps. American newspapers made little mention of these horrors. When the Russians and the Americans finally liberated the camps in 1945, the soldiers were shocked when they saw the condition of the survivors. Gen. Dwight D. Eisenhower, when he visited a camp, said, "The visual evidence of starvation, cruelty, and bestiality were so overpowering as to leave me a bit sick."

The Holocaust was the most inhumane act ever conceived by people in the history of the world.

The Cold War

The period of geopolitical tension that started at the end of World War II and lasted until the breakup of the USSR in 1991 was known as **the Cold War**. The United States and its allies went nose to nose with the Soviets and their beaten-down Neo-Communist friends. This was a very long-lasting threat.

Presidential advisor Bernard Baruch was credited with first using the phrase "Cold War" to describe American-Soviet relations. The USSR armies, moving westward into Germany in 1944 and 1945, marched through several European countries. They enjoyed the hospitality of these nations, and by war's end, the Soviets decided to stay. This Eastern Bloc consisted of Albania, Poland, Romania, Czechoslovakia, Bulgaria, Hungary, and East Germany.

The United States was very wary of Communism, and Truman did not trust Mr. Stalin and his goal of spreading Communism worldwide. The Soviets resented America's refusal to treat the USSR as part of the international community. Both sides played tit for tat—Stalin ordered the Berlin Blockade (tit), and Truman countered with the Berlin Airlift (tat). *Were the Russian tits bigger than the American tats?*

In 1949, **the North Atlantic Treaty Organization** (NATO) was founded to resist the Soviet presence in Europe. The United States and 11 other countries were the first members of the organization; currently, there are 30 members. To counter NATO, the Soviet Union and seven other followers soon established the Warsaw Pact.

Espionage was widespread in Europe. American operatives spied on Russian operatives and vice versa. There were spies, counterspies, and counter-counterspies. *Students in college were now majoring in espionage.*

Winston Churchill spoke of **the Iron Curtain**, the separation of Communist and non-Communist European lands. *Supposedly, he was rushed to the hospital with a hernia, created by his attempt to lift the curtain!*

The Chinese Civil War

An old joke about the situation in China:

"What do you think of Red China?"

"I think on a yellow tablecloth it will look great."

The Chinese Civil War was really not a joke. Starting in 1927, Mao Tse-tung and his Communist followers battled the Nationalists led by Chiang Kai-shek. From 1937–1945, the two opposing sides merged and fought side by side against the invading Japanese army. When World War II ended, the Communists and the Nationalists lined up again to battle each other. Finally, in 1949, after 22 years of almost constant battle, the Communists won, and the People's Republic of China was established. The Nationalists fled to the island of Formosa, now called Taiwan. The Chinese threat turned very real the next year in Korea. Chairman Mao said, "Politics is war without bloodshed while war is politics with bloodshed."

Today, no one jokes about the yellow tablecloth. *After all, it was probably made in China!*

Three April Deaths

For 30 years, the three most important political figures in the world were President Roosevelt of the United States, Der Führer Hitler of Germany, and Prime Minister Benito Mussolini of Italy. In a period of just 18 days in April 1945, all three men died.

On April 12, Roosevelt, age 63, died in Warm Springs, Georgia, of a cerebral hemorrhage.

On April 28, Mussolini, age 61, died in Northern Italy, at the hands of a firing squad.

On April 30, Hitler, age 56, died in Berlin, having committed suicide.

Ironically, none of these leaders were around to see the end of World War II, just days later, in May 1945.

The First - Jackie Robinson

Racial segregation was finally severely threatened in 1947 when Major League Baseball was integrated for the first time. Jackie Robinson of the Brooklyn Dodgers became the first African American to play in the major leagues. He opened the door for Black athletes to participate in all the major sports. Serena Williams, Willie Mays, Wilt Chamberlain, Arthur Ashe, Simone Biles, Jim Brown, Althea Gibson, Michael Jordan, Henry Aaron, Lebron James, Tiger Woods, and thousands of other African American athletes all owe a debt of gratitude to Robinson.

This author, an old Brooklyn Dodgers fan, saw Robinson play so many times—and No. 42 was terrific! He was the first in so many ways: he was Rookie of the Year in 1947; Most Valuable Player in 1949, leading the league in batting and stolen bases; a six-time All-Star; and was elected to the National Baseball Hall of Fame in 1962. *Truly, Jackie was the jack of all trades, and he was the master of all.*

Robinson said, "The most luxurious possession, the richest treasure anybody has, is his personal dignity."

Thurgood Marshall became the first African American justice of the US Supreme Court and Barack Obama became the first African American US president, but Robinson **was** the first!

Wars and Treaties of the 1940s

Besides World War II and the Chinese Civil War, 17 other wars, big and small, were fought this decade, all between 1945–1949. Battles were fought in Europe, Asia, and South and Central America. You would think that after the horrors of World War II, people would be tired of fighting.

Many treaties were signed in the 1940s. The first one signed at the beginning of the decade was the Tripartite Pact, which spelled out the mutual-assistance alliance among Germany, Italy, and Japan. Reading between the lines, it meant that when the Axis powers won the war, Japan would be given control of Eastern Asia, Italy would control the Mediterranean region, and Germany would control everything else in the world. *Wishful thinking!*

The most important agreement was the establishment of NATO and the signing of the United Nations Charter. Most of the treaties ended colonization and granted independence to several nations: the Philippines, Israel, and Transjordan. The charter of the Organization of American States was created, with 21 members.

The United States and Iceland signed a treaty in 1946, *I think dealing with ice!*

Important and Unimportant News of the 1940s

1940

1) The first peacetime draft in US history is signed into law. Sixteen million brave young men register.

2) In Japan, the Olympic Games are canceled because of the war.

3) The first McDonald's restaurant opens in California. *Is the Big Mac invented yet?*

4) In France, a Stone Age cave painting is discovered and is thought to be 17,000 years old, *give or take a few years.*

5) Nylon stockings make their debut; 5 million pairs are sold the first year. *Men are busy ogling ladies' legs.*

6) When the Nazis occupy Paris, French soldiers cut the cables to the Eiffel Tower's elevators. German soldiers use the stairs, and climb 1,000 feet, to hoist their swastika symbol.

7) Benjamin Davis is the first African American general in the US Army. Hattie McDaniel is the first African American to win an Academy Award. Booker T. Washington is the first African American depicted on a US postage stamp.

8) Leon Trotsky, a leader of the Soviet Revolution but not a close friend of Joseph Stalin, is assassinated in Mexico. The hatchet-man murderer is never arrested.

9) The Winter War takes place between the Soviet Union and Finland. It is over by springtime, and the Soviet army has performed poorly, incurring large losses.

10) Born this year are Speaker of the House of Representatives Nancy Pelosi, US Rep. John Lewis, actor Al Pacino, and golfer Jack Nicklaus.

11) Cartoon characters Tom and Jerry, Bugs Bunny, Woody Wood-pecker, and, lastly, Elmer Fudd, make their debuts.

12) It's a great decade for movies, starting with this year's *The Grapes of Wrath* and, to name just a few, *Citizen Kane, Casablanca, Going My Way,* and *The Best Years of Our Lives.*

13) In the NFL championship game, the Chicago Bears beat Washington, 73–0. *The game is not as close as the score indicates.*

14) *Scientists conclude that eating ice cream is the leading cause of the polio epidemic. They deduce that there are more cases of polio during the summer, when most ice cream is consumed. These brainy scientists did not win the Nobel Prize.*

15) Only 50% of the country has indoor plumbing. *The other half uses outdoor plumbing!*

1941

1) In FDR's State of the Union address, he speaks of the "four freedoms"—freedom of speech, freedom of worship, freedom from want, and freedom from fear.

2) American chemist Glenn Seaborg discovers the element plutonium.

3) The Atlantic Charter, signed by FDR and Mr. Churchill, provides a broad statement on war aims and post-war aims.

4) *V* symbolizes victory in Great Britain. In Nazi Germany, V is for villain.

5) Charles Lindbergh speaks at an America First rally in New York and is loudly criticized by President Franklin D. Roosevelt.

6) The US Congress approves the Lend-Lease Act to help Great Britain survive the Nazi menace.

7) British mathematician Alan Turing breaks the Enigma Code that the German military is using for secret communications. *Many people think that the Germans have a new, secret enema.*

8) Axis Sally, an American broadcaster working for Nazi Germany, makes her first propaganda broadcast to Allied troops in Europe. After the war, she is convicted of treason. *She is also known as the Bitch of Berlin.*

9) Cheerios (CherriOats) are introduced to the world. *Can Froot Loops be far behind?*

10) Two amazing feats take place in baseball. Yankees star Joe DiMaggio hits safely in 56 consecutive games. Red Sox great Ted Williams bats .406. He said, "Baseball is the only field of endeavor where a man can succeed three times out of 10 and be considered a good performer."

11) The cocker spaniel is America's favorite dog. *The least favorite is the German shepherd. I wonder why?*

12) In April, the Soviet Union and Japan sign a neutrality pact that lasts four years. In August 1945, Japan appears to have lost the war, and the Soviets then invade Japanese-occupied Manchuria and Korea.

13) An unbelievable quote from Senator Harry S. Truman: "If we see that Germany is winning, we ought to help Russia, and if Russia is winning, we ought to help Germany, and that way let them kill as many as possible."

14) To protect Iceland from a German invasion, the United States, though neutral, occupies the island nation for four years. *There are plenty of snowball fights.*

15) Some of the leading entertainers of the decade, to name a few: Humphrey Bogart, Billie Holiday, Gary Cooper, Judy Garland, Charlie Chaplin, Roy Rogers, and Cary Grant.

16) *Children's book character Curious George is named Zozo in the United Kingdom to avoid using King George's name on a monkey.*

1942

1) The first mass-produced helicopter is introduced in the United States.

2) Japanese American citizens (Nisei) are interned in concentration camps in the western United States. People still debate, was this the right thing to do?

3) Scrap drives begin. The public is encouraged to collect rubber tires, tin, aluminum, and other household products to be used in the war effort.

4) A fire in a Boston nightclub kills 491 partygoers because the doors open inward.

5) Ladies get into the act with the formation of the Women's Army Corps (WACs); the US Navy introduces the WAVES.

6) Actress Hedy Lamarr is granted a patent for radio-control torpedoes. Smart *and* beautiful!

7) Gas rationing begins, at three gallons per week. *That's enough to go from Brooklyn, New York, to the Bronx's Yankee Stadium and back.*

8) Daylight Savings Time goes into effect in the United States.

9) The five Sullivan brothers of Iowa are killed when a Japanese submarine sinks the USS *Juneau* in the Pacific Ocean.

10) Pinup girls are the rage for American GIs. Favorites are Betty Grable and Rita Hayworth, *but **not** Axis Sally.*

11) War bonds are introduced to the American public. The Voice of America is broadcast to Europe.

12) Irving Berlin composes "White Christmas," as sung by Bing Crosby. It becomes the biggest Christmas song in history.

13) Future President Joe Biden is born, as well as popular Brooklyn singers Barbra Streisand and Carole King. Boxing champ Muhammad Ali and philanthropist Mike Bloomberg make their debuts.

14) The British government asks its citizens to bathe in only five inches of water. *How can a person take a bath in a teacup?*

1943

1) A race riot in Detroit kills 34 people.

2) The Pentagon, the world's largest office building, opens in Arlington, Virginia.

3) There aren't enough players in the NFL because of the war, so the Steelers and the Eagles join forces and play that season as **the Steagles**. Their record is 5–4–1.

4) The Jefferson Memorial in Washington, DC, is dedicated. *Mr. Jefferson is busy and cannot attend.*

5) Rosie the Riveter, a feminist drawing by Norman Rockwell, appears on the *Saturday Evening Post*.

6) The Japanese attack and destroy John F. Kennedy's patrol torpedo boat, *PT-109*.

7) Wartime causes a shortage of copper. During this year only, the penny is made of steel. A few copper pennies are made. They now each could be worth $100,000!

8) Rodgers & Hammerstein have a plethora of Broadway hits this

decade, starting this year with *Oklahoma!* They follow up two years later with *Carousel*, and then in 1949 comes *South Pacific*.

9) The All-American Girls Professional Baseball League forms. *But it's difficult running the bases in high-heel shoes.*

1944

1) An earthquake in Argentina kills 10,000 people.

2) At Sing Sing Prison, three leaders of Murder, Inc. get the hot seat. *Obviously, not at the same time.*

3) The Bretton Woods Conference establishes the International Bank for Reconstruction and Development.

4) Because of the war, there is a scarcity of baseball players. Some players lose the best years of their career; others lose their lives. The St. Louis Browns are forced to use a player with one arm, Pete Gray. *He bats .218, and people wonder if he had two arms, would he bat .436?*

5) A fire at a circus in Hartford, Connecticut, kills 169 people, including 100 children.

6) The most important weather forecast of all time: Gen. Dwight D. Eisenhower's meteorologist sees a change in the weather pattern and urges D-Day be moved from June 5 to June 6. Ike agrees, and the invasion is a success.

7) An undersea oil pipeline between England and France is constructed.

8) Tennessee Williams writes *The Glass Menagerie*. Three years later, his greatest success, *A Streetcar Named Desire*, dazzles Broadway.

9) Great American band leader Glenn Miller disappears during a flight over the English Channel.

10) A plot to kill Adolf Hitler backfires, causing only minor injuries to Der Führer. The Gestapo arrests 7,000 people, then executes 500.

11) Germany launches rocket attacks against London, destroying large parts of this great city.

12) "Don't be a Paleface" is the new slogan of Coppertone suntan oil, which is now certainly politically incorrect.

13) Romania is at war with the Allies and the Axis powers at the same time. *That's called hedging your bets.*

14) Professional baseball player/US spy Moe Berg is sent to Europe to meet a Nazi scientist to determine if Germany is close to using the nuclear bomb. He is to murder the scientist if the bomb is a reality. The threat is not real and, the scientist is not killed.

15) During a battle, a British officer uses a bow and arrow to kill a German soldier. *He loves Western movies.*

16) British soldiers receive a daily ration of three sheets of toilet paper; American soldiers get 22 sheets. *The Allies hope to wipe out the enemy.*

1945

1) The Arab League is forms in Cairo, Egypt. *Nothing to do with baseball's American League. Who's pitching for Cairo?*

2) A US Air Force bomber crashes into the eightieth floor of the Empire State Building in New York City in dense fog, killing 14 people.

3) Princess Elizabeth, soon to be Queen Elizabeth II, becomes a truck driver/mechanic during the war effort. *I guess she needs the extra money.*

4) President Franklin D. Roosevelt founds an organization to find a cure for polio—the March of Dimes. After his death, his face is put on the 10-cent piece.

5) On March 27, Argentina declares war on Germany and Japan. *Better late than never!*

6) Brooklyn-born "Lord Haw-Haw," who broadcast Nazi propaganda to the United Kingdom, is convicted of high treason and later hung.

7) A Japanese submarine sinks the USS *Indianapolis* in the Philippine Sea, killing 883—the worst naval disaster in US history.

8) In April, Adolf Hitler marries longtime girlfriend Eva Braun. *The marriage lasts just one day! The next day, both are dead.*

9) German rocket scientist Wernher von Braun and 120 of his team members surrender to the United States . . . and then come to America to work on the US space program.

10) Fifty countries sign the United Nations Charter, and the United States happily joins.

11) The Nuremberg Trials, military tribunals held by the Allies to prosecute Nazis who participated in the Holocaust and other war crimes, begin after the war.

12) The first ballpoint pen is sold in Gimbels department store, for $12.50. *No more "Today I am a fountain pen."*

1946

1) The first meeting of the United Nations is held in London. Trygve Lie of Norway is the first secretary-general. The last meeting of the League of Nations occurs.

2) The United States makes an offer of $100 million to buy Greenland from Denmark. The offer is rejected, as there is *a new Danish plan to grow Greenland pineapples, but that is obviously unsuccessful.*

3) Violence between Hindus and Muslims in India kills 3,000.

4) After the war, a new rage in music appears: bebop. Charlie Parker and Dizzy Gillespie become the leaders of *bebop, which is not related to hip-hop.*

5) UNICEF and UNESCO make their debuts.

6) The United States bounces radar waves off the moon, launching the space age.

7) The Philippines gain their independence from the United States.

8) The NBA (BAA) makes its debut. Only the Celtics and the Knicks are still dribbling.

9) Ho Chi Minh is elected president of North Vietnam.

10) In Jerusalem, the King David Hotel is bombed, leaving 90

dead. Irgun leader Menachem Begin, who ultimately becomes prime minister of Israel, is arrested.

11) The Soviet Union gifts a statue to the US ambassador in Moscow. *Seven years later, it's discovered to have a bugging device that spies on the embassy.*

12) The US Atomic Energy Commission is established.

13) The first CARE package consisting of US Army rations is delivered to war-torn Europe.

14) The movie *It's a Wonderful Life* opens, and it's a box-office failure. Years later, it is everyone's favorite Christmas movie. *Things change!*

15) The bikini bathing suit is introduced in Paris. *It enables the classic movie Beach Blanket Bingo to reach great success in later years.*

16) The Flamingo, the first hotel and casino, opens in Las Vegas. *Blackjack!*

17) This was the year of the "baby boomer" president. Born are future Presidents Bill Clinton, George W. Bush, and Donald Trump, who said, "People love me. And you know what, I have been very successful. Everybody loves me."

1947

1) Pakistan, with a Muslim majority, is created as an independent country within India, which then gains independence from the British Empire.

2) Kon-Tiki, a wooden raft piloted by a Norwegian explorer, travels 4,300 miles across the Pacific Ocean in 101 days, from Peru to the Polynesian islands. *Is he looking for Norway?*

3) Princess Elizabeth, the future British queen, marries the Duke of Edinburgh in London. *Mazel tov.*

4) The House Un-American Activities Committee (HUAC) begins to investigate Communism in Hollywood.

5) The CIA, formerly called OSS, is created.

6) In Texas, a cargo ship explodes, killing 552 and injuring 3,000.

7) A shepherd discovers the Dead Sea Scrolls in Palestine. *He is disappointed because he was looking for a lost sheep.*

8) The Truman Doctrine is proclaimed to help deter the spread of Communism.

9) Six UFOs are supposedly sighted in Washington State, and an extraterrestrial spacecraft is found in Roswell, New Mexico. *Do you believe that?*

10) The ship *Exodus 1947* leaves France for Palestine with 4,500 Jewish Holocaust survivors aboard. *Actor Paul Newman, star of the movie, does not make the trip.*

11) Howdy Doody makes his TV debut. The puppet plays for 13 years in the Peanut Gallery.

12) Voice of America transmits radio broadcasts to Eastern Europe, and the Marshall Plan produces relief aid for Europe.

13) *Meet the Press*, America's longest-running TV show, makes its debut, hosted by Martha Rountree.

14) "Almost presidents" Mitt Romney and Hillary Clinton are born, as well as singer Elton John and basketball legend Kareem Abdul-Jabbar.

15) In the Yukon, the coldest temperature ever is recorded in North America: minus 63 degrees Centigrade, or minus 81 degrees Fahrenheit. *Where is global warming when we need it?*

16) *A New York City bus driver detours his bus and drives to Florida, just "to get away from it all." He becomes a hero of the working man!*

1948

1) The Israeli Declaration of Independence is signed, and Israel becomes a newly independent country. David Ben-Gurion is the first prime minister, and Chaim Weizmann becomes the first president. The very next day, Egypt, Transjordan, Syria, and Iraq invade Israel— the first Arab-Israeli War. Although vastly outnumbered, Israel defends itself. Finally, a truce is signed.

2) Mahatma Gandhi, leader of the Nationalist movement against British rule in India, is assassinated. He once said, "An eye for an eye only ends up making the whole world blind."

3) Racial segregation in the US Army ends. Apartheid in South Africa begins.

4) A former salesperson at Macy's in New York City becomes the queen of Romania. *Was the king working in Bloomingdale's?*

5) The first astronaut, a monkey named Albert, is launched into space from New Mexico. He doesn't survive the flight. *Too much monkey business.*

6) The Kinsey Report is introduced. It describes sexual behavior in the human male. *Ladies line up at the bookstores for illustrated copies.*

7) Hells Angels, the motorcycle gang, is founded in California. *Marlon Brando, the Wild One, gets an honorary membership.*

8) At the Democratic National Convention, Gen. Dwight D. Eisenhower's name is discussed as a presidential candidate. Four years later, he gets the Republican presidential nomination and wins the election.

9) In Daytona Beach, Florida, the first NASCAR race is held. *Hey, Bubba, want a beer?*

10) For the first time since 1936, the Summer Olympics are held, this time in London. Germany and Japan are not invited.

11) *In Munich, Germany, a parrot can only say two words: "Heil Hitler." Local authorities say the bird must go through denazification or else—Kentucky Fried Chicken!*

12) The first TV Western, *Hopalong Cassidy*, is introduced.
Question: What is the name of Hoppy's horse?
Answer: Topper

1949

1) This is the first year that no African American is lynched in the United States.

2) The Geneva Convention establishes standards of international

law for humanitarian treatment in war.

3) The first Volkswagen Beetle is produced, *but will The Beatles chip in and buy one?*

4) The first Emmy Awards are given for TV excellence. *Not too much competition, for The Howdy Doody Show is the big winner.*

5) Transjordan changes its name to Hashemite Kingdom of Jordan; Siam becomes Thailand. *No more Siamese twins, only Thai triplets.*

6) Uncle Joe Stalin starts a new campaign against "rootless cosmopolitans"—which means Soviet Jews.

7) Broadway loves writer Arthur Miller's *The Death of a Salesman*, which wins him a Pulitzer Prize for drama.

8) In West Germany, Konrad Adenauer becomes the first chancellor of the Federal Republic of Germany. In East Germany, the German Democratic Republic is founded.

9) A female stalker shoots and almost kills Phillies first baseman Eddie Waitkus in a hotel room. *She wanted to discuss balls and strikes!*

10) Tokyo Rose is found guilty of treason and serves seven years in a US prison, *deprived of sushi.*

11) The polio (infantile paralysis) epidemic hits the United States, and thousands die. *Camphor bags that children wear around their neck become a fashion statement.*

12) The City of Los Angeles buys the 725-acre Van Nuys Airport for $1. *I think they overpaid.*

13) George Orwell writes the great futuristic novel *1984*. Four years before, he wrote *Animal Farm*.

14) The first TV sitcom, *The Goldbergs*, is introduced and becomes a huge hit. *"You-hoo, Mrs. Goldberg."*

15) American Chuck Yeager breaks the sound barrier.

16) Last, but not least, "the **bigges**t story of the decade." Grady the Cow, a 1,200-pound Hereford, gets stuck inside a storage silo in Oklahoma. Before being rescued, the cow is milked, and then hoisted to freedom. *LIFE* magazine runs a big story on this big cow, which becomes an Oklahoma celebrity. *Some wanted Grady the Cow to run for the US Congress!*

Deaths This Decade of Notable People

- Lou Gehrig, 37. The Pride of the Yankees.
- George Herman Ruth, 53. The Babe was the best in baseball.
- Henry Ford, 83. American industrialist. "Failure is simply the opportunity to begin again, this time more intelligently."
- Margaret Mitchell, 48. Author of *Gone with the Wind*.
- George Washington Carver, 79. African American scientist and inventor.
- Kaiser Wilhelm II, 82. German emperor for 30 years.
- Gen. George Patton, 60. Commanded the US Army in World War II Europe.
- Tōjō Hideki, 63. Japanese leader during World War II.
- Anne Frank, 15. Holocaust victim who wrote a diary of her experiences hiding from the Nazis.
- Bill "Bojangles" Robinson, 72. Great American tap dancer and actor.
- Fiorello La Guardia, 64. Colorful mayor of New York City.
- Marcus Garvey, 52. African American political activist.
- Judge Kenesaw Mountain Landis, 78. First commissioner of baseball.
- Nickola Tesla, 86. Inventor and electrical engineer.
- F. Scott Fitzgerald, 44. American author of *The Great Gatsby*.
- W.C. Fields, 66. American humorist. *"A rich man is nothing but a poor man with money."*

Advances in Science this Decade

Britain's radar system – First nuclear chain reaction – DNA introduced (although discovered in 1869) – Streptomycin – Pap smear – Scuba –

German guided missile – DDT – Fluorides – Synthetic quinine – Digital computer – Jet plane – Cortisone – Napalm – Defibrillator – Hologram – Kidney dialysis – Ballistic missiles

Important Innovations of the 1940s

Nylon parachute – Electric blanket – Polaroid camera – Scrabble – Atomic clock – Jeep – Commercial TV – Synthetic rubber tires – Velcro – Microwave oven – New phonograph record speeds: 45 rpm and 33 rpm – Tupperware – Sunscreen – Elmer's Glue – Power steering – Tubeless tire – Silly Putty – Kitty litter – Polyester fabric – Slinky – M&M's

---

IN 1940, the population of the world was 2.3 3 billion people. The United States's population was 1 3 1 million people. The average life expectancy of Americans was 62 years.

What a relief! The decade of the 1940s was over. World War II was now a memory—to some, a terrible memory. Now we must go forward and hope and believe that there will never be a World War III.

6

1950–1959
THE COLD WAR GETS HOT

The last years of the decade of the 1940s saw the hot war turn cold; in the 1950s, *the Cold War got microwaved,* and many hot wars were ignited. Threats were everywhere! There were 27 different wars around the globe—wars in Asia, revolutions in Europe and Central America, and turmoil in Africa. There was a space race and problems with race relations in America. A US senator was convinced that all government employees were Communists; even the peacefulness of popular music was threatened by a new phenomenon: rock 'n' roll!

Presidential Elections of the 1950s

In 1952, President Harry S. Truman decided not to run for reelection, considering the fact that his approval rating was at 22%. *Many felt that Mickey Mouse would probably beat him in an election.*

Heading the Democratic ticket was Illinois Governor Adlai Stevenson II and his running mate, Alabama senator John Sparkman. Gen. Dwight D. Eisenhower and California senator Richard Nixon were the choice of the Republicans, and they won the election in a landslide. This was the first Republican presidential victory in 24 years.

1956 was more of the same. Eisenhower, our 34th president, and Vice President Nixon, in a bigger landslide than in 1952, again defeated Stevenson, this time with Tennessee senator Estes Kefauver as his running mate.

Korea

Peace was threatened, then shattered in June 1950 when the army of North Korea, using Soviet weapons and tanks, invaded South Korea. Historically, Japan had annexed Korea in 1910 and renamed it Chosen, and the country remained under brutal Japanese control until 1945. When Japan surrendered at World War II's end, Korea was divided at the 38th parallel, becoming North Korea and South Korea. China and the Soviet Union were to aid the North, while the South would become a US ally. Communist North Korea, the Hermit Kingdom, became a one-party system controlled by a dictator, Chairman Kim Il-Sung, who believed very strongly in concentration camps.

The United Nations, coming to the aid of South Korea, quickly formed an army consisting mostly of US troops and led by Gen. Douglas MacArthur. At first, the South was losing badly, but the tide quickly turned, and the North Koreans soon retreated, obviously to the north. US troops followed the enemy into North Korean territory and soon up to the China-North Korea border. Hundreds of thousands of Chinese soldiers poured over the border and pushed the Americans back.

MacArthur wanted to use nuclear weapons on mainland China. In April 1951, Truman was forced to remove his general for insubordination. The president's quote: "I didn't fire him because he was a dumb son of a bitch, although he was, but that's not against the law for generals. If it was, half to three-quarters of them would be in jail."

MacArthur made a farewell speech to the US Congress and tearfully said, "Old soldiers never die, they just fade away."

The Korean War went on until 1953, despite the frigid Korean winters, really ending in a stalemate. No peace treaty was signed, just an armistice for this police action, since the United States had never formally declared war on North Korea.

It seems Joseph Stalin and his Soviet generals gave permission to Kim to attack in 1950 because the USSR and China wanted to unify Korea as a Communist nation. Today, the economy of tiny South Korea is **the 12th-largest** in the world while North Korea languishes in **115th place**, behind Afghanistan and Iceland. The Russians are not laughing.

Vietnam

Farther to the south in French Indochina, war was real. France's colonial empire in Asia, established in 1887, was about to be toppled. In 1941, Japan invaded because they were in need of coal, tin, rubber, and rice. Chairman Ho Chi Minh was the leader of the local Indochinese, and with US aid, he battled the invaders. When World War II had ended, Ho declared independence from France and established the Democratic Republic of Vietnam. Ho said, "You will kill ten of our men, and we will kill one of yours, and in the end, it will be you who tire of it."

Between 1946–1954, the First Indochina War was fought. China and the Soviet Union aided Ho, while the US aided France.

The grueling battle at Dien Bien Phu, won by the Vietnamese, meant au revoir for the French. At the Geneva Conference in 1954, Vietnam was divided at the 17th parallel, the North becoming a Communist state, while South Vietnam became an American ally.

You may ask about the Second Indochina war, which actually started in 1955. This was the beginning of the Vietnamese War, which haunted the United States in the decades of the 1960s and 1970s. More to come!

The Middle East

The threat of war became a reality in the Middle East in 1956. **The Suez Crisis** was triggered by President Gamal Abdel Nasser of Egypt, who planned to nationalize the Suez Canal and close it to all Israeli shipping. Two-thirds of Europe's oil shipments came through the Suez Canal, so access to the waterway was vital to many countries.

The canal opened in 1869 and was controlled by the British. It was strategically important because it linked the Mediterranean Sea with the Indian Ocean. Mr. Nasser and Nikita Khrushchev were becoming fast friends, as the USSR wanted to control the Middle East and Egypt wanted to be the leader of the Arab world. Nasser said, "I have been a conspirator for so long that I mistrust all around me."

In a well-planned, secret strategy, Israel, the United Kingdom and France invaded Egypt and took control of the Suez Canal. Within a month, these three countries had militarily won this short-lived war. The Soviets, busy with the Hungarian Revolution, threatened military action while the United States attempted to mediate the situation.

When the dust—or desert sand—had finally settled, Israel now had to be regarded as a major power in the Middle East and was given use of the canal, the United Kingdom and France suffered politically at home, and Nasser was viewed as a hero in the Arab world.

Again, more to come in 11 years.

Hungary

As mentioned, the Soviet Union had problems of their own in some of the Eastern European countries that they had usurped after World War II. The Soviets rid these countries of the Nazis, *but they enjoyed Hungarian goulash and Romanian pastrami so much that they decided to stay* and set up their own puppet Communist governments.

In 1956, Poland became upset with the Soviet domination and staged massive protests around the country against the Communist regime. The army fired upon the protesters, with heavy casualties, before **Soviet** peace prevailed.

Very soon thereafter, in Hungary, the locals grew hungry and restless. Student protesters demanded a more democratic political system apart from Soviet oppression. The Communist government was quickly overthrown and a new liberal government established. The Hungarian Revolution was very short-lived, as the Soviet army invaded Budapest, with thousands of protesting Hungarians killed and others later executed. The Soviet-style government quickly returned. Soviet leader Khrushchev said, "Revolutions are not made for export."

TIME magazine's Man of the Year for 1956 was the Hungarian Freedom Fighter. Thirty-five years later, in 1991, Russian President Mikhail Gorbachev officially apologized to the Hungarian government for the Soviet actions in 1956. *Better late than never! More vodka with your goulash?*

Cuba

Closer to home, another violent revolution took place in the 1950s—this time in Cuba.

A dictator, Fulgencio Batista, ran Cuba for decades with the help of American organized crime. Several large, American companies controlled the corrupt government's economy.

A young, **anti-Communist** lawyer, Fidel Castro, led a new armed revolution, starting in 1952. Along with his brother Raul and Che Guevara, the Cuban rebels, hiding in the mountains and vastly outnumbered, were able to defeat the Cuban army. Castro proclaimed, "The revolution is a dictatorship of the exploited against the exploiters."

Happy new year! Feliz año nuevo! On January 1, 1959, Castro, at age 33, entered Havana and was greeted as a hero. *That morning, Señor Batista flew the coop to Santo Domingo with $300 million stuffed in his pockets.* Young Fidel ruled the country for only 49 years, until 2008, when old Fidel stepped down at age 82.

Castro visited the United States that April and was greeted as a celebrity. He met with Nixon, and both immediately disliked each other. At this point, the jury was out on whether Castro was a Communist or not.

For Castro and the Cubans (sounds like a rock group), the 1960s would become very eventful and threatening for the United States, the Soviet Union, Cuba, and the rest of the world.

Senator Joseph McCarthy

In the early 1950s, McCarthy ruled American TV. No, not Charlie McCarthy the puppet, but rather the conservative Republican senator from Wisconsin, Joseph McCarthy. He had a bad habit of making accusations of treason with no tangible evidence. McCarthy's **Red Scare** was an absolute threat to the country. Eisenhower remarked, "I will not get into the gutter with this guy!"

In a 1950 speech, McCarthy presented a list of alleged members of the Communist Party who worked in the US Department of State. Of course, these reckless accusations were unsubstantiated, and careers and reputations were badly damaged. Hundreds of Americans were accused of being Communists or Communist sympathizers. The senator proudly said, "McCarthyism is Americanism with its sleeves rolled."

In the days before Senator McCarthy came on the scene, the House Un-American Activities Committee (HUAC) targeted Hollywood's movie industry professionals. The HUAC was concerned with known or suspected membership in the Communist Party and wanted members of Hollywood to testify and name names. Most did not cooperate, and many were sent to jail. Certain actors, writers, and directors were blacklisted and suffered career and character assassinations.

McCarthy investigated the US Department of State and the CIA in his quest to uncover Communists but came up empty. His downfall occurred when he decided to investigate the US Army. These hearings were lengthy and appeared on national TV, where the senator came across as the bad guy. In a classic quote, Joseph Welch, attorney for the army, famously asked McCarthy, **"Have you no sense of decency?"**

McCarthy's coup de grâs came in 1954 when the US Senate voted to censure their colleague for conduct that had brought the Senate into dishonor and disrepute. Only nine other senators in American history have been censured, but McCarthy's case was the most famous. *His namesake, Charlie McCarthy, was not proud of him.*

The Space Race

The Cold War between the Soviet Union and the United States had many tentacles. One of these was **the Space Race**. *The competition between Communism and Capitalism now became sky high!*

In 1955, both countries announced that they were working on programs to launch a satellite. *The satellite, which was about the size of a basketball, was being constructed by the NBA champion Boston Celtics! (That's a joke.)*

The Soviets won the first round when, in October 1957, Sputnik I was put into orbit. Soon thereafter, Sputnik II was launched, this time carrying a dog named Laika. *In Moscow, every Russian puppy was renamed Laika.*

In December 1957, the Americans attempted to launch our first satellite, but the attempt failed. *The satellite was nicknamed **Flopnik**!* But a month later, in January 1958, Explorer I was successfully launched. The United States quickly sent into space the first communication satellite and then, in 1959, the first weather satellite.

The Soviets, being busy, launched a satellite that bounced off the moon. *American scientists wondered how high the satellite had bounced.* The Soviets then sent off a satellite that took photos of the far side of the moon. The space race was just getting started, preparing for the glory days ahead for America—**1969**!

Civil Rights

Speaking of race, the modern Civil Rights movement in the United States began in December 1955. In Montgomery, Alabama, Rosa Parks, an African American woman, refused to give up her seat to a White man on a city bus. She was arrested, and a boycott of the Montgomery bus system followed. The one-year boycott was led by an unknown 26-year-old, Dr. Martin Luther King Jr. Finally, the US Supreme Court ruled that segregated seating on public transportation was unconstitutional.

The 1954 case Brown v. Board of Education made segregation illegal in public schools. In 1957, Eisenhower sent federal troops to Little Rock, Arkansas, to escort nine Black high school students to class. The Civil Rights Act of 1957 stated that the act of preventing a person from voting was a federal crime. That same year, King founded the Southern Christian Leadership Conference, preaching nonviolence. Civil rights for Black Americans were just starting in the 1950s, but really grew in the 1960s.

Africa

In the 19th century, Africa was colonized by the powerful countries of Europe—Great Britain, France, Portugal, Belgium, Germany, Spain, and Italy. It has been said that the three motives of European colonization of Africa were the three G's—**God**, **gold**, and **glory**!

After World War II, the African colonies were tired of European economic exploitation. African Nationalism grew, and in the 1950s, several European-controlled colonies achieved their independence.

In 1951, Libya declared its independence from Italy. Then, in 1956, Sudan became independent from the United Kingdom. Tunisia followed, getting its independence from France, which then, along with Spain, granted independence to Morocco. The Gold Coast, which changed its name to Ghana, got its independence from the United

Kingdom in 1957. Guinea, known as French West Africa, became independent from France in 1958.

If seven colonies becoming independent seems like a lot, just wait until the 1960s, when **34 colonies** became independent countries!

The Soviet Union

The Cold War boiled down to a war between Communism and Capitalism. This frigid conflict took place between 1945–1991. It was not that Capitalism won the battle, but rather that Communism lost the war!

The United States felt that Communism needed to be contained—either by diplomacy, threats, or by force. Two Americans, husband and wife Julius and Ethel Rosenberg, were convicted of espionage. They were said to have passed atomic secrets to the Soviet Union in the 1940s, and they were executed in 1953.

Joseph Stalin, the Soviet dictator for 30 years, died in 1953 and was replaced by Georgy Malenkov, who was replaced by Nikolai Bulganin, who was replaced by Khrushchev. So the USSR was led by one man for 30 years and then had three different leaders over the next five years. *The busiest man in the Kremlin was the comrade who changed the locks on the private bathroom!*

There were many purges, as usual, during this decade in the USSR. The head of the secret police, *Lavrentiy Beria (not Yogi Berra)*, was arrested and later executed for being "an enemy of the people." Mr. Malenkov became manager of an electric plant somewhere, and Foreign Minister Vyacheslav Molotov was shipped off to Mongolia as an ambassador.

Mr. Khrushchev was a live wire. He was anti-Stalin and was busy replacing Stalin statues and portraits all over Moscow with his own likeness. *Khrushchev said that the Soviet Union had missile superiority over the United States and challenged America to "a missile shooting match." The United States refused because he wanted the match to be held over New York City—just kidding!*

The **"kitchen debate"** between Khrushchev and Nixon took place in 1959 and was broadcast around the world. Khrushchev's most famous quote to the United States was, **"We shall bury you."** Not a very nice thing to say, and five years later, he was just a memory, and not a very good one.

Rock 'n' Roll

A threat to popular music occurred this decade with the advent of **rock 'n' roll**! African Americans enjoyed rhythm and blues, or "race music," but it was not allowed to be played on mainstream White radio. A little-known disc jockey, Alan Freed, on WINS New York, coined the phrase and began to play this music for his White teenage fans. Soon, Perry Como, Patti Page, and Eddie Fisher were replaced by Ray Charles, Little Richard, and Chuck Berry, who once said, "Of the five most important things in life, health is first, education or knowledge is second, and wealth is third. I forget the other two."

Then in 1956, a new phenomenon appeared—**Elvis Presley**. For the first time, a White country performer who sang Black music became the country's biggest star. *Teenage girls cried when Elvis joined the US Army in 1959 and was issued blue suede combat boots!*

On Dick Clark's *American Bandstand*, Danny and the Juniors sang, "Rock 'n' roll is here to stay, it will never die!"

Wars and Treaties of the 1950s

The experts were wrong in thinking that the planet would be tired of military conflict after World War II, and 27 wars were fought. The Korean War (or police action) saw 1 million people die. And there was no winner because actually, in war, there are only losers.

The horrible Vietnamese War of the 1960s and 1970s actually started in 1955.

Civil War Gen. William Sherman said it best: **"War is hell."**

Twenty-five different treaties were signed this decade. The most notable was the Korean Armistice, which unofficially ended the Korean War.

The Southeast Asia Treaty Organization (SEATO) was important, as was the Australian, New Zealand, and United States Security Treaty (ANZUS).

On the Communist side, the Warsaw Pact was signed to counteract the NATO treaty.

Important and Unimportant News of the 1950s

1950

1) China and the USSR sign a mutual defense pact.

2) Eleven thieves steal $2 million from a Brink's armored car in Boston. *That's $181,000 per thief. Not a bad haul.*

3) Stasi, the East German secret police, forms.

4) The Brooklyn-Battery Tunnel opens. The toll is 35 cents one way. Today, it's just $10.17 round trip.

5) Two Puerto Rican Nationalists attempt to assassinate President Harry S. Truman in Washington, DC. *They miss.*

6) Race riots occur in South Africa as apartheid begins.

7) Diners Club begins operations in New York City. *The first credit card transaction is for dinner for two: $3.75!*

8) The Dalai Lama, at 15 years old, is enthroned in Tibet. *Well, hello, Dalai!*

9) For the only time in college basketball history, one team wins both the NIT and the NCAA tournaments the same year—CCNY.

10) There is a scandal among seven New York college basketball teams—point shaving. Thirty-two players are arrested, some are jailed, and others are banned from the NBA. *This is a blemish on college basketball that even Clearasil cannot help.*

11) A US Air Force bomber crashes in Canada, carrying a nuclear bomb. The bomb is never found.

12) Say hello to *Beetle Bailey* and *Peanuts*.

13) Residents of Guam are given the right to vote.

14) The Boston Celtics's Chuck Cooper integrates professional basketball as the first Black player. He opens the door for thousands of others, including Bill Russell, who plays 13 seasons for Boston and wins 11 championships.

15) Lazy Bones, from Zenith, is the *first TV remote control. But only men can use it!*

16) Commercial TV becomes very popular on 10-inch TV sets, even though only three networks and station patterns are available.

1951

1) The United Nations building Headquarters in New York City opens.

2) A nuclear test is carried out near Las Vegas. *Not one person in a casino is concerned.*

3) In a 96-hour operation, Chicago surgeons remove a giant ovarian cyst from a woman, *who loses half her weight. No need for Diet Pepsi.*

4) Prime Minister Liaquat Ali Khan of Pakistan is assassinated.

5) Heartbreak in Brooklyn, New York, as Bobby Thomson of the New York Giants hits a game-winning/pennant-winning home run in the final inning of the last playoff game to beat the Brooklyn Dodgers. It was "the Shot Heard 'Round the World."

6) The CBS Eye logo is introduced, as is *Dennis the Menace*.

7) Boxing champions Sugar Ray Robinson and Jake LaMotta fight each other six times. LaMotta jokingly said, *"I fought Sugar Ray so often, I almost got diabetes!"*

8) The 117-mile long New Jersey Turnpike has its grand opening. *Where does Tony Soprano live?*

9) *I Love Lucy* debuts. *The Milton Berle Show, Gunsmoke,* and *The Howdy Doody Show* are TV favorites.

10) J.D. Salinger's *The Catcher in the Rye* and Ernest Hemingway's *The Old Man and the Sea* are literary successes.

11) The first direct-dial, coast-to-coast telephone call is made, but nobody answers.

12) First Lady Dr. Jill Biden is born, as is comedian/actor *Robin Williams, who proclaims, "My mother's idea of natural childbirth was giving birth without makeup." Very funny!*

1952

1) The first successful open-heart surgery is performed in United States. About 500,000 surgeries are now done each year.

2) George Jorgensen becomes Christine Jorgensen in **first sexual reassignment operation**. No jokes here!

3) The US Special Forces is created.

4) "Night of the Murdered Poets"—13 Soviet Jewish poets are executed. It seems that Joseph Stalin does not care for Jews nor poetry.

5) The United States detonates first hydrogen bomb in the Pacific Ocean. *The H-bomb is not to be confused with the F-bomb.*

6) For the first time, Siamese twins are successfully separated, in a lengthy operation in Cleveland, Ohio.

7) President-elect Dwight D. Eisenhower goes to Korea after the election to visit American troops.

8) The United Kingdom announces that they have the atomic bomb. Join the club.

9) King Farouk of Egypt abdicates; King Hussein, at age 17, becomes the ruler of Jordan.

10) A Mau Mau uprising occurs in Kenya as martial law declared.

11) Because of alleged Communist affiliations, Charlie Chaplin is denied entry to the United States. He is allowed to return 20 years later to accept an Academy Award.

12) The first **DON'T WALK** sign appears in New York City. *People are confused and everyone starts running.*

13) The Great Smog of London, the worst air pollution in UK history, kills almost 12,000 and sickens 100,000.

14) Mrs. Putin gives birth to baby Vladimir, the future Russian leader.

15) *MAD* magazine publishes its first issue. *Alfred E. Neuman says, "What, me worry?"*

16) Lieutenant Sanders opens the first Kentucky Fried Chicken—where else?—in Kentucky. *He is later promoted to colonel after his heroics in the bird flu epidemic.*

17) Question: World-renowned scientist Albert Einstein is offered the presidency of what country?

Answer: If you said, "Outer Mongolia," you are wrong. The correct answer is Israel. He declined the offer.

1953

1) Dr. Jonas Salk in New York creates the polio vaccine. Monumental!

2) Princess Elizabeth is crowned Queen Elizabeth II of the United Kingdom.

3) MLB calls in the moving trucks as franchises move for the first time. The Boston Braves move to Milwaukee. In 1954, the St. Louis Browns become the Baltimore Orioles, and the next year, the Philadelphia Athletics move to Kansas City.

4) The CIA helps overthrow the government of Iran, aiding the Shah.

5) California Governor Earl Warren is appointed chief justice of the US Supreme Court, succeeding Fred Vinson.

6) James Bond, aka 007, makes his literary debut in Ian Fleming's *Casino Royale*. *Shaken, not stirred.*

7) Dag Hammarskjöld of Sweden is elected secretary-general of United Nations.

8) Just a few of the great, great movies of this decade: *From Here to Eternity, On the Waterfront, The Country Girl, 12 Angry Men*, and *The Bridge on the River Kwai.*

9) President Dwight D. Eisenhower makes his "Atoms for Peace"

speech.

10) The Royal Yacht *Britannia* is launched. It is 412 feet long, big enough for 250 guests. It is now retired and a popular tourist attraction in Scotland.

11) Sir Edmund Hillary climbs to the summit of Mount Everest, 29,000 feet—the highest point on Earth. *Going back down, he uses a snowboard.*

12) President Dwight D. Eisenhower signs an executive order that prohibits homosexuals from working in the federal government. Thousands of gay people lose their jobs and their careers. The ban is lifted in 1975.

13) The first issue of *Playboy* appears. The centerfold is Marilyn Monroe—nude! *She famously says, "It's not true I had nothing on, I had the radio on."*

14) Chinese leader Xi Jinping is born, as is UK Prime Minister Tony Blair.

1954

1) Marilyn Monroe marries Joe DiMaggio. *The Yankee Clipper has a Playboy subscription!*

2) The USSR wants to join NATO and is totally rejected.

3) Hurricane Hazel kills 1,000 in Haiti.

4) The USS *Nautilus*, the first nuclear-powered submarine, is launched.

5) The Communist Party is outlawed in the United States. Senator Joseph McCarthy is overjoyed.

6) Two words are added to "The Pledge of Allegiance: "Under God." The pledge was created in 1892.

7) Roger Bannister of England runs the first sub-four-minute mile—3:59:4. The fastest current world's record is 3:43:13.

8) German leader Angela Merkel is born.

9) A fire on the USS *Bennington* aircraft carrier kills 103 sailors.

10) Two smaller auto companies merge to form American Motors Corporation.

11) A mass vaccination of the American public of Dr. Jonas Salk's polio vaccine takes place.

12) Armistice Day has a name change—**Veterans Day**, a federal holiday celebrated on November 11, honoring military veterans.

13) Regarding countries becoming Communist, President Dwight D. Eisenhower speaks of *"the falling domino principle." Nothing to do with singer Fats Domino slipping on the ice.*

14) For 18 cents, you can buy a hamburger at the first Burger King franchise in Miami.

15) *The Tonight Show* debuts on NBC, hosted by Steve Allen. Some later hosts are Jack Paar, Johnny Carson, Jay Leno, and Jimmy Fallon.

16) After 2,956 "Hi-Yo, Silvers!," the last radio episode of *The Lone Ranger* is broadcast. Did you know that's the Lone Ranger's real name is John Reid?

1955

1) Sir Winston Churchill resigns as UK prime minister at age 80, succeeded by Anthony Eden. I'm sure you know that *Sir Winston's mother was born in Brooklyn. That's why Mr. Churchill spoke with a Brooklyn accent.*

2) The first—and certainly not the last—"advisers" are sent to South Vietnam.

3) Disneyland opens in Anaheim, California. *The Mickey Mouse Club* premieres on TV.

4) Argentine President Juan Perón is ousted and exiled for 16 years.

5) **"Wait till next year"** finally happens as the Brooklyn Dodgers win their first World Series after losing seven straight times, the last five to the hated Yankees.

Question: Who is the only person to play for the MLB Dodgers and the NHL New York Rangers the same year?

*Answer: Gladys Gooding **played the organ** at Ebbets Field for the Dodgers and at Madison Square Garden for the Rangers! A trick question.*

6) President Dwight D. Eisenhower suffers a heart attack, followed by a stroke months later. But he recovers nicely and is soon playing golf.

7) The AFL and the CIO merge, forming a giant labor union.

8) Marion Anderson is the first African American singer to perform at the Metropolitan Opera in New York City.

9) Two of the biggest names in technology are born this year: Apple founder Steve Jobs and Microsoft founder Bill Gates, who said, "It's fine to celebrate success, but it is more important to heed the lessons of failure."

10) Seat belts are offered in new cars as an option. Only 2% of buyers of new Fords choose this option. *A very smart 2%!*

11) *The Guinness Book of World Records* is published. Interesting trivia:

A) The smallest living dog is a Chihuahua, at 3.8 inches tall.

B) The world's largest rubber band ball contains 700,000 rubber bands and weighs 9,000 pounds.

C) The tallest professional female model is a Russian who stands 6 feet 8 inches tall.

12) *Kermit the Frog makes his debut; his significant other, Miss Piggy, makes her appearance in 1976. Piggy likes older frogs.*

1956

1) Two commercial airplanes collide over the Grand Canyon, killing 128. Interesting fact: There were hundreds of plane crashes in the 1950s. In the 2010s, there were just 49.

2) The Million Dollar Quartet records an album. *Who ever heard of Elvis Presley, Johnny Cash, Jerry Lee Lewis, and Carl Perkins? Nobodies!*

3) Syria and Lebanon sign a mutual defense pact.

4) New York Yankee pitcher Don Larsen pictures the first perfect game in MLB history during the World Series as the Yankees beat the Brooklyn Dodgers. This decade, the Yankees are champions six times. *A famous Yogi Berra quote regarding Mickey Mantle: "He hits from both sides of the plate. He's **amphibious**."*

5) Actress Grace Kelly of Philadelphia marries Prince Rainier of Monaco. *Philly cheesesteaks are served at the royal wedding.*

6) The Italian ocean liner *Andrea Doria* collides with the MS *Stockholm* in heavy fog near Nantucket, killing 51.

7) Althea Gibson becomes the first African American to win a Grand Slam tennis tournament. Victorious at Wimbledon, she commented, "Shaking hands with the queen of England was a long way from being forced to sit in the Colored section of the bus going into downtown Wilmington, North Carolina."

8) Singer Dean Martin and comedian Jerry Lewis end their successful relationship. Both become even bigger stars.

9) The first American U2 spy plane flies over the Soviet Union. *Do the Russians know?*

10) The transatlantic telephone cable is now in operation. How much is a call from New York to London?

11) *My Fair Lady* opens on Broadway to rave reviews, as does *West Side Story* the following year.

12) Soviet leader Nikita Khrushchev publicly denounces former leader Joseph Stalin. Can you imagine what would've happened to Mr. Khrushchev if he had done this in 1952? *Off with his head!*

13) Marilyn Monroe is busy: she divorces Joe DiMaggio and marries playwright Arthur Miller, *who now renews his Playboy subscription.*

1957

1) Over 100 Mafia leaders meet in an old farmhouse in Upstate New York to supposedly discuss agriculture. *Federal agents crash the*

party and arrest many of the gentlemen farmers.

2) François Duvalier, aka Papa Doc, assumes power in Haiti and remains dictator for 14 years.

3) **The Eisenhower Doctrine** proclaims the use of American military to combat Communist aggression in the Middle East.

4) Chairman Mao Tse-tung admits that 800,000 domestic "enemies" were liquidated between 1949–1954. If that's not bad enough, **the Asian flu** kills 1 million Chinese people and millions more around the globe.

5) Soon-to-be President John F. Kennedy wins the Pulitzer Prize for his book *Profiles in Courage.*

6) The European Common Market is established.

7) *As an April Fools' Day joke, the BBC broadcasts pictures of spaghetti growing on trees. People should know that only macaroni grows on trees, certainly not spaghetti.*

8) The Mad Bomber, George Metesky, is finally arrested after planting 30 bombs. *He would have been better off planting 30 flowers.*

9) *Atlas Shrugged* by Ayn Rand and *Doctor Zhivago* by Boris Pasternak are best-selling books.

10) *American Bandstand* makes its debut, and 42 years later, Dick Clark still looks like a kid.

11) South Carolina senator Strom Thurmond makes the US Senate's longest filibuster speech—24 hours—against the Civil Rights Bill.

12) In England, hand, foot, and mouth disease among animals is rampant, and 30,000 animals die.

13) Among the most popular entertainers are Frank Sinatra, Charlton Heston, John Wayne, Doris Day, Debbie Reynolds, Johnny Mathis, Gregory Peck, and Audrey Hepburn, who said, "Nothing is impossible, the word itself says, **'I'm possible.'**"

14) The Standard & Poor's 500 index is introduced.

15) *A Brazilian farmer claims that extraterrestrials abducted him. Authorities are not sure what he is farming.*

16) *A 42,000-pound hydrogen bomb accidentally falls from a US*

bomber over Albuquerque, New Mexico. Fortunately, it did not deto-nate. The pilot says, "Whoops."

1958

1) Egypt and Syria unite and form the United Arab Republic. The new country lasts for all of three years.

2) Brooklyn Dodger All-Star catcher Roy Campanella is in an auto accident that leaves him permanently paralyzed.

3) **The first Cod War** erupts between the United Kingdom and Iceland—*over fish and chips.*

4) On a trip to South America, Vice President Richard Nixon's car is attacked in Venezuela. *The attacker thinks that the vice president is a crook, but Mr. Nixon denies it.*

5) Bobby Fischer, at age 14, wins the US chess championship. Van Cliburn, at age 19, wins the International Piano Competition in Moscow.

6) The USS *Nautilus*, the first nuclear-powered submarine, *crosses the North Pole underwater while looking for Santa Claus, a scuba enthusiast.*

7) The great Chinese famine begins. Unbelievably, tens of millions die. **The Great Leap Forward** hopes for rapid industrialization.

8) Regarded as the greatest NFL game ever, in overtime, the Baltimore Colts defeat the New York Giants to win the championship. Because of TV coverage, professional football makes huge gains in popularity.

9) Ford Motor Company introduces the Edsel. *A colossal failure!*

10) The US Marine Corps is sent to Lebanon because of Christian and Muslim hostilities.

11) The beatnik movement flourishes, rejecting social conventions. Leaders are writer Jack Kerouac and poet Allen Ginsberg.

12) The first commercial transatlantic jet flight debuts, between New York and London. Smoking is allowed.

13) A sad year for New York baseball: the Giants leave town to pan

for gold in San Francisco, and the Dodgers vacate Brooklyn for the glamour of Beverly Hills.

14) A New York jeweler donates the 45-carat Hope Diamond to the Smithsonian Institute. *What a great tax write-off.*

15) The bossa nova dance craze is introduced in Rio de Janiero, performed by "The Girl from Ipanema." *"Tall and tan and young and lovely."*

1959

1) Alaska becomes the 49th state, and Hawaii becomes the 50th.

2) A chartered plane crashes, killing three young rock 'n' roll stars—Buddy Holly, Ritchie Valens, and the Big Bopper.

3) Queen Elizabeth II and President Dwight D. Eisenhower open the St. Lawrence Seaway.

4) Typhoon Vera kills 5,000 people in Japan.

5) The Guggenheim Museum, designed by Frank Lloyd Wright, opens in New York City.

6) The North American Aerospace Defense Command (NORAD) is established.

7) After taking nearly three years to build, the new capital of Brazil, Brasília, opens. Its population is now almost 5 million.

8) NASA, formed in 1958, introduces the first seven astronauts.

9) Rodgers & Hammerstein do it again—twice. *The Sound of Music* is a smash hit, as was *The King and I* eight years earlier.

10) Rebellion against Chinese Communist rule is crushed in Tibet. The Dalai Lama is forced to leave.

11) *The latest fad: phone-booth stuffing. Twenty-five South African students fit themselves into a phone booth. Does anyone have a dime? I have to make a phone call.*

12) Jacques Plante of the Montreal Canadiens becomes the first goalie to wear a protective mask, and not just on Halloween. His team wins the Stanley Cup six times this decade. Five of the wins are consecutive.

13) Big news for the ladies: pantyhose are introduced.

Deaths This Decade of Notable People

- Errol Flynn, 50. Hollywood star. "I like my whiskey old and my women young."
- "Shoeless" Joe Jackson, 64. Involved in the Black Sox Scandal of the 1919 World Series.
- W.C. Handy, 84. American musician who was considered Father of the Blues.
- Bill Tilden, 60. American tennis star.
- Charlie Parker, 34. Jazz saxophonist and leader of bebop music.
- King George VI, 56. King of England from 1936–1952.
- Henri Matisse, 84. French painter who led modernism and post-impressionism.
- Frank Lloyd Wright, 91. Famous American architect.
- Albert Einstein, 76. German-born physicist who developed the theory of relativity.
- Pope Pius XII, 82. Leader of the Catholic Church for 23 years.
- Al Jolson, 64. Known as the World's Greatest Entertainer.
- Jim Thorpe, 65. Native American athlete and Olympic gold medal winner.
- William Randolph Hearst, 88. American newspaper publisher known for "yellow Journalism."
- Humphrey Bogart, 57. American actor who starred in *Casablanca*.
- Billie Holiday, 44. Immortal American singer. *"Mom and Pop were just a couple of kids when they got married. He was 18, she was 16, and I was 3."*

Advances in Science This Decade

Heart ultrasound – Microchip – Human growth hormone – First nuclear power plant (in Moscow, not Chernobyl) – Tetracycline – First chemotherapy treatment – Antihistamines – Cardiac pacemaker – Birth control pills (finally)

Important Innovations of the 1950s

Univac (the first commercial computer) – Radial tires – Nonstick frying pan – Credit cards – Roll-on deodorant – Frozen TV dinners – Color TV – Frisbee – Diet soda – Atomic clock – Transistor radio – LEGOs – Telephone answering machine – Super Glue – Hula-Hoop – Disposable diapers – Portable TV sets – Videotape recording – 3D movies – Instant iced tea – Saran Wrap – Liquid paper – Stereophonic recordings – The cha-cha – Mr. Potato Head (now gender-neutral and called **Potato Head**.)

IN 1950, the population of the world was 2.5 billion people. The United States's population was 151 million people. The average life expectancy of Americans was 68 years.

The Nifty '50s were over. The country had survived the many threats that were imposed upon it and looked forward to the next decade. Good luck, America!

7

1960–1969

THE DECADE FROM HELL

O f the 10 decades of the 20th century, the **most** threatening decade to the United States was the 10-year period of the 1960s!

The Cold War with the Soviet Union was boiling hot, we were involved in a long-running war in Asia 9,000 miles away against an enemy who looked like the people we were protecting, and young Americans were rioting and protesting this most unpopular war.

Our leaders were being assassinated, White Americans and Black Americans were fighting and killing one another in the burning streets of America, and the United States was close to a nuclear disaster with a country that was only 90 miles away.

America's most reliable Middle Eastern ally was forced to fight a war against five countries that totally outnumbered them, and Africa had many wars occurring while the continent was being decolonized, all with the threat that the United States might have to make an appearance.

1968 is regarded as the most turbulent and traumatic year of the decade, perhaps even of the century. There was a bit of good news during the 1960s, though: an American man walked on the moon, The

Beatles invaded America, and the amazing New York Mets won the World Series!

Presidential Elections of the 1960s

In 1960, Massachusetts Democratic senator John F. Kennedy and Texas senator Lyndon B. Johnson narrowly defeated the Republican Vice President Richard Nixon and his running mate, United Nations Ambassador Henry Cabot Lodge. Mr. Kennedy, the first Roman Catholic ever elected president, participated in the first televised debate with Mr. Nixon. *Who says looks are unimportant in choosing a president?* Kennedy was handsome and well groomed; Nixon was unruly and needed a shave. Sadly, Kennedy (and his New Frontier) was only in office 1,036 days. The 35th president once said, "Forgive your enemies, but never forget their names."

Rumors persist that many of JFK's votes came from a Chicago cemetery, thanks to Chicago Mayor Richard Daley. Nixon was hospitalized for a few days in October before the election, and Kennedy, the nice guy, would not campaign until *Tricky Dick* was released. Would that happen in an election campaign today? I doubt it.

Nixon ran for governor in his home state of California in 1962 and lost to Governor Pat Brown. The former vice president famously said to the press, "You won't have Nixon to kick around anymore because, gentlemen, this is my last press conference."

However, he was wrong once again, *and over the next 12 years, Mr. Nixon was kicked around plenty—like an old, deflated football!*

In 1964, the newly sworn-in President Johnson and Minnesota senator Hubert Humphrey, in a total landslide, defeated conservative Republican senator Barry Goldwater of Arizona along with New York Rep. William Miller. What might have caused him to lose was this quote, as the right-wing Mr. Goldwater spouted, "I would remind you that extremism in the defense of liberty is no vice! And let me remind you also that moderation in the pursuit of justice is no virtue."

Vice President Humphrey later said, *"To this day I have a great deal of respect for Barry Goldwater and his running mate, what's-his-name."*

In 1968, the 36th president, LBJ, decided not to run for reelection because his approval ratings were very low, primarily because of his policy regarding the war in Vietnam. Johnson quipped, "If one morning I walked on top of the water across the Potomac River, the newspaper headline that afternoon would read, **'President can't swim.'**"

The Democrat Humphrey, along with Maine senator Edmund Muskie, were soundly beaten by guess who? Mr. Nixon was now heading back to Washington, DC, along with Maryland Governor Spiro Agnew. Alabama Democratic Governor George Wallace, a segregationist, ran as an independent and won five Southern states and 46 electoral votes.

The 37th president had a plan: stopping the war in Vietnam and, by using law and order domestically, stopping the anti-war protesting. I'm not sure if the plan worked.

The Cold War

The Cold War between the United States and the Soviet Union, which had become so heated in the 1940s and the 1950s, now became red hot (*let's change that to white hot*) in the 1960s and was a huge threat to this country. The decade got off to a rousing start when in May 1960, an American U-2 spy plane was shot down over Russia. The Soviets captured the pilot, Francis Gary Powers, when he parachuted to safety. *He was tried, found guilty of treason, and sentenced to 10 years in a luxurious, Russian prison. However, two years later, he was traded for a Russian spy and two draft picks.*

Soviet leader Nikita Khrushchev lost his cool in the United Nations's General Assembly that year. *Taking offense to a comment, he took off his shoe and pounded his table while other ambassadors stared in disbelief at the holes in his socks. Surely Joseph Stalin would have been wearing new, red argyle socks!* After his outburst, Mr. Khrushchev remarked, "I once said, 'We will bury you,' and I got into trouble with it. Of course, we will not bury you with a shovel. Your own working class will bury you."

A year later, the East Germans got into the act by constructing a wall that separated East Berlin from West Berlin, called the Anti-Fascist Protection Wall. Actually, this wall cut off West Berlin from the rest of Germany, and this Wall of Shame symbolized the Iron Curtain of Eastern Europe. The intent of the Berlin Wall was to keep the East Germans from escaping to West Berlin, although the Communists said the intent was to keep Western Fascists from entering East Germany. *That's like saying prisons have walls to prevent people from trying to get into jail!*

Newly elected President Kennedy perhaps wisely said, "A wall is a hell of a lot better than a war!"

Cuba

And then there was Cuba. In 1960, President Dwight D. Eisenhower and the CIA planned to arm Cuban refugees from Florida, Guatemala, and Nicaragua to invade Cuba and overthrow Fidel Castro's government. In April of the next year, the Bay of Pigs invasion took place and was a total failure. Due to information from the Russians, Señor Castro knew in advance about the invasion and was well prepared. Most importantly, the United States did not give their promised air support. Hundreds of the captured refugees were executed.

Obviously, Castro was no longer a best friend of Mr. Kennedy. The bearded one nationalized many American interests in Cuba—oil refineries, banks, sugar mills, Esso, Sears, and Coca-Cola. *It was rumored that the CIA was in talks with the Mafia about whacking Castro and his pal Che Guevara. There was talk of giving Castro a poison cigar to puff on!*

The Soviet Union quickly jumped into bed with Castro, promising him military hardware and economic aid. Castro declared Cuba a Socialist nation and abolished all elections. In a shift from the anti-

Communist 1950s, he now declared, "I am a Marxist-Leninist and will be one until the day that I die."

Now portraits of Karl Marx were displayed throughout Cuba while portraits of JFK were burned. The United States enacted many sanctions on Cuba and finally an embargo on all Cuban trade.

1962 was the year that the United States and the Soviet Union came closest to a nuclear war. An American spy plane flying over Cuba took photos of the construction of soccer fields. *The CIA realized that something was wrong because Cubans play baseball, not soccer, and Russians play soccer, not baseball.* They soon took photos of Soviet missile launchers being constructed, with missiles being aimed at Miami Beach. Kennedy, conferring with former Presidents Dwight D. Eisenhower and Harry S. Truman, ordered a naval blockade of Cuba and demanded that all missiles be dismantled. Our nation held its breath for several days until Soviet Premier Khrushchev backed down and agreed to remove the missiles. Actually, a secret deal was made, and the United States agreed to remove missiles from Turkey and Italy. *Phew! That was a very close call.*

Vietnam

From Europe to Latin America and finally to Southeast Asia, like a pandemic virus, the Cold War spread and threatened our country. The war in Vietnam started in 1955—although some say it began in 1945— and lasted until 1975. In the early 1960s, the Viet Cong, with weapons and supplies from the Soviet Union and China, secretly sent their troops from North Vietnam to South Vietnam. By 1964, our new president, Johnson, received congressional authority, the Gulf of Tonkin Resolution, to increase the US military presence in Vietnam. More troops were sent (by 1969, 550,000 were involved), and many more casualties were realized.

The My Lai Massacre in 1968 was the mass murder of 400 unarmed South Vietnamese civilians by US troops. This horrible war crime appalled the world.

The American public opposed the war, with students leading the protests, burning draft cards, and heading to Canada. The motto of the protesters was, **"Make love, not war."** *Even old Ho Chi Minh and his girlfriend liked this motto.*

The morale of the US soldiers deteriorated, their drug use was heavy, and the use of Agent Orange was mind-boggling. The Tet Offensive of 1968 was devastating to the American and South Vietnamese forces. Neighboring countries Laos and Cambodia became battlefields in the war. Finally, the 1970s saw the end to this conflict. More to come in the next chapter.

What a mess!

Assassinations

The 1960s appeared to be the **"decade of the gun."**

A day that has gone down as one of the saddest days in American history was November 22, 1963. In Dallas, Texas, Kennedy was shot to death at the age of 46. Vice President Johnson was immediately sworn in and became the 36th president of the country.

The assassin, allegedly Lee Harvey Oswald, was himself murdered two days later—this time on national TV. Rumors abounded about who had ordered Oswald to murder Kennedy. Could it have been the Soviet Union, or Cuba, or the Mafia, or the CIA, or a jilted girlfriend? We'll never know!

The Kennedy family's tragic legacy continued when, five years later, JFK's brother, New York senator Robert F. Kennedy, was assassinated. RFK, 42, was campaigning for the Democratic presidential nomination in 1968 and was far ahead in the polls. The former attorney general's widow and their 11 children mourned his passing.

The senator once said, "There are those who look at things the way they are and ask why . . . I dream of things that never were and I ask why not."

Another horrible assassination also took place in 1968 when Dr. Martin Luther King Jr. was murdered. King, 39, was the leader of the

Civil Rights movement in America and believed in nonviolent resistance. He won the Nobel Peace Prize in 1964 for combating racial inequality. In the years to come, he would be greatly missed. A famous quote: "We must learn to live together as brothers or perish together as fools."

Several other notables met violent deaths:

1961: Patrice Lumumba, 35, was the prime minister of the Republic of the Congo. He helped achieve Congolese independence from Belgium.

1961: Rafael Trujillo, 69, was the dictator of the Dominican Republic. He led the country for 31 years and was a polarizing figure in the Caribbean region.

1963: Ngo Dinh Diem, 62, was the president of South Vietnam who was deposed during a military coup with assistance from the CIA.

1965: Malcolm X, 39, was a controversial African American who opposed Martin Luther King's racial philosophy on civil rights. At one time, he was a leader of the Nation of Islam. He said, "If you're not ready to die for it, put the word 'freedom' out of your vocabulary."

1966: Hendrik Verwoerd, 64, was the prime minister of South Africa. He was known as the Architect of Apartheid and was not well liked by the Black majority.

1967: Che Guevara, 39, was a leader of the Cuban Revolution, along with Castro. He wanted worldwide Communist revolutions, but the CIA did not let him succeed. He once said, "Cruel leaders are replaced only to have new leaders turn cruel."

1967: George Lincoln Rockwell, 49, founded the American Nazi Party. He denied the Holocaust, loved Adolf Hitler, and favored segregation. *He should not be invited to a Shabbat dinner!*

The Six-Day War

In sports, upsets are rare, but well remembered—the underdog New York Jets beating the favored Baltimore Colts in the 1969 Super Bowl, the "Miracle on Ice" US hockey team beating the Soviets in the 1980

Winter Olympics, and 42–1 underdog Buster Douglas knocking out world heavyweight champion Mike Tyson in 1990.

In the real world, a tiny nation the size of New Jersey with a population of less than 3 million going to war with **five countries** with a total combined population of 47 million seems laughable. But in June 1967, Israel, the nation of David, soundly and quickly defeated Goliath —Egypt, Iraq, Syria, Jordan and Lebanon—in what is known as **the Six-Day War**.

In May of that year, President Gamal Abdel Nasser of Egypt closed the Straits of Tiran to Israeli shipping, meaning Israel would be without oil imports. Nasser also mobilized Egyptian armed forces on the Egypt-Israel border as a prelude to war. Realizing that conflict was imminent, Israel had no choice but to cast the first stone. In a surprise air attack, they **destroyed** the Egyptian, Iraqi, Syrian, and Lebanese air forces without the enemy ever getting one plane off the ground! The Israeli army routed the Egyptians in the Sinai Peninsula, Jordan was defeated in the West Bank, and the Syrian army surrendered the Golan Heights. Most importantly, Jerusalem was liberated and now was an Israeli city, with the Western Wall having great religious significance! Israel lost 1,000 soldiers, while the Arabs lost 20,000.

The United States and France had been Israel's biggest providers of aid; the USSR was the Arabs' benefactor. A cease-fire was declared, and Nasser resigned his presidency in shame, although he was quickly reinstated. He proclaimed, "The genius of you Americans is that you never make clear-cut stupid moves, only complicated stupid moves."

As a result of the war, Israel retained the Golan Heights, the Gaza Strip, the Sinai Peninsula, and the West Bank of the Jordan River. Israel's economy flourished with oil transported from the Sinai Peninsula and tourism starting to boom. American Jews were now proud and supportive of Israel, and Jewish people from many nations emigrated to the country. President Kennedy beautifully said, "Israel was not created in order to disappear—Israel will endure and flourish. It is the child of hope and the home of the brave. It can neither be broken by adversity nor demoralized by success. It carries the shield of democracy, and it honors the sword of freedom."

At the end of the war, Israel offered to return the Sinai Peninsula and the Golan Heights in exchange for a permanent peace agreement. At the next Arab summit meeting, the response was, "No peace, no negotiation, and no recognition of the Zionist state."

As usual, the Arabs goofed!

Civil Rights and Race Riots

In life, the concept of good is associated with love, happiness, justice, and charity. The civil rights movement in the 1960s was good.

The concept of bad or evil is associated with deliberate wrongdoing, discrimination, humiliation, destructiveness, and indiscriminate violence. The race riots of the 1960s were bad.

The civil rights movement, which started in the 1950s, continued into the 1960s and through today, with **Black Lives Matter**. The goal of the movement was to end racial discrimination of African Americans and racial segregation. Ruby Nell Bridges, at age 6 in 1960, was the first African American child to integrate a Southern school. The 1960 sit-ins at Southern lunch counters and other public facilities proved useful. Freedom Rides in the Deep South by civil rights activists challenged segregation of public buses. Voter registration for Black Americans in the South was also accomplished.

The Big Six Black leaders of the civil rights movement were King, US Rep. John Lewis, Whitney Young, A. Philip Randolph, James Farmer, and Roy Wilkins. In 1963, King organized the March on Washington, and 300,000 followers, Black and White, met at the Lincoln Memorial. King made his famous "I Have a Dream" speech, and this was the defining moment of the civil rights movement. The speech was a classic!

Johnson made civil rights his highest priority, as he signed the Civil Rights Act of 1964 and then the Voting Rights Act of 1965. He declared, "We have talked long enough in this country about equal rights. It is time now to write the next chapter—and to write it in the books of law."

The murder of three civil rights workers by the Ku Klux Klan made national headlines, as well as the Bloody Sunday police violence against protesters in Selma, Alabama. The infamous KKK dynamited a Black church in Birmingham, Alabama, in 1963, killing and injuring many children.

On April 3, 1968, in Memphis, Tennessee, King made his last speech, "I've Been to the Mountaintop." One day later, he was dead.

Inner-city poverty, discrimination, racial profiling, unemployment, and poor relations with the police department—all were valid complaints by African Americans in the 1960s, as well as today. Provoked by the police, rioting occurred in the summer of 1964 in the Harlem section of New York City; in Rochester, New York; and in Philadelphia. In 1965, the Watts Riots in Los Angeles involved 30,000 people and left 34 dead, 1,000 injured, and 4,000 arrested. The Watts section where the rioters lived was burned to the ground and totally destroyed.

The "long, hot summer" of 1967 was the year of 159 race riots, including the deadly Newark, New Jersey, riot, where 26 people were killed and hundreds were injured. Detroit's riot was especially devastating: 43 dead, 1,200 injured, 7,200 arrested, and 2,000 buildings destroyed. After King's murder in 1968, terrible rioting occurred in Washington, DC; Chicago; and Baltimore.

The Kerner Commission Report, established by LBJ, concluded that the chief causes of violence and rioting in the 1960s by African Americans was White racism and lack of economic opportunity. The report sadly warned, "Our nation is moving toward two societies, one Black, one White—separate and unequal."

In total, the 1960s saw over **750 race riots** that killed 228 people and injured 12,000. This was not just bad—this was a horrible threat to our nation.

The 1968 Democratic Convention

No American political convention was as confrontational as the Democratic National Convention in August 1968, held in Chicago. In the aftermath of the assassination of Senator Robert F. Kennedy, the Democrats nominated Vice President Humphrey for the top spot on the ticket. Minnesota senator Eugene McCarthy ran a close second.

Outside in the streets, thousands of young anti-war demonstrators protested against the conflict in Vietnam. Mayor Daley, the law-and-order mayor, called in the Illinois National Guard to augment the Chicago police force. Six hundred protesters were arrested, 1,100 were injured, and 200 police were injured. The kind-hearted mayor said, "The police are not here to create disorder, they are here to preserve disorder."

This was a week of hate, as Chicago was under siege. The protesters chanted, "Hey hey LBJ, how many kids have you killed today?"

The Anti-War Movement

Opposition to the war in Vietnam began in 1964, with many demonstrations being held. Young people opposed the military draft, and *many young men openly burned their draft cards while young women burned their bras (after taking them off).*

McCarthy was an outspoken critic of the war policy and became the hero of student activism. McCarthy said, "It is dangerous for a national candidate to say things that people might remember."

The country became polarized over the concept of the war—the left, the "doves," felt that the war was immoral, while the right, the "hawks," supported it, believing in stopping "the falling domino principle," the spreading of Communism to the world.

Many different groups were active in this anti-war movement: students—Students for a Democratic Society (SDS) emerged at Columbia University—as well as environmentalists, musicians, African

Americans, clergy, soldiers, teachers, Asian Americans, artists, etcetera. There were mass demonstrations at many universities; in 1969, the largest protest ever was held as 15 million Americans demonstrated nationwide against the war.

Muhammad Ali, once known as Cassius Clay, was the world heavyweight champion, and he refused to be drafted into the US Army. The country was outraged, and he was sentenced to five years in prison, although this was ultimately overturned. He was banned from professional boxing for three years, but later, he was regarded as a hero. With humility, he said, *"My only fault is that I don't realize how great I really am."*

Book Excerpt

Here is an excerpt from my first book, *Funny Things Happened: From Brighton to Boca*. This is a first hand humorous look of what was actually happening during this chaotic period. The title of this vignette is **"Come the Revolution."**

 The year 1968 was one of the worst years in the history of our country. Two assassinations shocked the nation - first, Martin Luther King, Jr. and then Robert F Kennedy.

The war in Vietnam was escalating, and there was tremendous opposition in the United States to this unpopular war. Young people opposing government policies, rioted at the Democratic National Convention in Chicago, causing many deaths and injuries.

Times were indeed bad!

One morning, I was in a taxi going to see a client in downtown Manhattan (Uber was still 40 years from being created). I was neatly dressed, wearing a suit with a shirt and tie. I started a conversation with my young taxi driver, who was not wearing a shirt and tie, but proudly displayed a tattoo on his burly forearm. He was an angry young man, talking about the injustices in our country and especially about the war in Vietnam.

Unbelievably, he growled at me, "**When the revolution starts, we're going to get people like you!**"

"**Me?**" I responded nervously, sounding like Woody Allen. "I'm just a nice Jewish boy from Brooklyn. I'm wearing a suit because my mother dressed me this morning. I hate the Vietnam War, I hate the Democrats, and hate the Republicans, and love the Cubans, the Russians, and the PLO."

I figured I had to touch all the right bases.

I wonder whatever became of that revolutionary taxi driver. Possibly after the revolution, he went to work for Goldman Sachs!

The Decolonization of Africa

When World War II was finally over, several European countries were deeply in debt and could not afford the luxury of keeping their African colonies. African leaders sensed this and realized that after hundreds of years of subjugation, the many colonies of Africa could become independent nations. As previously discussed, the 1950s witnessed several former colonies becoming independent. Kwame Nkrumah, who became the first president of Ghana, said, "We prefer self-government with danger to servitude in tranquility."

1960 was the Year of Africa, as 17 colonies achieved their independence. France, the United Kingdom, Belgium, and Italy all gave up large parts of their colonial empires. New countries with new names appeared—Mali, Senegal, Chad, and Gabon. Harold Macmillan, the British prime minister, famously said in South Africa, "The wind of change is blowing through this continent."

Starting in 1954 and lasting eight years, France was involved in a war with Algeria, a French colony since 1834. Hundreds of thousands of casualties occurred during this long war, and finally, in 1962, France granted Algeria its independence.

During the rest of the decade, 13 more European colonies achieved their independence—Zimbabwe, Zambia, and Botswana, to name a few. The process was very unorganized, and much political turmoil and violence took place. Who's counting, but there were at least 24 wars/conflicts in Africa in the 1960s. The United States and the Soviet Union were competing for influence during that decade on that continent. I'm not sure if there was a winner.

Question: What two African countries were never colonized?

Answer: Ethiopia and Liberia. Did you know that?

The Space Race

The 1950s Space Race, with the Soviets leading, continued into the 1960s. In April 1961, Yuri Gagarin, a Russian cosmonaut, became the first human to be launched into space. One month later, Alan Shepard followed as the first American in space. 1962 saw John Glenn, who later became a US senator, become the first American to orbit Earth. The astronaut proclaimed, "I don't know what you could say about a day in which you have seen four beautiful sunsets."

Not everything was peaches and cream in the race for space. In 1967, a fire killed three American astronauts during a ground test.

In 1962, President Kennedy famously said, "We choose to go to the moon." Although he never lived to see it, on July 20, 1969, Apollo 11 landed on the moon after a three-day journey. Astronaut Neil Armstrong was the first person to set foot on the moon, and in one of the most famous quotes of all time, he proclaimed for the world to hear, **"That's one small step for man, one giant leap for mankind!"**

Nothing can beat that quote!

Wars and Treaties of the 1960s

The decade was heavy with battles, 35 in total. In the war in Vietnam, 2 million people died. In Algeria, the War of Independence killed 184,000. The Six-Day War in the Middle East was deadly, while the war in the Philippines lasted from 1969–2017. The Football War between Honduras and El Salvador was not fought over touchdowns and field goals, but rather over land reform and immigration.

Twenty-eight treaties were signed this decade. One hundred and ninety countries signed the 1968 Nuclear Non-Proliferation Treaty dealing with nuclear weapons. Israel, North Korea, India, Pakistan, and South Sudan did not sign it. Indonesia and Malaysia signed a peace treaty ending their three-year war. *The Outer Space Treaty was signed by 190 countries, but Mars and Venus refused to sign.*

Important and Unimportant News of the 1960s

1960

1) In Egypt, construction begins on the Aswan High Dam. *However, Israel doesn't give a damn.*

2) A coal mine collapses in South Africa, killing 435 workers.

3) France tests its first atomic bomb—*hopefully, not over Paris.*

4) Iran, Iraq, Kuwait, Saudi Arabia, and Venezuela establish the Organization of the Petroleum Exporting Countries (OPEC).

5) The most powerful earthquake ever recorded, magnitude 9.5, occurs in Chile, causing a tsunami that kills 5,700.

6) Great reading this decade includes *To Kill a Mockingbird, Catch-22, The Spy Who Came in from the Cold, The Godfather,* and *Portnoy's Complaint.*

7) The first 50-star American flag is flown, in Philadelphia. *Predictably, Phillies fans boo the flag!*

8) *A US Army pilot parachuted from a balloon at a height of*

102,000 feet - 19 miles! He landed uninjured except for a sprained pinkie.

9) The musical *The Fantasticks* opens in New York City to terrible reviews. *It soon closes—42 years later!*

10) The Israeli Mossad capture infamous Nazi torturer Adolf Eichmann in Argentina.

11) Golfers Arnold Palmer and Jack Nicklaus each win six major tournaments this decade. *Fore! (No—six.)*

12) Elvis Presley returns to the United States after two years of army duty in Germany. He declares, "After a hard day of basic training, you could eat a rattlesnake."

13) The CIA implants a listening device in a cat to spy on the Soviets. When the cat is released in Washington, DC, to do its spy job, a taxi immediately runs it over. *Not a yellow cab, but a Red cab.*

14) Two commercial jet planes collide over New York City, killing 128 people. So many plane crashes—hundreds in the 1950s and 1960s. What is wrong with the airlines?

15) Margaret Court wins 16 Grand Slam tennis tournaments this decade. Fellow Australian Roy Emerson is victorious 12 times.

16) Queen Elizabeth II gives birth to Prince Andrew, the first child born to a British sovereign in over 100 years.

17) Several MIT students are so busy with their studies that they create an icicle that is four stories high. *Obviously, this is not summer school.*

18) The Boston Celtics create an NBA dynasty by winning nine championships this decade, seven of them in a row.

19) The FDA approves the first birth control pill. Millions cheer!

1961

Did you know that the year 1961 is a **strobogrammatic number**? If you turn this book upside down, the number 1961 will appear. Do you know when the next strobogrammatic year will occur? If you guessed **6009**, you are absolutely right!

1) President Dwight D. Eisenhower, making his farewell address, warns of a "military-industrial complex." *Whatever that means.*

2) At President John F. Kennedy's inauguration, our new leader proclaims, "Ask not what your country can do for you, ask what you can do for your country."

3) The USSR detonates a 58-megaton H-bomb, the largest bomb explosion ever. *They ask permission to explode it over North Carolina, but the United States says no.*

4) The United States severs diplomatic relations with Cuba. They are restored 54 years later.

5) President John F. Kennedy establishes the Peace Corps. *"How's your cousin Seymour? Seymour joined the Peace Corps."*

6) The Soviet city Stalingrad is renamed Volgograd. Russian ballet dancer Rudolf Nureyev requests asylum in France.

7) Who was born this year? President Barack Obama, Princess Diana, hockey star Wayne Gretzky, and actor George Clooney.

8) The United Arab Republic, consisting of Egypt and Syria, *ends their marriage of three years, citing incompatibility—no alimony involved.*

9) Ernie Davis of Syracuse University becomes the first African American to win the Heisman Trophy. He is selected first in the NFL draft, but unfortunately never plays a minute of professional football, as he sadly dies of leukemia at age 23.

10) The 23rd Amendment is passed, giving Washington, DC, residents the right to vote.

11) Roger Maris hits 61 home runs, breaking the record of 60 set by fellow Yankee Babe Ruth in 1927.

12) U Thant of Burma becomes secretary general of the United Nations, succeeding Dag Hammarskjöld, who was killed in a plane crash. The human rights organization Amnesty International is founded in London.

13) *An original painting by Henri Matisse, displayed at the MoMA in New York City, is discovered to be hanging upside down, but only for 47 days.*

14) The Barbie doll has a boyfriend, as Ken is introduced. *Rumors persist that Barbie is expecting.*

15) *The Misfits* is the last movie made by Clark Gable, 59, and Marilyn Monroe, 36, for both die in the early 1960s. Costars Montgomery Clift, 45, and Thelma Ritter, 66, die later in the decade. A bad-luck movie.

16) The Green Bay Packers are the class of the NFL, winning five championships. Coach Vince Lombardi expounds, *"Show me a good loser and I'll show you a loser."*

1962

1) JFK gives a great quote when 49 Nobel Laureates are invited to dinner at the White House: "I think this is the most extraordinary collection of talent, of human knowledge, there has ever been gathered at the White House with the possible exception of when Thomas Jefferson dined alone."

2) After 307 years, Jamaica, Trinidad, and Tobago become independent from the United Kingdom.

3) The first of James Bond's 27 movies, *Dr. No*, debuts. Who played the role of Bond the most? If you said, "Sean Connery," you are wrong. Roger Moore played 007 seven times.

4) A newspaper strike in New York City lasts 114 days. *Subway riders are forced to talk to one another.*

5) The first Walmart store opens in Arkansas, the first Kmart opens in Michigan, and the first Target opens in Minnesota. Everyone is looking for a bargain.

6) In a welterweight championship fight, Emile Griffith knocks out Benny "Kid" Paret, who is hospitalized and soon dies.

7) The ultimate Nazi, Adolf Eichmann, is found guilty of crimes against humanity and executed in Israel.

8) Johnny Carson becomes host of *The Tonight Show* and sits at same desk for 30 years. *Here's Johnny!* Other big TV shows were *Bonanza, The Beverly Hillbillies,* and *Rowan & Martin's Laugh-In.*

9) The attempted assassination of Charles de Gaulle of France fails. He survives more than 30 assassination attempts over the years. He said humbly, "I was France."

10) A flood in Barcelona, Spain, kills 440; an earthquake in Iran kills 12,000.

11) Wilt Chamberlain of the Philadelphia Warriors unbelievably scores 100 points in a single game. For the season, he averages 50 points per game, along with 25 rebounds, while playing every minute of every game. Wilt the Stilt leads the league in scoring seven straight years, averaging 39 points per game. In my opinion, he was the best!

12) Leonardo da Vinci's *Mona Lisa* leaves Paris for a tour of the United States. First Lady Jacqueline Kennedy is responsible for the visit.

13) Marilyn Monroe, in her last public appearance, sings "Happy Birthday" to President John F. Kennedy at Madison Square Garden.

14) The United States and Cuba make a trade—Cuba returns 1,100 prisoners from the Bay of Pigs invasion in exchange for food and medicine.

15) In one of the great blunders of the decade, The Beatles audition for Decca Records—and are **rejected**!

1963

1) After 53 years, the demolition of Penn Station in New York City begins. It soon becomes the new Madison Square Garden.

2) Nuclear submarine the *USS Thresher* sinks, killing 129 sailors.

3) Alcatraz, the federal prison in San Francisco Bay, is closed. *It was once the home of Al Capone, Machine Gun Kelly, and other fashionable socialites.*

4) The Moscow-Washington hotline is installed. Known as "the red phone" in Washington, DC, *maybe in Moscow it is known as the red, white, and blue phone!*

5) Pope Paul VI succeeds Pope John XXIII. He is leader of the Catholic Church for the next 15 years.

6) Malaya, Singapore, North Borneo, and Sarawak merge to form the country of Malaysia. Singapore is expelled from Malaysia in 1965 and remains independent.

7) Five hundred African students demonstrate in Moscow's Red Square. *Nikita Khrushchev is seen throwing his shoes at the protesters.*

8) The Great Train Robbery in England, by a gang of 15, nets 2.6 million pounds. Most of the robbers are apprehended, while most of the money is never found.

9) Andy Warhol paints his classic Campbell Condensed soup cans. *Mmm mmm good.*

10) The ZIP code is introduced. ZIP stands for "Zone Improvement Plan."

11) Doctors tell brilliant scientist Stephen Hawking, 21, that he has two years to live. *He proves them wrong by living another 53 years.*

12) Winston Churchill becomes an honorary citizen of the United States. He once said to a lady, *"I may be drunk, miss, but in the morning, I will be sober, and you will still be ugly."*

1964

1) President Lyndon B. Johnson's first State of the Union Address declares war on poverty.

2) The US Surgeon General reports that smoking may be hazardous to one's health. *The **understatement** of the decade!*

3) By far, the most important musical event of the decade, perhaps of the century, is the British Invasion. We're not talking about the War of 1812, but rather The Beatles! These four boys from across the pond create a sensation in music never before seen. Hit after hit, album after album, were huge successes. The Beatles appear on *The Ed Sullivan Show, and 73 million people want to hold their hand.*

4) The great Alaskan earthquake, the largest in North America, registers at magnitude 9.2.

5) The Polo Grounds, the old home of the New York Giants, is demolished. *Brooklyn Dodger fans remember 1951 and continue crying.*

6) A revolving door in Moscow as Nikita Khrushchev is out and Leonid Brezhnev is in. Alexei Kosygin waits in the wings.

7) Riots break out at a soccer game between Peru and Argentina over a referee's decision, and 300 die. *Hopefully, not the referee.*

8) Tickets for Broadway shows are in great demand this decade. So many hits: *Fiddler on the Roof, Man of La Mancha, Hello, Dolly!, Camelot, The Odd Couple, The Great White Hope,* and, lastly, *Hair.*

9) The New York World's Fair opens in Queens, as does the Verrazano-Narrows Bridge, connecting Brooklyn and Staten Island.

10) *A chimpanzee's painting, using a pseudonym, is hung in a Swedish art gallery. Critics love the painting, and it is supposedly sold for a bunch of bananas.*

11) The Warren Commission Report says that Lee Harvey Oswald acted alone in killing President John F. Kennedy.

12) South African anti-apartheid leader Nelson Mandela is sentenced to life imprisonment. He is released after 26 years and then becomes president of the country.

13) In a great boxing upset, newcomer Cassius Clay, soon to be known as Muhammad Ali, defeats world heavyweight champion Sonny Liston.

14) The Boston Strangler is finally captured after killing 13 women. *A career boost for actor Tony Curtis.*

15) Sidney Poitier becomes the first African American actor to win an Oscar, for his role in *Lilies of the Field.*

16) Born this year are Boris Johnson, the British prime minister; baseball's Barry Bonds; and First Lady Michelle Obama, who said, "There are still many causes worth sacrificing for, so much history yet to be made."

17) The most embarrassing moment in NFL history: Jim "Wrong Way" Marshall of the Minnesota Vikings *recovers a fumble and runs 66 yards—**the wrong way**, to his own end zone.*

18) Fidel Castro's sister defects from Cuba to Mexico. He feels badly about losing his sister but feels worse *when he finds out that she has been spying on Cuba for the United States for many years.*

1965

1) An electrical blackout in the Northeast causes turmoil for 13 hours. *Nine months later, there's a baby boom.*

2) The Chevy Impala becomes the biggest-selling car in US history.

3) Tokyo officially becomes the largest city in the world, surpassing New York City. *But who has better sushi?*

4) The Beatles perform at Shea Stadium in New York before 55,000 screaming fans. *It was **a hard day's night**.*

5) Anyone convicted of burning his draft card is sentenced to five years in prison. *How many years for burning a bra?*

6) The Astrodome opens in Houston; the Gateway Arch in St. Louis is completed. McDonald's is happy.

7) Besides The Beatles, there is other music this decade. Diana Ross, Stevie Wonder, The Jackson 5, Smokey Robinson, and Motown Records are all major successes.

8) West Germany establishes diplomatic relations with Israel. Immediately, all Arab countries sever relations with West Germany.

9) The Cultural Revolution begins in China. The Chinese hope to spread revolution around the world against the United States and Western Europe.

10) A Soviet cosmonaut takes the first walk in space. *They are still looking for him.*

11) Los Angeles Dodgers pitcher Sandy Koufax refuses to pitch the opening game of the World Series because of Jewish holiday Yom Kippur. *With God watching, the Dodgers lose.*

12) The Great Comet of 1965, Ikeya-Seki, is discovered. If you missed it, just wait 600 years for its return.

13) Pope Paul VI visits New York City and holds Mass at Yankee Stadium. *He hits a home run as the Cardinals beat the Yankees.*

1966

1) Two US Air Force planes collide off the Spanish coast, while refueling at 30,000 feet. Now the bad news: Four H-bombs were on board one plane and were dropped over Spain. Fortunately, the bombs were not detonated and were recovered. ***The planes in Spain fall mainly on the plains.***

2) Edward Brooke of Massachusetts becomes the first African American elected to the US Senate since the days of Reconstruction.

3) The National Organization of Women (NOW) is established. *Men are welcome.*

4) Indira Gandhi, daughter of the late Prime Minister Jawaharlal Nehru, becomes prime minister of India. She is assassinated in 1984.

5) A sniper with a rifle at the University of Texas kills 14 and wounds 32 students.

6) The Black Panther Party is founded in Oakland. *None of the founders appear in the 2018 superhero movie.*

7) The groundbreaking is held for the World Trade Center in New York City. The Metropolitan Opera House opens at Lincoln Center for the Performing Arts.

8) *Star Trek* makes its debut. The *New York Herald Tribune* ends its publication after 42 years.

9) The Miranda warning comes into effect, and suspects must be informed of their rights. *You've seen this on TV so many times.*

10) The Aberfan disaster in South Wales, a mudslide caused by heavy rain, kills 144, including 116 children.

11) Los Angeles Dodger All-Star pitcher Sandy Koufax wins 27 games and then announces his retirement at age 30. Also retiring this decade are baseball greats Ted Williams, Stan Musial, Warren Spahn, and Mickey Mantle, who said, "If I knew I was going to live this long, I would have taken better care of myself."

12) Eventual President Ronald Reagan, an actor, is elected governor of California. Originally a liberal Democrat, he switches hats

and becomes a conservative Republican. He made 69 movies, including the famous *Cowboy from Brooklyn.*

13) Pop art, psychedelic art, and minimalism are highlights of the art world. Leaders include Andy Warhol, Jackson Pollock, Mark Rothko, and Roy Lichtenstein.

14) "The housewife revolt" takes place across the country as women protest the high cost of food. Ladies get their way, as food prices soon drop.

15) The Salvation Army celebrates its 100th birthday. Merry Christmas to all.

1967

1) Thurgood Marshall becomes the first African American justice of the US Supreme Court. *"I have a lifetime appointment and I intend to serve it. I expect to die at 110, shot by a jealous husband."*

2) A Brussels, Belgium, department store burns down in a devastating fire, killing 323.

3) The 25th Amendment is ratified, which details presidential succession and disability.

4) The NHL expands from six teams to twelve. The Montreal Canadiens take five Stanley Cups this decade, while the Toronto Maple Leafs win four times. O Canada!

5) Joseph Stalin's daughter defects to the United States from the Soviet Union, *looking for a capitalist career on Wall Street. Quite a switch!*

6) Canada celebrates its 100th anniversary of Confederation. Charles de Gaulle visits Canada and endorses a separatist movement. "Vive le Quebec libre."

7) An explosion on the aircraft carrier *USS Forrestal* kills 134 sailors in Vietnamese waters.

8) President Lyndon B. Johnson has a summit meeting with Soviet Premier Alexei Kosygin in New Jersey. *The Russian leader wants to stroll the boardwalk in Atlantic City and eat saltwater taffy.*

9) Dr. Christiaan Barnard, a South African surgeon, performs the world's first human heart transplant. "On Saturday, I was a surgeon in South Africa, very little known. On Monday, I was world renowned."

10) The Summer of Love is proclaimed in San Francisco in the counterculture movement.

11) **Thirty-six million** gallons of crude oil are spilled off the British coast, the worst oil spill in UK history.

12) The US Supreme Court rules that interracial marriage is constitutional.

13) Canadian soldiers testing Agent Orange are told the chemical is completely safe, and they spray it on one another. It's unclear how many died of cancer.

14) Albania is the first and only constitutionally atheist country to exist. All religious practices are officially banned between 1967–1991.

15) *James Bedford of California becomes the first person to be cryopreserved. He dies in 1967 but could be defrosted at any time.*

16) Elvis Presley and Priscilla Beaulieu get married in Las Vegas. *He wears his "Blue Suede Shoes," and they honeymoon at "Heartbreak Hotel" with their "Hound Dog."*

1968

1) In January, an Israeli submarine is lost in the Mediterranean Sea. The next day, France also loses one in the Mediterranean. In March, a Soviet submarine sinks in the Pacific Ocean. In May, a US nuclear submarine is lost in the Atlantic Ocean. In total, hundreds are killed. *Sounds like something from a James Bond movie.*

2) North Korea seizes the *USS Pueblo* in territorial waters. After 11 months, the 83-man crew is released, *but North Korea keeps the ship, which is now a tourist attraction for anyone wishing to vacation in North Korea.*

3) Former First Lady Jacqueline Kennedy ("One must not let oneself be overwhelmed by sadness") marries business tycoon Aristotle

Onassis. David Eisenhower, presidential grandson, marries Julie Nixon, presidential daughter.

4) The USSR invades Czechoslovakia with 650,000 soldiers to combat Czech liberalism and the end of Prague Spring.

5) An Israeli commando raid at Beirut Airport destroys 13 Arab planes as reprisal for a terrorist attack on an Israeli plane.

6) The Pennsylvania Railroad Company and the New York Railroad Company merge to establish the Penn Central Transportation Company, which goes bankrupt in two years.

7) The new Madison Square Garden opens in New York City. *The Knicks and Rangers lose again.*

8) The Paris Peace Talks regarding ending the war in Vietnam are held, but unfortunately, they fail. It appears that President Richard Nixon had a hand in "monkey-wrenching" the results before the election.

9) The Zodiac Killer starts his deadly spree in California, murdering about 30. *Lock your doors; he has never been caught.*

10) Some of the many celebrities of this decade include Elizabeth Taylor, Steve McQueen, Julie Andrews, Jack Lemmon, Rock Hudson, Dean Martin, Bob Dylan, Janis Joplin, Simon & Garfunkel, James Brown, Mick Jagger, and Truman Capote, who said, "Life is a moderately good play with a badly written third act."

11) At the Mexico City Summer Olympics, African American athletes give the Black Power salute at the medals ceremony, upsetting many Americans.

12) The Hong Kong flu makes it deadly debut, killing about 1 million people globally.

13) Denny McLain of the Detroit Tigers wins 31 games, a hard-to-beat record.

14) *60 Minutes* makes its TV debut, the waterbed is introduced, and the first Big Mac is sold for 49 cents. Burp!

15) Yale University announces that it will now admit women, *but they will not be allowed to play Ivy League football.*

1969

1) Golda Meir becomes the first female prime minister of Israel. *"Let me tell you something that we Israelis have against Moses. He took us 40 years through the desert in order to bring us to the one spot in the Middle East that has no oil!"*

2) Woodstock Music Festival takes place in Upstate New York, where 300,000 stoned people sleep in the mud.

3) The Soviet Union and China battle on the Manchurian border. Chairman Mao Tse-tung is ready to use nuclear weapons but relents.

4) Yasser Arafat is elected chairman of the Palestine Liberation Organization (PLO). "We plan to eliminate the state of Israel and establish a purely Palestinian state."

5) Senator Ted Kennedy drives off a bridge in Chappaquiddick, killing his female assistant. He does not report the incident to police until much later. *He says that he will cross that bridge when he comes to it.*

6) *The Saturday Evening Post*, after being in the magazine business for 147 years, publishes its last weekly edition. *Artist Norman Rockwell is looking for a job.*

7) North Korea shoots down a US Navy reconnaissance plane, killing 31 aboard. Why no reaction from America?

8) Warren Burger succeeds Earl Warren as chief justice of the United States. Lots of Warrens want to interview for a job: Warren Beatty, Warren Buffett, and Elizabeth Warren.

9) A decade of great movies, including *West Side Story, Lawrence of Arabia, The Longest Day, Cleopatra, A Man for All Seasons, The Graduate, The Sound of Music*, and, of course, *My Fair Lady*.

10) The Stonewall Riots in Greenwich Village, New York City, are the start of the modern gay rights movement. Commemorating the 50th anniversary of the riots in 2019, the NYC police commissioner apologizes for the police action.

11) There is religious civil rights strife in Northern Ireland between Protestants and Catholics; 1,000 British soldiers get involved.

12) 1969 was the year of New York City. "Broadway Joe" Namath leads the New York Jets to an upset victory over the Baltimore Colts in the Super Bowl. The winning quarterback wisely said, "When you win, nothing hurts."

13) The Amazing New York Mets, an expansion team, behind Tom Seaver, beat the Baltimore Orioles to win the World Series. Perennial losers, the New York Knicks win the NBA championship, defeating the Los Angeles Lakers.

14) Project Blue Book, a comprehensive study by the US Government, concludes that there is no evidence of UFOs. *But I saw one last week!*

15) Rocky Marciano dies in a plane crash. He is the only world heavyweight champion to finish his career undefeated, 49–0.

16) Student anti-war riots close many college campuses across the country. *Students must bring a note from their mother for missing classes.*

17) *Sesame Street* debuts. Kids are happy. Bert and Ernie must be taking the right vitamins—*after all these years, they haven't aged one bit.*

18) Englishman John Fairfax rows across the Atlantic Ocean, from the United Kingdom to Miami, in only 180 days. Two years later, he rows across the Pacific Ocean. *He tries to get a job tending the rowboats in Central Park Lake but is rejected because of lack of experience.*

Deaths This Decade of Notable People

- Herbert Hoover, 90. Thirty-first US president. 1929-1933. "Blessed are the young for they shall inherit the national debt."
- Dwight D. Eisenhower, 78. Thirty-fourth US president. 1953-1961.
- Ho Chi Minh, 79. North Vietnam leader.
- Nat "King" Cole, 45. Unforgettable American singer.
- Winston Churchill, 90. British prime minister during

World War II. "The pessimist sees difficulty in every opportunity. The optimist sees opportunity in every difficulty."

- Yuri Gagarin, 34. Soviet cosmonaut was the first man in space.
- Gary Cooper, 60. American actor who starred in *High Noon* and *Sergeant York.*
- Ty Cobb, 74. Held MLB's highest career batting average.
- Pope John XXII, 81. Catholic Church leader, 1958–1963.
- Jawaharlal Nehru, 74. First prime minister of India, 1947–1964.
- Robert Frost, 88. Leading American poet.
- Helen Keller, 87. Author and disability rights advocate despite her loss of sight and hearing.
- Edward R. Murrow, 57. American broadcast journalist.
- Eleanor Roosevelt, 78. Former First Lady. "A woman is like a tea bag—you can't tell how strong she is until you put her in hot water."
- Walt Disney, 65. Mickey Mouse and Minnie Mouse's father.
- Spencer Tracy, 67. Bright Hollywood star.
- Judy Garland, 47. Actress in *The Wizard of Oz.* "I was born at the age of 12 on an MGM lot."

Advances in Science This Decade

The chemical makeup of DNA– the oral polio vaccine – Vaccines for mumps and measles– The first in vitro fertilization of a human egg cell – The pulsar is discovered – The US Government removes the artificial sweetener cyclamate from the market, citing links to cancer – Thalidomide causes congenital deformities in 7,000 babies – The tranquilizer Valium – The weather satellite – The first human eye transplant – Ibuprofen – The optical fiber laser – Kevlar – The internet

Important Innovations of the 1960s

Halogen lamp – Audio cassette – Handheld calculator – Astroturf – Nondairy creamer – Permanent-press fabric – Soft contact lenses – Computer video game – Smoke detector – Golf ball typewriter – Automatic teller machine (ATM) – Pampers – Electric toothbrush – Jacuzzi – Aluminum cans – 911 emergency number – Compact disc – Miniskirt – Skateboard – New Hampshire Lottery – Sharpies – Chubby Checker and the Twist – Touchtone phones – And, happily, silicone breast implants

---

In 1960, the population of the world was 3 billion people. The United States's population was 179 million people. The average life expectancy of Americans was 70 years.

The Swinging '60s of the hippies were over. The revolution in music, drugs, clothing, sexuality, and so many other things dealing with the counterculture had just begun. The threats that we have discussed were widespread—the anti-war movement, student protests, the civil rights movement, feminism, and the gay rights movement all emerged this decade. This truly was **the decade from hell**!

The country and the world (and you, dear reader) were now ready for the threats of the 1970s.

8

1970–1979
THE ME DECADE

Writer Tom Wolfe, author of *The Bonfire of the Vanities*, coined the phrase **"the Me Decade"** to best describe the period of the 1970s. He felt that individualism had become more important, as people became disenchanted with the wars and politics of the previous decades.

There were plenty of threats in the 1970s, but not nearly the same as the crazy 1960s. The Cold War had cooled off a bit, thankfully. We had a domestic hot war in Washington, DC, the threat being an almost constitutional crisis. Our dependency on foreign oil imports caused a huge threat as the spigots from the Arab world were quickly turned off.

The war in Vietnam continued, as did the anti-war protests, a major concern. A huge threat was the concept of international terrorism, which reared its ugly head for basically the first time. A terrible economic climate also gripped the country as inflation heated up for the first time in a long while.

Our closest Middle Eastern ally became involved in another war that threatened to include us. And finally, a revolution in a country previously friendly to us became a huge threat as the new rulers who regarded America as Satan took many US citizens hostage.

Presidential Elections of the 1970s

In 1972, Republican President Richard Nixon and Vice President Spiro Agnew were reelected in a landslide. Democratic South Dakota senator George McGovern and his running mate, US Ambassador to France Sargent Shriver (JFK's brother-in-law) were soundly defeated. *It was rumored that Sargent Shriver would be demoted and become* **Corporal** *Shriver.*

Then things got worse for the administration when, in 1973, Agnew was forced to resign in disgrace. He was accused of suspicion of bribery, extortion, and tax fraud while payments were supposedly made to him when he was in office. *Nothing too serious, though!*

He made this infamous quote that nobody could understand, "In the United States today, we have more than our share of the nattering nabobs of negativism." *What the heck does that mean? He should have resigned just for making that quote.*

Question: Who was the first vice president to resign?

Answer: That's easy—John C. Calhoun in 1832.

Nixon replaced Agnew with Republican Gerald Ford of Michigan, who had served 24 years in the House of Representatives.

As a result of the Watergate scandal (of which you will soon become apprised), Nixon, in August 1974, became the only US president to resign his office. Ford became the 38th president, and he selected New York Governor Nelson Rockefeller as his veep.

In the 1976 election, Ford and his running mate, Kansas Republican senator Bob Dole, lost in a very close race. The new president, No. 39, was the Democratic governor of Georgia, Jimmy Carter. The new vice president was Walter Mondale, a longtime senator from Minnesota.

Did you know that Ford was the only person who became both a vice president and president of the United States **without ever being elected** to either office?

The Cold War

The biggest threat of the last four decades, the Cold War with the Soviet Union, became less of a threat in the 1970s. The magic word was **"détente,"** a French term meaning "release from tension." The United States and the Soviet Union launched a joint space flight docking a US Apollo spacecraft with the Soviet Soyuz.

Question: Nixon traveled to China in 1972, but who was the first president to visit the country while he was not in office?

Answer: Former President Ulysses S. Grant in 1878.

China and the Soviets had border disputes and philosophical problems, and the United States cheered from the sidelines. By 1979, America and China had normalized relations. By the end of the decade, East Germany and the United States were engaged in diplomatic relations. The 1972 Strategic Arms Limitation Talks (SALT) *had nothing to do with sodium intake but rather with strategic ballistic missile launchers. The Cold War was turning into a Warm Peace.*

Watergate Woes

The scandal began in June 1972, when five "plumbers" burglarized the Democratic National Committee's headquarters in the Watergate Office Building in Washington, DC. *The five perps (sounds like a vocal group of the 1950s) had cash on them that was connected to the Committee to Re-elect the President, known as* **CREEP**—*a perfect name for the Nixon campaign.*

Over the next two years, it was shown that *Tricky Dick* and his close allies had known about this operation and did their best to cover it up. *Washington Post* reporters Bob Woodward and Carl Bernstein uncovered invaluable evidence from **Deep Throat**, implicating Mr. Nixon and all the president's men. Nixon famously declared, **"I'm not a crook."**

National TV coverage of the US Senate Watergate hearings revealed that the cover-up was "a cancer on the presidency." A smoking-gun audio tape showed that Nixon was involved in the cover-up from the very beginning. The US Congress was ready to impeach and remove the president from office—a huge constitutional threat.

On August 9, 1974, Nixon sorrowfully resigned. He had once said, "A man is not finished when he is defeated. He's finished when he quits." *Nixon was finished!*

Attorney General John Mitchell, Ehrlichman, Haldeman, Kleindienst and about 20 other Nixon compatriots, spent many of the next several months luxuriating in federal prison.

The next month, Ford issued a full and unconditional pardon of Nixon, calling the situation "an American tragedy." The American public was not in favor of the pardon, and this ultimately could have been the deciding factor in Ford's defeat in the 1976 election. *He once said, "I watch a lot of baseball on the radio." He must have been friends with Yogi Berra!*

Vietnam and Anti-War Protests

Nixon had a plan to end the war, which he emphasized in his 1972 campaign. He began to reduce the number of American forces in the war-torn area—the concept of Vietnamization. US troops in 1969 numbered 549,000; by 1972, the troop count was down to 69,000.

In 1970, Secretary of State Henry Kissinger began secret peace negotiations with the North Vietnamese in Paris. The talks failed, but at least it was a first step in ending the war. Mr. Kissinger did win the Nobel Peace Prize in 1973 for his efforts in stopping this most unpopular conflict.

Meanwhile, at home, the threat of the anti-war movement of the 1960s continued. A horrible event took place in May 1970 at Kent State University in Ohio. At a peace rally, National Guard soldiers fired into a crowd of unarmed protesters, killing four students and wounding nine others. The country was in a turmoil over the shootings, and millions of students walked out of school in an organized strike. "Stop the war and feed the poor" was heard throughout the country.

US Army veterans came to Washington, DC, and threw away their prized medals on the steps of the US Capitol building.

Meanwhile, back in Vietnam, the United States bombed and invaded neighboring countries Laos and Cambodia. In 1972, the Vietcong launched the Easter Offensive against the south. Finally, in January 1973, Nixon signed the Paris Peace Accords, officially ending US physical involvement in Vietnam. In a speech, he stressed, "Peace with honor."

In 1975, Saigon fell to the Vietcong; there was a mass evacuation, and South Vietnam surrendered. Finally, North Vietnam and South Vietnam were unified as a new independent nation, the Socialist Republic of Vietnam.

After so many years of fighting, with 58,000 American soldiers dying in a losing war, the question remains: "Was it worth it?"

I think not.

The Yom Kippur War and the Oil Crisis

The Arab world was humiliated by their stunning defeat to Israel in the Six-Day War of 1967. Shortly thereafter came the War of Attrition, small conflicts between Israel and Egypt and the other Arab countries. Israel's experienced pilots, called *"Moshe's Marauders" (named for Moshe Dayan),* bombed very close to Cairo.

Egyptian President Gamal Abdel Nasser died in 1970 and was succeeded by Anwar Sadat. Egypt's economy was in a shambles, and the clever Egyptians believed that war was a necessity for survival. Syria mobilized their army, confident that they could win the next conflict with Israel. The Arab countries planned their war for three years. Israel knew that it was coming but did not know exactly when. *Israel received valuable information from a spy in Egypt who happened to be Mr. Sadat's son-in-law.*

October 6, 1973, was Yom Kippur, the holiest day of the year for the Jewish people. This was the day that Egypt and Syria launched a surprise attack on Israel. The invaders were aided by a group of countries: Cuba, Morocco, Saudi Arabia, Jordan, Iraq, Libya, Tunisia, Algeria, and the USSR. Israel was aided by their only friend, the United States.

Egypt crossed the Suez Canal unopposed into the Sinai Peninsula while Syria invaded the Golan Heights. For three wonderful days for the Arab countries, Israel was losing. Then the tide turned as Israel counterattacked the invaders. Egypt's forces were cut off in the Sinai Peninsula, and Syria paid a heavy toll in the Golan Heights. The Israeli army advanced into Syria, only about 10 miles from the capital city of Damascus.

A cease-fire was agreed to on October 28. Israel suffered major casualties, but not nearly as many as the Arab countries endured. Kissinger proclaimed, "The security of Israel is a moral imperative for all free peoples."

In the aftermath, there was a repercussion and a huge threat to the United States. Immediately, the Arab members of OPEC declared an oil embargo on the United States and Israel. Oil prices then skyrocketed 400% in one year. American domestic production of oil could not keep pace with the huge demand, and gasoline was being rationed. The six-month embargo led to a global recession and the stock market crash of 1973-1974. Because of the rising price of black gold, the oil-exporting nations accumulated vast wealth.

The major oil companies began searching for new ways to increase oil supplies. Exploration in areas never thought of before (underwater, for example) were now being utilized. Conservation to reduce consumption and alternative energy sources—nuclear, fossil fuels, and solar energy—were all very important during the oil crisis.

The rest of the world was totally dependent on Arab oil. While the United States imported just 12% from this part of the world, Western Europe imported 80%, and Japan imported 90%. There was now a need for smaller cars, not the gas guzzlers on the highways in the 1970s.

The Threat of Economic Crisis

The years following World War II, and lasting until the early 1970s, brought a period of economic expansion and prosperity. But due to the Arab embargo, *the oil hit the fan,* and there was now limited economic growth. A recession began in November 1973 and lasted until March 1975. Inflation rose dramatically and coincided with high unemployment and stagnant growth, causing **stagflation**. The stock market in 1973 and 1974 crashed, losing 45% of its value. Other countries had it worse: the London Stock Exchange lost 73%.

When Nixon initiated price controls in 1971, it fueled inflation in the coming years. Inflation soared from 3% in 1972 to 12% in 1974. It calmed in the mid-1970s, but by 1979, inflation reached 13%. In 1975, inflation in the United Kingdom reached 25%.

New York City was in bad financial shape in 1975, experiencing a severe cash shortage and near bankruptcy. New York Governor Hugh Carey and NYC Mayor Abraham Beame went to Washington, DC, to ask Ford for federal help. The headline of the October 30 edition of the *New York Daily News* said it all: **"Ford To City: Drop Dead."**

The next energy crisis occurred in 1979, caused by the Iranian revolution and decreased oil production. Oil prices rose, and the cost of gasoline, when it was available, hit the roof. More to come on this subject.

Terrorism

The definition of terrorism is "the unlawful use of premeditated violence and intimidation, especially against civilians, usually in the pursuit of political aims." Terrorism in one form or another has been around for almost 2,000 years. A terrorist wears many hats, as there are at least five different forms of the activity: state-sponsored, dissent (against the government), political ideology, religious, and criminal.

Sadly, the 1970s were the golden age of terrorism. The tactics that terrorists used were assassinations, suicide bombings, kidnappings, airline hijackings, taking hostages, and armed assaults. Unfortunately, the terrorists became very good at doing their bad deeds. Almost 10,000 incidents occurred, leaving nearly 7,000 dead. Threats were everywhere!

A great many of the attacks involved the Palestinians and the Palestine Liberation Organization (PLO). The most heinous took place at the 1972 Summer Olympics held in Munich, Germany, when the Black September Palestinians murdered 12 Israeli athletes. Also in 1972, the Japanese Red Army killed 26 Puerto Ricans at the Israeli airport on behalf of the PLO. *Still trying to figure that one out!* All through the 1970s, the PLO targeted Israel, killing hundreds of civilians, including school children. Planes were hijacked and blown up.

In the United States, there were many terrorist attacks. The Black Panthers were responsible for 24 bombings, the Jewish Defense League conducted 44 bombings, the Puerto Rican group Fuerzas Armadas de Liberación Nacional (FALN) planted 82 bombs, and the Weather Underground was responsible for 25 bombings until they finally blew themselves up.

Terrorism was active in Europe, especially in Northern Ireland and England. Carlos the Jackal was No. 1 on the Most Wanted list throughout Europe. *He currently resides in France, safely behind bars.*

The USSR and Afghanistan

In 1978, a revolution in the Asian country of Afghanistan took place that was decidedly pro-Soviet. The next year, the US ambassador was kidnapped and murdered, presumably by government forces. Relations between Afghanistan and the United States now became hostile.

America began aiding the rebel forces, known as the mujahideen, while the Soviets gave aid to the government forces, creating the threat of a proxy war. Finally, in the last days of 1979, the USSR invaded Afghanistan, installing a very pro-Soviet government. This invasion lasted 10 years, was very unsuccessful, and ultimately led to the demise of the Soviet Union. The invasion was a huge blunder. How ironic that the rebels that the United States supported in the 1980s morphed into the Taliban that America fought for the next three decades.

Iran

By 1971, the Persian Empire was 2,500 years old. Now called Iran, the non-Arab (Aryan) country was ruled by the Shah, who was a tough guy. His secret police, SAVAK, were brutal, oppressive, and corrupt. Nevertheless, the United States and Iran were best friends. With no humility, the Iranians later declared, "Shah is a kind of magic word with the Persian people."

Iran was a huge producer of oil, and with the price of oil skyrocketing in the 1970s, zillions of dollars were being made. Almost all of this income went to the Shah and his family. *They were not on Persian food stamps.*

Taking no nonsense, a Muslim Shia leader, Ayatollah Khomeini, who opposed the government, was sent into exile in 1963. Because of inflation, anti-government protests and general strikes broke out in 1978, and martial law was declared. The Islamic Revolution had begun.

In early 1979, the Ayatollah returned to Iran and declared the country to be an Islamic republic. *The Shah and his family packed their belongings (aka money) and flew the coop.* The new Iranian government now hated Westernization and canceled all treaties with the United States, the USSR, and everybody else. The United States froze all Iranian assets and created an economic embargo.

Meanwhile, the Shah was dying and came to America for treatment. The Ayatollah demanded that the Shah be returned to Iran to be executed, but the United States refused. In anger, 500 revolutionaries stormed the US embassy in Tehran and took 66 American diplomats as hostages and held 52 of them for 444 days. The price of oil skyrocketed again, creating gasoline shortages and soaring fuel prices. The second energy crisis of the decade had begun.

It was said of the new Iranian leader, "When the Islamic Revolution began, it aroused considerable admiration in the Arab Street. It deposed one of the region's most tyrannical regimes. The people discerned in this revolution new hope for freedom and change."

Author Christopher Hitchens said of the Iranian crisis, "The US moved from the age of the Red Menace to the epoch of the Holy War."

For the next several decades, Iran truly became a great threat to the United States and its allies.

Wars and Treaties of the 1970s

There were plenty of wars this decade. Actually, 55 different ones were fought. Twenty-six wars ended; 29 started this decade but finished later. The Vietnam situation was a 30-year ordeal that killed 2 million people. The Chinese Cultural Revolution lasted nine years and also killed 2 million.

The two Cod Wars were fought in the 1970s between the United Kingdom and Iceland. *Snowballs were used as weapons.*

Many important treaties were signed. The Paris Peace Accords ended US involvement in Vietnam at long last. The Camp David Accords, brokered by Carter, produced the peace treaty that Israel and Egypt signed in 1979—a monumental event. Sadat wisely said, "Russians can give you arms but only the United States can give you a solution."

The 1972 signings of the Anti-Ballistic Missile (ABM) Treaty and the SALT treaty were also very important to the world.

Important and Unimportant News of the 1970s

1970

1) The wreck of a Confederate submarine is found near Charleston, South Carolina, after 100 years. *The captain of the old sub cannot believe that the Civil War is over.*

2) Construction workers in New York City attack student protesters in what are called The Hard Hat Riots. *New York University fraternities will not allow hard hats to be worn at the senior prom, causing the uproar.*

3) The World Trade Center opens. At the time, the Twin Towers are the tallest buildings in the world.

4) The NFL and the AFL merge; the championship game is now called the Super Bowl.

5) United Airlines has "men only" flights, with free cigars and other amenities. *The stewardesses must ask, "Coffee, tea, or me?"* A lawsuit ends the flights.

6) A rocket-powered car breaks the land speed record of 622 mph. *The driver gets a ticket for speeding, as the limit is 55 mph.*

7) Thirty-seven members of Wichita State University's football team are killed in a plane crash. Another crash claims the lives of 75 members of Marshall University's football team.

8) Born this year was Senator Ted Cruz, actor Matt Damon, and First Lady Melania Trump, who said, "I am not a 'yes' person. No matter who you are married to, you still need to lead your life." And lastly, future Triple Crown winner Secretariat.

9) Anti-war protesters **the Chicago Seven** are found guilty and sentenced to five years in jail. The conviction is overturned two years later.

10) The United States sinks 418 containers of nerve gas near the Bahamas. *Sharks in the area become very nervous.*

11) The US Army gets its first two female generals. *The new army menu features quiche and kale.*

12) The Weather Underground accidentally blows up a luxury townhouse in New York City.

13) The first New York City Marathon is held, with 127 runners. In 2019, 53,000 runners finish the race.

14) Riots in Poland over high food prices leave 300 dead.

15) A national post office strike lasts two weeks. *President Richard Nixon, chased by a dog, delivers Washington, DC, mail.*

16) The biggest news: The Beatles break up! Worldwide, they sold 600 million albums and singles. Band member George Harrison said, "The Beatles saved the world from boredom." And John Lennon famously proclaimed, "We are more popular than Jesus now; I don't know which will go first—rock 'n' roll or Christianity."

1971

1) Cigarettes are banned from being advertised on radio and TV. *What will happen to the Marlboro Man and Willy the Penguin?*

2) The 26th Amendment is ratified. *Now 18-year-olds can vote, but they cannot drink—oh sure!*

3) *The New York Times* publishes the Pentagon Papers—the United States's involvement in Vietnam from 1945–1967.

4) Haitian President François "Papa Doc" Duvalier dies. He's succeeded by his 19-year-old son, Jean-Claude "Baby Doc" Duvalier.

5) Mystery man D.B. Cooper parachutes from a commercial flight over Oregon with $200,000 in ransom money. He is still missing after all these years.

6) Oil production from the North Sea begins in Norway.

7) Riots in Attica Correctional Facility in New York State leave 42 dead.

8) The United Arab Emirates are established, gaining independence from the United Kingdom. *There are seven Emirates—Dubai, Abu Dhabi, and five that you have never heard of.*

9) A new stock market index called NASDAQ makes its debut in New York City.

10) Detroit Lions wide receiver Chuck Hughes, 28, becomes the only player in NFL history to die on the field.

11) Idi Amin takes control of Uganda and becomes a notorious dictator.

12) Hollywood has an enormous decade. Some of the biggest movies are: *The Godfather, Rocky, Jaws, Annie Hall, The Exorcist,*

Patton, One Flew over the Cuckoo's Nest, Saturday Night Fever, and definitely *Star Wars.*

13) Fred Baur invents the Pringles can. *When he dies 37 years later, his cremated remains are put into one.*

14) The first Starbucks coffee shop opens in Seattle. *I guess it was successful!*

15) The Fight of the Century occurs when Joe Frazier beats Muhammad Ali. In 1974, Ali beats George Foreman in the Rumble in the Jungle. Then, in 1975, Ali beats Frazier in the Thrilla in Manila.

16) In Washington, DC, the John F. Kennedy Center for the Performing Arts opens.

17) The US ping-pong team travels to China to take part in the *annual "Lo Mein" Bowl.*

18) UCLA, led by Bill Walton and coached by John Wooden, establish a college basketball dynasty, winning the NCAA tournament seven consecutive times. Over three years, UCLA wins 88 straight games. Coach Wooden said, "Failure to prepare is preparing to fail."

19) Walt Disney World opens in Orlando, Florida. *The personnel department is looking to hire a mouse with big, round ears.*

1972

1) Because of a leap day and two leap seconds, 1972 is **the longest year** in history.

2) Shirley Chisholm, the first African American woman to be elected to the US Congress, announces her candidacy for president. She does not win, but says, *"Tremendous amounts of talent are being lost to our society just because that talent wears a skirt."*

3) The Miami Dolphins become the only NFL team to have a perfect season, winning all 17 games, including the Super Bowl. Coach Don Shula wisely said, "The superior man blames himself. The inferior man blames others."

4) Segregationist Governor George Wallace of Alabama is shot at a political rally. He is paralyzed for the rest of his life: 26 years.

5) A big year for the ladies—The Boston Marathon allows women to run. The FBI now has female agents. Sally Priesand becomes the first US female rabbi.

6) American Bobby Fischer defeats Russian Boris Spassky in the championship chess match, held in Iceland. *This match was **really** a cold war!*

7) Ceylon becomes independent from the United Kingdom and changes its name to Sri Lanka.

8) At the Summer Olympics, American swimmer Mark Spitz wins seven gold medals. *After he takes off his bathing suit, he enters the real estate business.* At the 1976 Summer Games, 14-year-old Nadia Comaneci of Romania wins three golds in gymnastics. *Later in life, she appears on The Celebrity Apprentice TV show, where Donald Trump fires her.*

9) Actress Jane Fonda tours North Vietnam, leading critics to dub her "Hanoi Jane." *This is not the high point of her illustrious movie career.*

10) HBO begins and DDT ends.

11) Death claims baseball legend Jackie Robinson at age 52. Plane crashes kill MVPs Roberto Clemente and New York Yankees captain Thurman Munson in 1979.

12) The Iran Blizzard kills 4,000 as 26 feet of snow falls over a week.

13) *Pong* is the first video game to be commercially successful. *Ping is a failure.*

14) *A Quaker does not want his tax dollars to fund wars, so on his tax return, he claims 3 billion dependents, the population of the world. The IRS does not agree, and he is sent to jail.*

15) A Japanese soldier from World War II is found hiding in the jungles of Guam. *After 27 years, he demands that America surrenders.*

1973

1) Despite being out of office for 18 years, Juan Perón is elected president of Argentina.

2) The US Supreme Court overturns state law against abortion in the Roe v. Wade case, making the procedure legal. Pro-choice advocates celebrate.

3) CBS sells the New York Yankees to George Steinbrenner and friends for $10 million. *Forty-seven years later, the team is worth $5 billion. Not a bad investment!*

4) Yankee pitchers Fritz Peterson and Mike Kekich announce that they have swapped wives and children. *Do they also swap earned-run averages?*

5) In a switch, Israel accidentally shoots down a Libyan jetliner, killing 108 on board. Israel apologizes and pays compensation to the families of the victims.

6) Two hundred Native Americans occupy Wounded Knee in South Dakota. *After 71 days, the group surrenders to **an orthopedic surgeon**.*

7) The Sears Tower in Chicago opens. At the time, it is the world's tallest building.

8) The great racehorse Secretariat wins the Triple Crown, the first time a horse is awarded the title in 25 years. He retires at age 3 and spends the rest of his years happily producing future racing champions.

9) The first US space station, Skylab, launches. The crew of three is in orbit for almost six months.

10) The first phone call is made from a handheld cellular phone. *It goes to voice mail.*

11) Billie Jean King defeats Bobby Riggs in three sets at the Battle of the Sexes tennis match. Ninety million watch—the most-viewed tennis match in history.

12) The Trilateral Commission forms to foster political and economic dialogue among the United States, Western Europe, and Japan. A lots of heavy hitters are involved.

13) Golda Meir, prime minister of Israel, confers with Pope Paul VI at the Vatican. *She brings bagels and lox to the Pontiff.*

1974

1) The Symbionese Liberation Army kidnaps newspaper heiress Patty Hearst. Brainwashed, she becomes a bank robber before she is captured.

2) A news anchorwoman in Sarasota, Florida, commits suicide by shooting herself on live TV.

3) The Franklin National Bank of Long Island goes under, the largest bank failure on record at the time. Fraud and mismanagement does it every time.

4) A French acrobat walks for 45 minutes on a tightrope connecting the Twin Towers of the World Trade Center. *He is 1,300 feet above the ground, and he only falls once. Just kidding—he does fine.*

5) Golda Meir resigns as Israeli prime minister. Yitzhak Rabin replaces her. *Rumor has it that the pope did not like the bagels.*

6) The barcode is used for the first time at an Ohio supermarket on a package of Wrigley's chewing gum. The gum costs 5 cents.

7) Haile Selassie is removed as emperor of Ethiopia after only 58 years on the throne. The country becomes a Socialist state.

8) Hank Aaron breaks Babe Ruth's career home-run record of 714. He retires two years later with 755 homers. His record remains unbroken until Barry Bonds hits 762. "Hammering Hank" also holds the career record for RBIs.

9) Salaries soar in baseball as free agency begins. The first free agent is Jim "Catfish" Hunter, who signs with the Yankees.

10) India becomes the sixth nuclear power, peacefully exploding the bomb.

11) The 3-million-year-old skeleton of Lucy the dinosaur—*not to be confused with I Love Lucy*—is discovered in Africa.

12) Bjorn Borg of Sweden wins eight tennis Grand Slams this

decade, while Australian Margaret Court is victorious seven times, finishing her career with a record 24 titles.

13) The Native American Kootenai Tribe of Idaho declares war on the United States. *The tribe receives 12.5 acres from the government, and the war ends.*

14) After 29 years of turmoil, East Germany and the United States establish diplomatic relations.

15) Stephen King's first novel, *Carrie*, is published to great success, followed by dozens more. Other big books of the 1970s include *Love Story*, *The Winds of War*, *Ragtime*, and *The French Lieutenant's Woman*.

16) PLO Chairman Yasser Arafat shocks the United Nations's General Assembly by proclaiming, "I have come bearing an olive branch and a freedom fighter's gun. Do not let the olive branch fall from my hands."

1975

1) Construction begins on the 800-mile-long Trans-Alaska Pipeline.

2) President Gerald Ford survives two assassination attempts within 17 days. *The female shooters were not very good shots.*

3) After eight years, the Suez Canal is reopened to every country but—you guessed it—Israel.

4) Union leader Jimmy Hoffa is reported missing. After all these years, he still has not been found. *Try the end zone at Giants Stadium.*

5) President Gerald Ford restores full citizenship rights to Gen. Robert E. Lee, after only 110 years. *Lee is not there for the ceremony.*

6) *Saturday Night Live* debuts, with George Carlin as the first host. *Wheel of Fortune* makes its first spin.

7) Born this year: golfer Tiger Woods, baseball All-Star Alex Rodriguez, actress Angelina Jolie, and soccer star David Beckham.

8) Saudi Arabian Prince Faisal bin Musaed bin Abdelaziz assassi-

nates his uncle, King Faisal. *His defense is that he is insane and had lost his head. After a quick trial, the prince actually does lose his head!*

9) A religious civil war breaks out in Lebanon between Christians and Muslims that lasts 15 years.

10) Disco gets everyone dancing. Other musical favorites include Neil Diamond, Bette Midler, the Eagles, the Bee Gees, Linda Ronstadt, and Michael Jackson.

11) Hall of Famer Frank Robinson becomes the first African American manager of a baseball team, guiding the Cleveland Indians.

12) Two young men, Bill Gates and Paul Allen, start a new company called Microsoft. *It is moderately successful.*

1976

1) Happy birthday! The United States of America turns 200 years old.

2) In New York City, the Son of Sam kills his first victim. Over the next year, before being captured, he terrorizes the Big Apple as he kills five more and wounds seven others.

3) The NBA and the ABA merge; three years later, **the three-point shot** becomes a reality, and basketball is changed.

4) Israeli commandos successfully rescue 103 hostages being held at Entebbe International Airport Kampala in Uganda by pro-Palestinian terrorists.

5) A monster earthquake in China kills 650,000 people.

6) Scientists realize that liquids in aerosol cans reduce the ozone layer. *Deodorant manufacturers start sweating.*

7) The two-dollar bill is introduced. Whose picture is on it? If you said, "Thomas Jefferson," you are right.

8) Twenty-nine people mysteriously die at an American Legion convention in Philadelphia. The deaths are traced to the air-conditioning system and given the name **legionnaires' disease**. *Suppose it was a convention of proctologists. Then what would the disease be called?*

9) Racial violence in South Africa kills hundreds, and thousands are injured.

10) Broadway has a successful decade. Standouts include *Annie, Chicago, The Wiz, Grease,* and *A Chorus Line.*

11) In Argentina, a military coup deposes Isabel Martinez de Perón as president. *She was the first female president in the world, not counting Wonder Woman.*

12) Steve Jobs and two friends found Apple Computer. Jobs said, "Of all the inventions of humans, the computer is going to rank near or at the top as history unfolds and we look back. It is the most awesome tool." *One of the friends sells his 10% share of the company for $800. Today, the 10% would be worth about $35 billion. He is still kicking himself!*

13) New Jersey approves legalized casino gambling in Atlantic City. Roll those bones!

1977

1) Two jetliners collide on the ground in the Canary Islands, killing 528 people. It is the worst aviation disaster in history.

2) During the coldest US January on record, snow falls in Miami for the first time in recorded history, and Alaska has the warmest January. *Go figure.*

3) A helicopter falls off the roof of the PanAm Building in New York City, killing five. That's the end of choppers landing on top of buildings in the Big Apple.

4) A fire in a Kentucky restaurant kills 165. A fire at the Beverly Hills Supper Club also kills 165 people.

5) *Roots* becomes a TV classic, winning nine Emmy Awards. Other boob-tube favorites include *Marcus Welby, M.D.; All in the Family; Happy Days* and *Laverne & Shirley.*

6) British Airways flies its Concorde from London to New York in 3.5 hours, compared with a regular flight of eight hours. Its speed exceeds 1,300 mph.

7) *"Elvis has left the building"*: Singing legend Elvis Presley dies at age 42 of an apparent heart attack.

8) Violence and looting occur during a summer electrical blackout in New York City that lasts 24 hours.

9) In France, a convicted murderer is executed by guillotine, the last person to be lawfully beheaded in the Western world. *Quit while you're a head.*

10) The first home computer, the Commodore PET, debuts for $795. Commodore declares bankruptcy in 1994.

11) Two Los Angeles Dodgers players create the high-five handshake. *But who invented the fist bump?*

12) Spain holds its first democratic elections in 41 years. *Spanish dictator Francisco Franco, who has been dead for two years, does not win.*

13) Everybody's favorite comic strip, *Li'l Abner*, ends after 43 years. *Daisy Mae and all the Yokums in Dogpatch are so disappointed.*

14) A Virginia park ranger is struck by lightning for the seventh time and again survives. *He is known as the Human Lightning Rod.*

15) A man from Queens, New York, climbs the South Tower of the World Trade Center, in almost four hours. *He is fined $1.10: one penny for each floor climbed.*

16) A British lady voluntarily stays awake for 449 hours (18 days). *Supposedly, she then slept for 449 straight hours.*

17) In November, President Anwar Sadat of Egypt visits Jerusalem, the first Arab leader to officially come to Israel. I made my first visit to Israel that monumental week, and many years later, I still remember the incident vividly.

1978

1) Cleveland, Ohio, becomes the first major US city to default on its debt since the Great Depression. *"Brother, can you spare a dime?"*

2) Jim Jones leads the mass murder-suicide of 909 Americans in

Jonestown, Guyana. Sales of the drink Flavor-Aid plummet because people think that it's Kool-Aid.

3) The Camp David Accords begin between President Anwar Sadat of Egypt and Prime Minister Menachem Begin of Israel. Both leaders share the Nobel Peace Prize of 1978. Begin said, "We want a full peace, normalization in all fields."

4) The United States grants Panama the right to control the Panama Canal, starting in 1999.

5) Charlie Chaplin's body is stolen and held for ransom. His wife refuses to pay because "Charlie would have thought it ridiculous." *Needless to say, Charlie is dead at the time.*

6) The rainbow flag of the LGBT movement flies for the first time in San Francisco. The city mourns the mayor and the city supervisor, who have both been assassinated.

7) The neighborhood of the Love Canal, located near Niagara Falls, New York, becomes a huge environmental disaster when it is discovered that it is a toxic chemical dump site. Thousands of residents suffer severe health problems.

8) The Catholic Church has three popes this year: Pope Paul VI, John Paul I, and Pope John Paul II.

9) The first test-tube baby is born in England and makes the cover of *TIME* magazine.

10) Ninety-eight percent of all American homes have TV sets. *The other 2% are very smart people.*

11) The Bulgarian secret police assassinate a Bulgarian defector with a poisoned umbrella tip. *What would've happened if it wasn't raining?*

12) Before 1978, the National Weather Service used only female names for hurricanes because the storms were "unpredictable and dangerous." *How about Hurricane Andrew?*

13) Hip-hop/rap music is born in the Bronx, New York. *Seniors check the obituaries to see if this music has died.*

14) Mavis Hutchison, at age 53, becomes the first woman to run

across the United States. *The sprint takes 69 days, and people ask, who is chasing her?*

1979

1) Margaret Thatcher becomes the first female prime minister of the United Kingdom. *Queen Elizabeth II is happy and now has a doubles partner for tennis.*

2) The United States and China establish full diplomatic relations. *President Richard Nixon and the US ping-pong team deserve all the credit.*

3) A female shooter goes on rampage in a San Diego school, killing and wounding many. Her reason: "I don't like Mondays."

4) An American Airlines flight crashes in Chicago, killing 271 people.

5) The Susan B. Anthony silver dollar is introduced. *The coin is now worth 100 cents.*

6) An accident at the Three Mile Island Nuclear Generating Station in Pennsylvania causes a radiation leak. Ironically, the movie *The China Syndrome*, starring Jane Fonda, opens the same week. *She's blamed for the accident.*

7) Nicaraguan dictator General Somoza resigns the presidency and flees to Florida as the Sandinistas take control. *He says there are no early-bird specials in Nicaragua.*

8) A government loan guarantee bails out Chrysler Corporation, which is facing bankruptcy.

9) Entertainers in the spotlight include Clint Eastwood, Barbra Streisand ("I was known as the kid who had a good voice and no father"), Burt Reynolds, Paul Newman, Robert Redford, Dustin Hoffman, Al Pacino, Aretha Franklin, Elton John, Paul Simon, Diana Ross, James Taylor, Jack Nicholson, and Robert De Niro.

10) The first British nudist beach is established in Brighton. *This is **not** Brighton Beach in Brooklyn.*

11) A computer malfunction causes a NORAD nuclear false

alarm. *It seems the Microsoft bill was not paid that month. The NORAD bookkeeper is then fired.*

12) President Jimmy Carter is attacked while fishing—not by an assassin, but by a swamp rabbit. *Is the rabbit a Republican?*

Deaths This Decade of Notable People

- Lyndon B. Johnson, 64. Thirty-sixth US president. 1963-1969
- Harry S. Truman, 88. Thirty-third US president. 1945-1953
- Charles de Gaulle, 79. French president, 1959–1969.
- David Ben-Gurion, 87. First prime minister of Israel, 1948–1963.
- Charles Lindbergh, 72. First person to pilot a plane across the Atlantic Ocean.
- Duke Ellington, 75. American composer and jazz bandleader.
- Pablo Picasso, 91. Spanish painter whose *Guernica* depicted the horrors of the Spanish Civil War.
- John Wayne, 72. Legendary American actor known as Duke.
- Charlie Chaplin, 88. English comic actor whose career spanned 75 years.
- Mao Tse-tung, 82. Chairman who led China for 27 years.
- Bing Crosby, 74. American actor and singer who immortalized "White Christmas," the greatest Christmas song ever.
- Louis Armstrong, 69. American jazz trumpeter Satchmo was also a TV star.
- Lord Louis Mountbatten, 79. British statesman and uncle of Prince Philip, duke of Edinburgh.
- Norman Rockwell, 84. American illustrator who created

The Saturday Evening Post covers for five decades.

- Vince Lombardi, 57. Iconic NFL coach. *"If it doesn't matter who wins or loses, then why do they keep score?"*
- Ed Sullivan, 73. American TV personality for 23 years.
- Groucho Marx, 86. American funnyman. *"I refuse to join any club that would have me as a member."*

Advances in Science This Decade

The Voyager program – Space station – Space shuttle – Birth of computers – Hip replacements – MRI – Eradication of smallpox – Vaccines for chicken pox, pneumonia, and meningitis – Skylab – Tommy John surgery – Heimlich maneuver – Concept of global warming – Test for dementia – Ebola outbreak – Bulimia – Genetic engineering – Artificial human heart – DNA sequencing –

Gene splicing – Liposuction – Fiber optics – L-Dopa – Acupuncture – Marijuana use for glaucoma – Heart valves from pigs – Cloning – Japanese self-driving car – Lithium battery

Important Innovations of the 1970s

Sony Walkman – Digital camera – Digital watch – Laser printer – Post-it note – Atari – Rubik's Cube – Disposable lighter – Federal Express – Airbags – Home VCR – Hamburger Helper – Nike swoosh – Fajita – Folding umbrella – Resealable plastic bags – Salad bar – Crock-Pot — Light beer – NPR – Ben & Jerry's Ice Cream – Car tape deck – Karaoke – Yellow tennis balls – Egg McMuffin – Computer mouse

IN 1970, the population of the world was 3.7 billion people. The United States's population was 203 million people. The average life expectancy of Americans was 71 years.

The Me Decade was over. The country survived the Watergate mess in Washington, DC, with Nixon resigning. The oil crisis and the recession, inflation, and the high unemployment rate that followed were all confronted. Anti-war protests led to the end of the long, unpopular war in Vietnam, and terrorism showed its ugly face. Finally, we endured the Iranian hostage situation and ultimately overcame it.

The 1970s were bad. Hopefully, the 1980s will be better!

9

1980–1989

THE WALL CAME TUMBLING DOWN

The decade of the 1980s, **the Information Decade**, as usual, was loaded with threats. The good news was that by 1989, the threat that had haunted the United States for seven decades was finally gone.

The country was threatened by a new, mysterious illness that affected a certain section of the population. Terrorism was in full swing, an addictive drug was threatening young people, and assassinations and assassination attempts were widespread. *As the Cold War began to cool, global warming started to heat up.*

Economically, international recession threatened the world. The Savings and Loan Crisis was devastating, and Black Monday destroyed the stock portfolios of millions of people.

Washington, DC, had a scandal involving a Central American country and a Middle Eastern enemy of ours that threatened the presidency. There were numerous natural disasters, a devastating space disaster, and a Soviet internal nuclear disaster.

The good news was that the Red Menace was gasping its last breath and was about to be stuffed into Vladimir Lenin's tomb in Moscow.

Presidential Elections of the 1980s

In 1980, the Republican governor of California and one-time Hollywood B movie star (remember *Bedtime for Bonzo?*), Ronald Reagan, became the 40th president of the nation. Alongside his running mate, former head of the CIA George H.W. Bush, the Republican pair, in a landslide, easily defeated incumbent President Jimmy Carter and Vice President Walter Mondale. Republican Rep. John Anderson came away with 6% of the popular vote.

The 1984 presidential election was the nation's 50th, covering 200 years. In that year, the Reagan-Bush ticket easily defeated the Democrat Mr. Mondale and New York Rep. Geraldine Ferraro, the first woman to be on a major party's presidential ballot. Ms. Ferraro said, "You don't have to have fought in the war to love peace."

Did you know that Reagan was the first divorced American president? He was married to actress Jane Wyman, and they starred in a movie together, *Brother Rat*.

Reagan once said, "The greatest leader is not necessarily the one who does the greatest things. He is the one that gets the people to do the greatest things."

In 1988, Vice President Bush (now president No. 41) and his running mate, Indiana senator Dan Quayle, easily beat the Democratic governor of Massachusetts, Michael Dukakis, and Texas senator Lloyd Bentsen. *In a campaign speech, Mr. Quayle profoundly said, "It's wonderful to be here in the great state of Chicago."*

The Cold War

The first half of the decade saw the Cold War heat up as the new administration took an aggressive stance toward the USSR. The 1970s policy of détente was scrapped in favor of the hard-line Reagan Doctrine. There was tit for tat regarding the Olympics, as the United States refused to go to Moscow in 1980 and the Soviets opted out of the 1984 Summer Games in Los Angeles.

In a 1983 speech, Reagan referred to the Soviet Union as "**the Evil Empire**." During a NATO military exercise in 1983, the Soviets thought that this was a prelude to war and put their armed forces on alert. Fortunately for the world, nothing happened.

Meanwhile, there was a revolving door in the Kremlin. Within 29 months, the Soviet Union had **four** different leaders. Leonid Brezhnev, who had led the country since 1964, died in 1982 and was replaced by Yuri Andropov, who lasted two years and was replaced by Konstantin Chernenko, who died in 1985. Then Mikhail Gorbachev took the reins and guided the country until 1990. *You definitely can't tell who the Soviet leaders are without a Russian scorecard.*

Gorbachev was a moderate leader who believed in glasnost, or government transparency. He wanted to withdraw from Afghanistan, begin a policy of liberalization, ration vodka, and revive the Soviet economy (perestroika). Trying to be funny, said, "What we need is Star Peace, not Star Wars." He met with Reagan several times, and tensions begin to ease between the two superpowers. When Gorbachev met with Bush in 1989 at the Malta Summit, it marked the **beginning of the end** of the Cold War.

At the conclusion of the decade, things got really bad for the Soviet Union. After 10 years of fighting, with thousands of casualties, the USSR withdrew from Afghanistan. There were Nationalist movements in several Soviet Republics—everyone wanted their independence. Latvia, Estonia, and Lithuania wanted to be free. There were riots in Central Asia, rebellions in Caucasus, and unrest in Ukraine and Belarus. Poland, after martial law, elected a non-Communist government. Romanian dictator Nicolae Ceaușescu and his wife were executed on live TV. Communist regimes were ousted in Hungary and Czechoslovakia—the Velvet Revolution. And finally, East Germans and West Germans began tearing down the hated Berlin Wall. In 1987, in Berlin, Reagan famously requested, **"Mr. Gorbachev, tear down this wall!"**

After 44 years, the Cold War was finally over!

Chernobyl

As things were spiraling downward and out of control for the USSR, an incident in 1986 exemplified this. The worst nuclear disaster in history occurred at the Chernobyl Nuclear Power Plant in Ukraine. A huge amount of radioactive contamination was released into the air—400 times more than that released by the atomic bombs over Hiroshima and Nagasaki in 1945. Wide areas of the Soviet Union were affected, and 100,000 people were evacuated. The accident occurred during a safety test with inadequately trained personnel. When will the affected area be habitable again? Some say not for **hundreds** of years. *What a mess!*

AIDS

In 1981, a strange phenomenon started occurring among gay men, drug users, and blood-transfusion recipients. An unusual cluster of rare pneumonia cases began to appear in New York City and San Francisco. The disease was named acquired immune deficiency syndrome, or **AIDS**, and is caused by the human immunodeficiency virus, or **HIV**. So basically, a person contracting HIV can develop AIDS, which is stage 3 HIV.

The disease supposedly originated in chimpanzees in Africa and traveled from the Congo to Haiti to New York. By 1983, AIDS was found in women and infants. *The New York Times* reported that by 1984, 1,450 cases had been diagnosed and 558 were dead. The next year, there were 7,600 cases, and 3,600 people had died. It appeared that by 1986, half of the people who had been diagnosed were dead.

The great pity of this disease was that it affected so many young, vibrant, and creative people. Rock Hudson, Roy Cohn, Peter Allen, Arthur Ashe, Liberace, Alvin Ailey, Perry Ellis, Rudolf Nureyev, and Keith Haring were among the famous people who died of this dreaded disease. It is estimated that almost 700,000 Americans have died of AIDS.

Fortunately, the medication AZT was discovered to help curb HIV, and many people diagnosed with the disease are alive today. Diana, Princess of Wales, became an advocate and helped celebrate Worlds AIDS Day in 1989.

Drugs

The early 1980s witnessed the start of a severe drug epidemic in the United States. The Medellín cartel from Colombia was a highly organized criminal cartel that brought drugs into the United States. Miami was the main entry point, as well as the Mexican border. The drug du jour was cocaine, and it is estimated that the cartel made $60 million per day—not a bad haul.

First Lady Nancy Reagan established a new program for the war on drugs: **"Just Say No."**

Crack cocaine, which was introduced in the mid-1980s, was cheap, potent, and highly addictive. Minority neighborhoods were bombarded with this new drug.

In 1986, All-American basketball star Len Bias died of a drug overdose at age 22. There was a cocaine-related scandal in baseball, and many top players were suspended and fined.

The drug problem caused the United States to invade Panama in 1989 to oust President Manuel Noriega, who was suspected of being a kingpin in the drug trade. *At his trial, he was convicted and sentenced to 40 years in jail, with the promise that he would not sell cocaine to his fellow inmates.*

Terrorism

All around the globe, the terrorists were having a field day, threatening everyone. From Italy to Kenya, from London to Guatemala, from India to Peru, from Barcelona to Colombia, terrorism was everywhere.

In 1983, Arab suicide bombers blew up the US Marine Corps barracks in Beirut, Lebanon, killing 300 American and French fighting men. The US Embassy in Beirut was also targeted, and 63 were killed.

There were continuous terrorist attacks on Israel this decade, mostly by Palestinian suicide bombers. Israel was complicit in the Beirut massacre of 1982, allowing a Christian Lebanese militia to kill hundreds of Palestine Liberation Organization (PLO) fighters.

Terrorists successfully used suicide bombers, detonated explosives on trains, and hijacked and bombed airplanes. The 1988 Libyan terrorist bombing of Pan Am Flight 103 over Lockerbie, Scotland, killed 273 people.

Bottom line, terrorism was a major threat to the world in the 1980s. There were hundreds of attacks, and thousands were killed.

Assassinations

The decade was filled with assassinations and assassination attempts. In 1980, John Lennon of The Beatles was murdered in New York City. His famous quote: "Reality leaves a lot to the imagination."

Egyptian President Anwar Sadat was killed in 1981. He famously said, "There can be hope only for a society which acts as one big family, not as many separate ones."

Liberian President William Tolbert was murdered, as well as Olof Palme, the Swedish prime minister. Indira Gandhi, leader of India, was assassinated by her bodyguards in 1984. Before her death, she proclaimed, "Forgiveness is a virtue of the brave."

There were assassination attempts on several international leaders that failed. In 1981, Reagan was shot in Washington, DC; Pope John Paul II was almost killed in Vatican City; and Prime Minister Margaret Thatcher of the United Kingdom survived an assassination attempt in 1984. She said, "What Britain needs is an iron lady." Thatcher had been referred to as "an iron fist in a silk glove." *Fortunately for these three leaders, the shooters were not good shots.*

The Iran-Contra Affair

A political scandal rocked the Reagan administration in the 1980s. Our enemy, Iran, was engaged in a deadly war with Iraq and badly in need of armaments and spare parts. Iran was subject to an embargo of arms sales, creating a problem. Senior government officials worked out a plan where Israel would supply the arms to Iran. Iran would then have Hezbollah militants in Lebanon release seven American diplomatic hostages.

Now it gets interesting. The proceeds from the sale of the weapons to Iran would go to fund the rebel Contras in Nicaragua who were fighting the Sandinistas. These Sandinistas were Socialist revolutionaries working closely with the Communist government in Cuba.

The clandestine affair started in 1981 but was exposed in 1986. The CIA and Lt. Col. Oliver North were involved in this operation. In 1987, Reagan took full responsibility and admitted that this was a huge mistake. Thirteen senior officials were convicted, and many were later pardoned. As the investigations were being conducted, *Mr. North said, "I'm trusting in the Lord and a good lawyer."*

Global Warming

The concept of climate change that ultimately could threaten and destroy the planet started to become widely discussed in the 1980s. Because of human influence, especially fossil fuel burning and greenhouse gases, scientists were shocked to see that average temperatures around the world were dangerously rising. Heat waves were causing wildfires, and more intense storms were occurring. A 1988 summer heat wave killed 17,000 in the United States. 1989 was deemed the warmest year in recorded history.

The increase in temperatures was greatest in the Arctic and Antarctica. Glaciers were melting, which could cause a devastating rise in sea levels, possibly inundating coastal cities. People were talking about an underwater Miami and ocean-front property in Chicago.

Exxon and Shell Oil warned of potential catastrophic events. Their scientists claimed that the American Midwest could become desertlike.

The Montreal Protocol, an international treaty that aimed to protect the ozone layer in Antarctica, was ratified by 197 United Nations members. *Rumors persisted that Antarctic penguins were going blind. Sunglasses for the penguins was a must!*

The Economy

The most severe global recession since World War II occurred between 1980–1983. The 1979 energy crisis, which led to a disruption of the oil supply to the United States, Europe, and Japan, was the catalyst for this recession. Inflation was high, as were interest rates, and there was widespread unemployment. The United Kingdom was hit particularly hard.

In the United States, there were many bank failures at this time. The country's seventh-largest bank, Continental Illinois National Bank and Trust Company, failed in 1984—the largest in American history. Wide-sweeping tax reform was initiated in 1986.

Stagflation was a major problem. The government applied the response of Reaganomics, which lowered taxes and decreased regulations, as well as government spending and tightening the money supply. These policies were also known as supply-side economics and trickle-down economics. Democrats called the policy "voodoo economics."

Starting in 1986, over 1,000 savings and loan associations (S&Ls) failed nationwide. Some of them used highly speculative investment strategies, including unsound real estate investing. The high interest rates of the 1980s hurt the S&Ls, and losses mounted. After investigating, it was found that fraud was rampant. In 1989, the US Congress finally passed reform legislation, making sure that this fiasco would never happen again.

The Stock Market

Silver Thursday was an event that occurred in the US silver commodity market on Thursday, March 27, 1980, following an attempt by the Hunt brothers to corner the market on silver. The price of silver had skyrocketed and the Hunts controlled one third of the world's silver supply. The COMEX rules on margin purchase were immediately changed, the Hunts were forced to sell most of their silver holdings, silver prices plummeted and a panic in the financial markets occurred. Soon thereafter, the Hunt brothers bankruptcy was one of the largest ever.

The Lone Ranger to his talking horse: "What day is today?"
Silver: "Thursday."

Black Monday took place on October 19, 1987. *No, this was not a racial issue.* Since 1982, the stock market had tripled in value, until this fateful day when the market crashed. The Dow Jones average fell 508 points, or 22.6%, the largest one-day percentage drop in history. World-wide losses exceeded $1 trillion.

What caused the crash? Some Monday morning quarterbacks blamed it on computer program trading, portfolio insurance, and derivatives. These concepts were all new to Wall Street and caused investors to panic as they faced margin calls and were forced to sell their holdings. At this time, hospitals saw a spike in admissions because of Black Monday stress.

After the crash, the stock exchanges implemented trading curbs and circuit breakers. Out of the ashes of this debacle arose the longest and strongest bull market in American history.

Disasters

Natural and unnatural disasters were plentiful in this decade, starting with the massive eruption of a volcano in Washington State. The Mount St. Helens eruption was the deadliest and most economically destructive in US history. *Did you know that there are 169 active volcanoes in America? Hopefully, your house is not sitting on one.*

The ground was shaking during this 10-year period, as there were 36 major earthquakes, with thousands dying around the world. The Loma Prieta earthquake of 1989 disrupted a World Series game between the San Francisco Giants and the Oakland Athletics, aka the Battle of the Bay, that Oakland ultimately won.

There were countless hurricanes, cyclones, mud slides, and wildfires, causing much grief. In 1988, fire destroyed one-third of Yellowstone National Park.

Two ships collided near the Philippines and killed over 4,000 people. The world's worst industrial disaster took place in 1984 in Bhopal, India, at a Union Carbide pesticide plant when a poisonous gas leak killed 4,000 and injured 500,000. Union Carbide paid India $470 million related to the disaster. In 1989, the *Exxon Valdez* created a gigantic oil spill in Alaska when 11 million gallons of oil was released.

A space disaster occurred in 1986 when the US space shuttle *Challenger* broke apart just after launch. Seven astronauts died as the world watched on live TV. No one will ever forget this devastating accident.

Wars and Treaties of the 1980s

There were plenty of wars fought around the globe in the 1980s—69 if you're counting. The Iran-Iraq War, lasting eight years, had 644,000 fatalities. The long-running civil war in Afghanistan resulted in over 500,000 dead. Wars in Lebanon, Ethiopia, and Angola killed hundreds of thousands of people. The Coconut War fought in Vanuatu in 1980 featured the rebels *using bows and arrows.*

Many treaties were signed this decade; the most important was the 1987 Intermediate-Range Nuclear Forces (INF) Treaty between the United States and the Soviet Union. *The China-Australia Migratory Bird Agreement (CAMBA) was for the birds!*

Important and Unimportant News of the 1980s

1980

1) At long last, Israel and Egypt establish diplomatic relations. *The hora is danced in the streets of Cairo.*

2) The FBI creates a sting operation targeting members of the US Congress regarding corruption. **Abscam** nets seven representatives, who are all convicted.

3) Rosie Ruiz wins the Boston Marathon, but—wait a minute—she cheated, and the title is taken away. She only ran the last half mile.

4) In Saudi Arabia, 63 insurgents lose their heads, literally, in the country's largest public execution.

5) Operation Eagle Claw, the commando mission to rescue the American hostages in Iran, is aborted because of mechanical issues in our helicopters.

6) The word "yuppie"—which stands for "young, urban professional"—is used for the first time, in a magazine article. *Newsweek* later declares 1984 "the Year of the Yuppie."

7) A derecho hits Wisconsin. (*What the heck is a derecho? A fast-moving wind storm.*)

8) The New York Islanders win hockey's Stanley Cup for four consecutive years. Wayne Gretzky and the Edmonton Oilers also win four titles. The Great One said, "You miss 100% of the shots you don't take."

9) The United States defeats the USSR in hockey at the 1980 Winter Olympics in Lake Placid, New York in the Miracle on Ice.

Question: What country participated in the 1980 Olympics that does not exist anymore?

Answer: Yugoslavia

10) A race riot in the Liberty City section of Miami kills 18 people.

11) A *Playboy* magazine Playmate of the Year is murdered by her jealous husband.

12) Fidel Castro releases thousands of Cuban criminals, mentally ill people, and prostitutes in the Mariel Boatlift. *Miami's population soars.*

13) Queen Juliana of the Netherlands abdicates the throne after ruling for 32 years. The new queen is her oldest daughter, Beatrix.

14) *The US Air Force unveils the stealth bomber, but no one can find it.*

15) The *Voyager I* spacecraft makes its closest approach to the planet Saturn, just 77,000 miles. *A multitude of photos are sent back to NASA, and the drugstores of Houston are kept busy for weeks developing photos.*

16) A New York man is released from prison after serving **68 years**, since 1912, for a second-degree murder charge, the longest prison term ever. *Immediately, he sends a letter to **President Woodrow Wilson** thanking him for his release.*

1981

1) As soon as President Ronald Reagan is sworn into office, the 52 American hostages being held by Iran are released. Thank goodness.

2) Prince Charles and Lady Diana Spencer are married in London as 750 million people watch on live TV. The prince said, "I learned the way a monkey learns—by watching his parents."

3) Sandra Day O'Connor becomes the first female justice of the US Supreme Court. *There are problems with the bathrooms.*

4) Two elevated walkways collapse at the Kansas City Hyatt Regency Hotel, killing 114.

5) Born this year are tennis stars Roger Federer and Serena Williams, singer Beyoncé, quarterback Eli Manning, and celebrities Ivanka Trump and Meghan Markle, the Duchess of Sussex.

6) Hosni Mubarak is elected president of Egypt, succeeding the murdered Anwar Sadat.

7) In a daring move, the Israeli air force destroys a nuclear reactor in Iraq. The world is stunned but happy.

8) Air traffic controllers nationally go on strike; President Ronald Reagan fires 11,000 workers.

9) An undiscovered Mozart symphony that he had written at age 9 is revealed. *It may be the first rap symphony.*

10) Martina Navratilova wins 15 tennis Grand Slam events this decade; Chris Evert and Steffi Graf are right behind.

11) Pablo Picasso's greatest painting, *Guernica*, is moved from the Museum of Modern Art in New York City to Madrid.

12) British Honduras changes its name to Belize.

13) *China announces that it has cloned a fish, a golden carp—not to be confused with the author George Karp.*

14) Mao Tse-tung's fourth wife, Jiang Qing, is sentenced to death in China. *Rumor has it that she burned his breakfast toast.*

1982

1) *TIME* magazine's Man of the Year is the computer.

2) In one of the largest antitrust cases in US history, AT&T agrees to divest its assets, creating seven Baby Bells.

3) The Falklands War between the United Kingdom and Argentina begins on April 1 and ends on June 14. *Initiating the war was a big mistake for Argentina, for it comes in second.*

4) An intruder breaks into Buckingham Palace and winds up in Queen Elizabeth II's bedroom. *Thankfully for the United Kingdom, the queen is wearing royal pajamas.*

5) The world's largest oil rig, *Ocean Ranger*, sinks in the North Atlantic Ocean, along with its crew of 84.

6) In Chicago, Tylenol capsules are laced with cyanide. Seven victims, with headaches, are dead.

7) The first CD player is sold, perhaps playing Michael Jackson's *Thriller* album.

8) Mexico cannot pay its foreign debt, starting an economic crisis that involves Latin America.

9) *The first president of Zimbabwe, Canaan Banana, passes a law*

that outlaws jokes about his name. Was he concerned about Canaan or Banana?

10) A New York City nuclear disarmament rally in Central Park brings together 750,000 protesters. A slogan: *"You can't hug your child with nuclear arms."*

11) PLO Chairman Yasser Arafat is forced to leave Lebanon and is exiled to Tunis. He returns after a year but is booted out again.

12) In the United Kingdom, 20 million trees die from Dutch elm disease. *People wonder if trees in the Netherlands will die from English elm disease.*

13) The Vietnam Veterans Memorial is dedicated in Washington, DC.

14) *Call the police!* Rickey Henderson of the Oakland Athletics steals 130 bases. The future Hall of Famer is the leader in career stolen bases.

15) *The ugliest doll ever, the Cabbage Patch Kid,* goes on sale and is a huge success.

16) Lawnchair Larry becomes an instant celebrity as he rises 16,000 feet in the air in a lawn chair that has balloons attached. *NASA offers him a big job, when and if he returns to Earth.*

1983

1) Prime Minister Menachem Begin of Israel resigns after six years in office. Mr. Begin, winner of the Nobel Peace Prize, said, "The Palestinian Arabs will have their autonomy, we will have our security. We shall live together." *Should only be!*

2) The United States invades the tiny island nation of Grenada to remove Cuban influence. The war lasts a total of four days.

3) The Detroit Pistons beat the Denver Nuggets, 186–184, in the highest-scoring game in NBA history. *Both defensive coaches should retire.*

4) After 70 years, the gold medals that Jim Thorpe won in the 1912

Summer Olympics are returned to his family. Native Americans rejoice.

5) A German newspaper publishes the Hitler Diaries, which turns out to be fake news and a Hitler hoax.

6) Dr. Martin Luther King Jr. Day becomes a federal holiday every January. Thirty-eight years later, Juneteenth (June 19th) becomes a federal holiday.

7) The series finale of *M*A*S*H* is watched by 125 million people. The US population is about 200 million. *The other 75 million are doing their homework.*

8) The Social Security system, approaching bankruptcy, is reformed. *Now senior citizens can still have their early-bird special.*

9) Sally Ride becomes, at age 32, the youngest—and the first American female—astronaut in space.

10) Millions die in Ethiopia as a result of famine.

11) The Rock and Roll Hall of Fame opens in Cleveland, Ohio. First-year inductees include Elvis Presley, Chuck Berry, Sam Cooke, and the Everly Brothers.

12) Singer Diana Ross gives a concert in Central Park in New York City. *Only 800,000 people attend.*

13) The lowest temperature ever recorded on Earth, minus 128 degrees Fahrenheit, occurs in Antarctica. *Even the penguins wear earmuffs.*

1984

1) The United Kingdom, which has controlled Hong Kong since 1842, and China reach an agreement to return Hong Kong to China in 1997.

2) Apple Computer runs a TV ad on Super Bowl Sunday for the new Macintosh personal computer. The powerful ad is never shown again.

3) After 266 years, William Penn is made an honorary US citizen.

The founder of Philadelphia is rumored to be the inventor of the Philly cheesesteak.

4) Upper Volta in Africa changes its name to Burkina Faso. *Everyone knows its capital is Ouagadougou.*

5) Great baseball movies are released this decade: *Field of Dreams, Bull Durham, Eight Men Out,* and *The Natural.* Other great flicks are *Raging Bull, Raiders of the Lost Ark, Gandhi, E.T. the Extra-Terrestrial, Wall Street, Driving Miss Daisy,* and *Rain Man.*

6) An explosion on a warship is the worst Soviet naval disaster ever, with hundreds killed.

7) *During the longest game in MLB history—25 innings in eight hours—the Chicago White Sox beat the Milwaukee Brewers as their third baseman falls fast asleep on the field.*

8) An Arkansas man who was in an automobile accident awakens from a coma after 19 years. *He must be very hungry.*

9) Using a jet pack, astronauts conduct the first untethered space walk. *What happens if the jet pack runs out of fuel?*

10) Born this year are basketball star LeBron James, Facebook's Mark Zuckerberg, actress Scarlett Johansson, and Prince Harry, the Duke of Sussex. His brother, Prince William, the Duke of Cambridge, is born two years earlier.

11) A goof by President Ronald Reagan: Without knowing that his microphone is on, he jokingly says about the Soviet Union, "We begin bombing in five minutes."

12) An air force colonel flies solo across the Atlantic Ocean in a helium balloon from Maine to Italy. The 3,500-mile flight takes 86 hours. *If the wind had shifted, he could have wound up in South America.*

1985

1) President Ronald Reagan and Russian President Mikhail Gorbachev meet for the first time in Geneva. *They soon become BFFs.*

2) Philadelphia Mayor Wilson Goode orders police to raid the

headquarters of radical group MOVE. In desperation, he has a bomb dropped from a helicopter onto the roof, killing many people and destroying many homes. *Goode did not make a good decision.*

3) The RMS *Titanic* is discovered in the North Atlantic, 12,000 feet down. *The iceberg has melted.*

4) No smoking in Aspen, Colorado, restaurants. *Depends on what they are smoking.*

5) Japan launches its first interplanetary spacecraft, *Sakigake*. The next year, it flies by Halley's Comet.

6) Coca-Cola introduces New Coke, to negative response. Old Coke comes back in a flash.

7) John Gotti becomes the leader of the Gambino crime family after the murder of two Mafia bigwigs outside a New York City steakhouse. *A homicide well done.*

8) The first internet domain name is used: symbolics.com.

9) In baseball, Pete Rose sets the all-time hit record, with 4,256 hits. In 1989, he is indefinitely banned from baseball for betting on games on teams that he manages.

10) President Ronald Reagan causes a major uproar in the United States when he attends a memorial service at a West Germany cemetery where SS troops from World War II are among the dead.

11) *Super Mario Brothers* is introduced; Microsoft releases the first Windows program.

12) Forty-five famous singers record "We Are the World" to raise money for famine relief.

13) A drug scandal rocks baseball, with many star players suspended.

14) *A little-known fact: From 1942–1985, dentists use uranium in making porcelain dentures because of its natural color. As a result, many people have radioactive teeth.*

15) A Japan Airlines plane crashes into a mountain, killing 520 people—the largest number of deaths in a single accident.

16) A 13-year-old girl becomes the youngest graduate of the University of Oxford in England. *But she does not make the rugby team.*

1986

1) Pope John Paul II visits the Great Synagogue of Rome, the first time a modern pope has visited a synagogue. *He loves the chopped liver.*

2) American Jonathan Pollard, age 31, pleads guilty to espionage for selling top-secret military intelligence to Israel and is sentenced to life in prison.

3) Haitian president Jean-Claude "Baby Doc" Duvalier is overthrown and flees the country with stuffed pockets, ending 28 years of family rule.

4) Among the important books this decade are *The Handmaid's Tale*, *The Color Purple*, *The Bonfire of the Vanities*, and loads of Stephen King novels.

5) One of the longest wars in history ends when the United Kingdom and the Netherlands sign a peace treaty, ending the Three Hundred and Thirty-Five Years' War. This was not even really a war since no shot was ever fired. But peace is better than war.

6) A cargo ship leaves Philadelphia carrying 14,000 tons of toxic waste. It wanders the sea for 16 months, finally dumping the waste in the waters off Haiti.

7) To raise money to fight hunger and homelessness, 5 million people form a human chain by holding hands, reaching from New York City to Long Beach, California, during the Hands Across America event. *A lady in Kansas breaks the chain when she has to sneeze!*

8) *Voyager 2* has its first encounter with the planet Uranus, only 1.7 billion miles away, give or take a few. It discovers the planet's 11 moons.

9) The United States bombs Libya because Libya is sponsoring terrorist organizations.

10) Broadway is booming with standout shows *The Phantom of the Opera*, *Les Misérables*, *Cats*, *Brighton Beach Memoirs*, *Glengarry Glen Ross*, and *Dreamgirls*.

11) Mad cow disease is discovered in the United Kingdom. *It is not related to angry horse disease.*

1987

1) During a televised press conference, the state treasurer of Pennsylvania, having been found guilty of four charges, shoots himself.

2) To celebrate the 50th anniversary of the Golden Gate Bridge in San Francisco, 800,000 people turn out. *Did they have to pay a toll?*

3) The first intifada, or Palestinian protests, take place in Gaza and the West Bank. The protests last six years, and hundreds die.

4) Iraq drops mustard gas bombs on residential areas in Iran, killing and injuring thousands.

5) An FBI agent is assigned the task of finding a mole in the FBI who is working with the KGB. *The agent **is** the spy, is caught, and is serving life imprisonment. This is the worst intelligence disaster in US history.*

6) France and the Walt Disney Company sign an agreement to build a Disneyland in Paris. *Mickey Mouse, Minnie Mouse, and the gang are now studying French.*

7) The first National Coming Out Day is celebrated.

8) The art world was booming. Leading artists are Keith Haring, Jean-Michel Basquiat, Jeff Koons, Willem de Kooning, Roy Lichtenstein, and Andy Warhol, who said, *"Art is anything you can get away with."*

9) The first Kentucky Fried Chicken restaurant opens in Beijing as Colonel Sanders becomes a Chinese national hero.

10) The world has to reset their watches as 1987 turns back the clock—by one second.

11) A businessman buys a lifetime unlimited first-class American Airlines ticket for $250,000. *He flies 10,000 times over the years, costing the company $21 million. What a deal!*

12) Iraqi missiles attack an American warship, supposedly by accident, and kill 37 sailors. Iraq apologizes and later pays dearly.

13) An 18-year-old West German amateur pilot lands his private plane on Red Square in Moscow, near the Kremlin. *The Soviet security people were all taking a coffee break, or probably a vodka break.*

1988

1) The United States demolishes its own embassy building in Moscow because the phone lines were bugged and the Kremlin was listening in on every phone call.

2) The first McDonald's opens in a Communist country—Belgrade, Yugoslavia (now Serbia). *How do you say "Big Mac" in Serbian?*

3) The world's biggest turtle washes up in Wales. Estimated to be 100 years old, it is nine feet long and weighs over 2,000 pounds. *Definitely could not beat the rabbit in a race.*

4) Medical waste is found on beaches in the New York area. Maybe from the waste dumped near Haiti.

5) Benazir Bhutto is elected prime minister of Pakistan, the first woman to lead an Islamic country.

6) Some of the brightest stars of the decade are Madonna, Prince, Whitney Houston, Tina Turner, Phil Collins, Paul McCartney, Bruce Springsteen, Tom Cruise, Harrison Ford, Michelle Pfeiffer, Gene Hackman, Jane Fonda, Eddie Murphy, and Sylvester Stallone.

7) A new terrorist organization, al-Qaeda, forms in Afghanistan, by a group led by Osama bin Laden. Among other horrible acts, al-Qaeda is responsible for the 9/11 catastrophe.

8) After eight years, the Iran-Iraq War ends, with over 1 million dead.

9) The first Worlds AIDS Day is held to raise awareness of the AIDS pandemic.

10) In the election for mayor of Rio de Janeiro, *the mayor is so unpopular that a monkey receives 400,000 votes. Just kidding—actually, an elephant won.*

11) The first transatlantic fiber-optic cable is laid. It can simultaneously carry 40,000 telephone calls. *Teenagers are jumping for joy.*

12) German tennis star Steffi Graf becomes the only person to achieve the Golden Slam by winning all four major tournaments plus the Olympic gold medal in the same calendar year.

13) The antidepressant Prozac is introduced. *Woody Allen once said that he doesn't take tranquilizers because they make him nervous.*

1989

1) Nathan's Famous of Coney Island, Brooklyn, opens in Moscow. *Russians claim they invented the hotdog.*

2) US Gen. Colin Powell becomes the first Black chairman of the Joint Chiefs of Staff. David Dinkins becomes the first African American mayor of New York City.

3) Five New York City teenagers are convicted of assaulting the Central Park Jogger. After 13 years, the five are released from jail, and the case is vacated after another man confesses to the crime.

4) In Beijing, 1 million people protest in Tiananmen Square demanding greater democracy. One protester, the Tank Man, becomes an international celebrity by standing in front of a big, approaching Chinese tank.

5) The wreck of the German battleship *Bismarck* is located in the Atlantic Ocean. Sunk in 1941, it became a popular song and movie in 1960.

6) *Seinfeld*, a TV show about nothing, makes its debut. *The public likes shows about nothing, and the program becomes really something.*

7) Other popular TV shows are *Cheers, Family Ties, The Cosby Show, Miami Vice, L.A. Law,* and everyone's favorite, *The Golden Girls.*

8) Salman Rushdie publishes *The Satanic Verses*, and the Supreme Leader of Iran issues a fatwa, an assassination of Mr. Rushdie. *I guess he did not like the book.*

9) An asteroid passes by Earth, only missing by 425,000 miles. *If you missed it, it will return in 2051.*

10) In Paraguay, a coup d'état occurs and Alfredo Stroessner, the dictator since 1954, is ousted. *Supposedly, he had invented fettuccine Alfredo.*

11) According to the official news agency in the Soviet Union, a UFO landed in Russia.

12) Deion Sanders did something that no one has ever done before and probably no one ever will. Sanders hit a home run for the New York Yankees and scored a touchdown for the Atlanta Falcons, all in the same week! He is the only person to play in the World Series and also in a Super Bowl!

13) Looking for their independence from the Soviet Union, people of Estonia, Latvia, and Lithuania join hands and form a human chain that's 372 miles long.

14) Apartheid in South Africa is finally ending as new Prime Minister F.W. de Klerk takes office.

15) In the Great Pyramid of Giza in Egypt, a 4,400-year-old mummy is found. *They are still looking for Daddy.*

16) New York real estate mogul Leona Helmsley, the Queen of Mean, is convicted of tax fraud. She famously said, *"We don't pay taxes. Only the little people pay taxes."*

17) A financial scammer in Thailand is found guilty of many financial crimes *and sentenced to 141,000 years in jail. With good behavior, he can get out in **80,000 years**.*

Deaths This Decade of Notable People

- Alexei Kosygin, 76. Premier of the Soviet Union, 1964–1980.
- Emperor Hirohito, 87. Ruled Japan from 1926–1989.
- Ayn Rand, 77. Conservative author of *Atlas Shrugged* and *The Fountainhead.*
- Irving Berlin, 101. America's greatest songwriter composed "God Bless America" and hundreds of other great songs.
- Joe Louis, 66. World heavyweight champion for 12 years.
- Jimmy Durante, 86. America's favorite entertainer for 50 years.

- Jesse Owens, 66. Olympic gold medal winner made Adolf Hitler squirm in 1936.
- Benny Goodman, 77. Jazz musician and bandleader; the King of Swing.
- Alfred Hitchcock, 80. English filmmaker dubbed the Master of Suspense.
- Ethel Merman, 76. The First Lady of the musical comedy stage for 50 years.
- Marc Chagall, 97. The quintessential Jewish artist of the 20th century.
- Georgia O'Keeffe, 98. The mother of American modernism.
- Ansel Adams, 82. American landscape photographer renowned for black-and-white images of the West.
- Grace Kelly, 52. Academy Award-winning star of *The Country Girl* became the Princess of Monaco.
- Cary Grant, 82. Hollywood's most debonair leading man for over 30 years.
- Moshe Dayan, 66. Israeli military leader and politician.
- Fred Astaire, 88. The best dancer in Hollywood for 76 years.
- Henry Fonda, 77. Legendary actor who won the Academy Award in 1981 for his final film, *On Golden Pond*.
- Jack Dempsey, 87. The Manassa Mauler was the world heavyweight champion from 1919–1926.
- Lucille Ball, 77. All of America loved *I Love Lucy*.
- Laurence Olivier, 82. Great English actor of stage and screen who earned three Academy Awards.
- Tennessee Williams, 71. Legendary American playwright wrote *A Streetcar Named Desire*, among other productions.
- Secretariat, 19. One of the great racehorses of all time won the Triple Crown in 1973.

Advances in Science This Decade

Rings of Neptune discovered – Gene therapy – Computer virus – Ozone layer hole – DNA fingerprinting – Wreck of the RMS *Titanic* – Space Shuttle – Nicotine patch – Synthetic skin – Abortion pill – Artificial insulin – First triple transplant (heart, lung, and liver)

Important Innovations of the 1980s

Cell phone – Personal computer – High-definition TV – Disposable camera – Disposable contact lenses – The Clapper – Virtual reality – Computer printer – Soft soap – Chicken McNuggets – Air Jordans – Digital audio tape – Red Bull – Depends – Lean Cuisine – Nintendo Entertainment System – PAC-MAN – Fax machine – MTV – Frequent flyer miles – Swatch watch – Email – Laptop computer – GPS (Global Positioning System)

IN 1980, the population of the world was 4.4 billion people. The United States's population was 227 million people. The average life expectancy of Americans was 74 years.

The clock is ticking toward the end of the 20th century. The world survived the 1980s and coasted into the 1990s. I think the next decade will be a positive one, finally.

10

1990–1999
THE GOOD DECADE

The end of the 20th century is finally in sight. It began with a relatively peaceful, nonthreatening decade, the 1900s, and ended with another relatively peaceful decade, the 1990s.

But, as usual, there were a multitude of threats to our nation during this 10-year period. The United States, along with our allies, became involved in a Middle Eastern war that, a decade later, became a quagmire. A war in the Balkans and an African genocide brought the possibility of our involvement.

Terrorism, both international and now domestic, was a major threat to our tranquility. The Hermit Kingdom was starving, and disasters, both natural and man-made, were all around us. The United States experienced a banking crisis, and for the first time in 130 years, a US president was impeached. The use of steroids threatened the integrity of our national pastime, baseball.

But if there is such a thing as a nonthreat, it occurred during this decade. After 46 years of so many threats, the Cold War had melted and was finally over, as the Evil Empire had become extinct!

Presidential Elections of the 1990s

The 1992 election saw the incumbent president, Republican George H.W. Bush, and Vice President Dan Quayle easily defeated. The Comeback Kid, Arkansas Democratic Governor Bill Clinton, became president No. 42, with Senator Al Gore of Tennessee becoming his vice president.

Anybody know who Gore's roommate was at Harvard? If you said, "George W. Bush," you are wrong. *It was actor* **Tommy Lee Jones**.

The independent candidate, Ross Perot, actually got 19% of the popular vote. *I'm not sure who his college roommate was. I'm not sure if he even went to college.*

Clinton said, "Strength and wisdom are not opposing values."

In 1996, the Clinton-Gore ticket easily beat the Republican candidate, Kansas senator Bob Dole, whose running mate was New York Rep. Jack Kemp, a former NFL quarterback. *The Republicans should have punted.*

The Cold War

1991 marked the dissolving of the Union of Soviet Socialist Republics, realistically ending the Cold War. Formed in 1917, the Soviet Union had disintegrated, and 14 independent republics emerged: Armenia, Azerbaijan, Belarus, Estonia, Georgia, Kazakhstan, Latvia, Lithuania, Moldova, Russia, Tajikistan, Turkmenistan, Ukraine, and Uzbekistan. *As my friend Neil Sedaka sang, "Breaking up is hard to do."*

The Soviet economy had broken down, as the gross domestic product fell 40% between 1990–1995. Lithuania, Latvia, and Estonia were the first to secede from the USSR. There was a failed coup attempt in 1991 to overthrow President Mikhail Gorbachev. The surest sign that Communism was dead in Russia was when, in 1997, *Gorbachev did a TV commercial for Pizza Hut. Joseph Stalin would have been very upset—he liked Domino's pizza.*

Boris Yeltsin became the first democratically elected president of Russia in 1991 and resigned eight years later. *He loved his vodka.*

A relatively unknown KGB officer, Vladimir Putin, succeeded Mr. Yeltsin as the new Russian leader. He once proclaimed, "Spying has always gone on since ancient times."

Russia is the largest country of the new post-Soviet group, both geographically and population-wise. It also possesses the world's largest stockpile of nuclear weapons. As a final slap in the face to the old Soviet Union, Estonia, Latvia, Lithuania, and neighboring Poland now all belong to NATO.

The First Gulf War

Another member of the Evil Empire, Iraq, became aggressive, and in 1990 invaded and annexed its Arab neighbor Kuwait. Iraq's dictator, Saddam Hussein, proudly said, "We are not intimidated by the size of the armies or the type of hardware the US has brought."

He miscalculated!

He declared that Kuwait was stealing oil from Iraq's oil fields and that they must be punished for this economic warfare. Fearing that Iraq was supporting terrorist groups and might attack Saudi Arabia and Israel, the United States put together a coalition of 35 nations, including several Arab states, to combat the Iraqi strongman. In February 1991, the First Gulf War, aka **Operation Desert Shield**, began with air bombardment and then a ground assault. A few weeks later, a cease-fire was declared as Iraq dumped 400 million gallons of crude oil into the Persian Gulf and set fire to 700 oil wells in Kuwait, causing widespread pollution. Not a pretty sight.

The First Gulf War was the first heavily televised conflict, as CNN broadcast from the front lines. New and sophisticated technology munitions were used. US soldiers came home with Gulf War syndrome, a medical condition with serious consequences. *Ten years later, things really heated up in Iraq—and not just the summertime temperatures in Baghdad.*

The Balkans War

In the early 1990s, the Balkan countries had become a hot spot. Let's go back to 1918 and the end of World War I. The Kingdom of Serbs, Croats, and Slovenes was part of the Ottoman Empire and the Austro-Hungarian Empire. From this hodgepodge of countries, in 1918, the nation of **Yugoslavia** was established. It became an independent Communist government in 1946 under Marshal Josip Broz Tito, but did not follow the lead of the Soviet Union. In 1991, Yugoslavia imploded, and seven new nations appeared: Slovenia, Serbia, North Macedonia, Montenegro, Kosovo, Croatia, and Bosnia and Herzegovina.

There were separate wars now, in Croatia, Bosnia, and Kosovo. Serbia engaged in "ethnic cleansing," a genocide killing 140,000 Muslims in Bosnia. Millions of refugees and displaced persons scattered throughout Europe as the economies in these Balkan nations were destroyed. Finally, in 1995, the Dayton Peace Agreement, negotiated by the United States and NATO, formally ended the Balkan Wars.

Rwanda

A civil war broke out in Rwanda, a newly independent African country, in 1990. Who knows the capital city of Rwanda? *You're pretty smart if you said, "Kigali."*

Rwanda was not controlled by the majority Hutus, but rather by the minority Tutsis. (*Not to be confused by the Dustin Hoffman film Tootsie.*) In 1994, the Hutus went ballistic and, in a three-month period, slaughtered **1 million** Tutsis. Sadly, the United Nations did nothing, and no country intervened to stop this genocide. Not wanting to get involved, the United States looked the other way.

North Korea

North Korea, always a threat to the United States and our Asian allies, went through some terrible times in the mid-1990s. Because of the loss of Soviet support, the North Korean economy became a disaster. Mass starvation occurred, and 3 million people died. Citizens were ordered to eat only two meals a day, when they could, and there were reports of cannibalism. Floods and then a severe drought further destroyed the country. The Great Successor, Kim Jong Un, became North Korea's leader, when his father, Kim Il-Sung, died in 1994, *surely not of starvation.*

Hypocritically, Kim Jong Un said, "We want to have many good friends in the United States."

Terrorism

Domestic terrorism became a very real threat to the United States in the 1990s. The deadliest such attack in US history occurred in April 1995 when a truck bomb destroyed the Alfred P. Murrah Federal Building in Oklahoma City. One hundred and sixty-eight people were killed, including many children, and almost 700 were injured. The main perpetrator, Timothy McVeigh, hated the US government and was executed for his misdeed.

In 1993, as a prelude to September 11, 2001, a truck bomb was detonated in a parking garage beneath the World Trade Center, killing six and injuring 1,000. Arab terrorists who hated the United States and Israel were arrested and convicted.

A 1999 attack in a high school in Columbine, Colorado, by two students awoke the nation to mass shootings. Twelve fellow students were killed, and many others were injured. Sadly, over the next 20 years, many other such massacres took place in schools around the country.

For 17 years, an American domestic anarchist (a former college professor) terrorized the country. Nicknamed the Unabomber, he detonated at least 16 bombs.

Since 1977, many doctors have been targeted at American abortion clinics. Pro-life extremists have carried out bombings, murders, and kidnappings.

International terrorism was rampant during this peaceful decade. A mysterious Saudi Arabian millionaire, Osama bin Laden, declared war on the United States and the West in 1996, and this was a precursor of things to come. He unbelievably said, "We love death. The US loves life. That is the difference between us two."

All around the world this decade, terrorism occurred. In Buenos Aires, the Asociación Mutual Israelita Argentina Jewish community center was bombed, as well as the Israeli Embassy, killing 100. Hezbollah was blamed for the bombings, and Israel retaliated in the West Bank. Arab terrorists conducted many suicide attacks on Israel, killing many innocent civilians.

A poison gas attack by terrorists in a Japanese subway killed several commuters and sickened 5,000. An Ethiopian jet was hijacked and crashed, killing 127. Terrorist bombings in Russia killed 158 comrades. A truck bomb in Saudi Arabia killed and wounded hundreds, including 19 American soldiers. An EgyptAir plane crashed in the ocean off Nantucket, killing 217 passengers. Did the Egyptian pilot purposely crash the plane?

The only good news was that notorious terrorist Carlos the Jackal was finally caught after 20 years and sentenced to life in prison. *He spends his days terrorizing his cellmate.*

Disasters

The decade was loaded with natural disasters. Just to name a few, Hurricane Andrew destroyed South Florida in 1992, perhaps the most costly hurricane to hit the United States. In 1994, a major earthquake shook Los Angeles. Japan suffered a devastating earthquake in 1995, which killed 5,500 people and caused $200 billion worth of damage. *A* cyclone—*not the roller coaster in Coney Island, Brooklyn*—killed 138,000 people in Bangladesh. *I could go on and on, but I don't want to ruin your day.*

In finance, the Savings and Loan Crisis of the 1980s continued into the 1990s. To fix this debacle, the Resolution Trust Corporation was established, as the total loss was $160 billion.

A Connecticut hedge fund, Long-Term Capital Management, collapsed in 1998, and almost $5 billion vanished. Around the globe, there were many economic crises: Norway, Finland, Sweden, Peru, Venezuela, Russia, Argentina, and Ecuador all had problems, but ultimately, everyone survived.

The Impeachment of President Bill Clinton

A word not heard for 130 years popped up in 1998—*"impeachment"—and it was not a Baskin-Robbins ice cream flavor.* The US House of Representatives impeached Clinton for lying under oath and obstruction of justice. Mr. Clinton, age 52, had a consensual sexual relationship with Monica Lewinsky, a 22-year-old White House intern. Quoting Mr. Clinton, he "did not have sexual relations with that woman, Ms. Lewinsky." The US Senate acquitted him of both charges in 1999.

President Andrew Johnson was the only other president at that time to have been impeached. In 1868, the US House of Representatives impeached him, but the US Senate acquitted him in a very close vote. He left the White House in 1868 and did something no other president has ever done. Anybody know what it was? He was elected to the US Senate in 1875, from his home state of Tennessee. *Many senators have become president, but only Johnson became a senator after being president.*

Steroids

Our national pastime, baseball, was threatened this decade by one word: **"steroids."** Baseball banned performance-enhancing drugs (PEDs) in 1991, but players looking to get an edge in competition secretly took them. Offensive production, such as home runs and runs batted in, skyrocketed. Great players of the 1990s were allegedly involved with steroids—Barry Bonds, Mark McGwire, Sammy Sosa, Roger Clemens, and Jose Canseco, just to name a few. The situation grew worse at the end of the 1990s and peaked in the early 2000s. Hitting the nail on the head, Bonds stated, "I never stop looking for things to try and make myself better."

After these superstar players retired, because of their alleged connection to PEDs, none were elected to the National Baseball Hall of Fame. Steroids left a black mark on the legacy of baseball.

Wars and Treaties of the 1990s

Many wars were fought—58 in total. The Civil War in Afghanistan killed 546,000, the war in Rwanda killed over 500,000, and the First Gulf War killed 25,000, mostly Iraqis.

Many treaties were also signed this decade: 42. In 1990, the United States and the USSR signed the Chemical Weapons Accord. The Maastricht Treaty established the European Union. Israel and the Palestine Liberation Organization (PLO) signed the Oslo Accords.

The Chemical Weapons Convention, ratified by 165 countries, outlawed the production, stockpiling, and use of chemical weapons. The Kyoto Protocol discussed the reduction of greenhouse gas emissions. The North American Free Trade Agreement (NAFTA) among the United States, Canada, and Mexico became a reality.

Important and Unimportant News of the 1990s

1990

1) President George H.W. Bush breaks his pre-election promise of "Read my lips—no new taxes." Those lips and those new taxes come back to haunt him in the 1992 election. *He said, "I do not like broccoli. I'm the president of the United States and I'm not going to eat any more broccoli."*

2) A global ban on the trade of ivory is introduced. *Does that mean that Ivory Soap is in trouble?*

3) Prince Akihito becomes the new emperor of Japan, succeeding his late father, Emperor Hirohito.

4) The first page of the World Wide Web—the internet—is written. It now contains billions of pages.

5) Baseball legend Pete Rose, the career hits leader, goes to jail for tax evasion. *He tries out for the prison team, but doesn't make it.*

6) A Boston art museum is robbed of 12 paintings that are worth over $300 million. *The next day, a security guard is hired.*

7) A well-preserved Tyrannosaurus rex specimen is discovered in South Dakota. *It is named Sue. Why not Sam?*

8) Communism is officially over, as a McDonald's restaurant opens in Moscow. On the menu is the Egg McStalin.

9) The Hubble Space Telescope is deployed. Monumental information will be gathered in the future.

10) After 27 years in a South African prison, Nelson Mandela is finally released. "The greatest glory in living lies not in never falling, but in rising every time we fall."

11) Industrialized nations of the world agree to stop dumping waste in the ocean. *But they don't say what they are going to do with it.*

12) Smoking is banned from all US domestic flights. Only drinking is allowed.

13) A stampede in Mecca, Saudi Arabia, kills 1,400 Muslim pilgrims.

14) *The Simpsons*—Homer and family—make their TV debut. *First Lady Barbara Bush calls it "the dumbest thing I've ever seen."*

15) This decade, Steffi Graf wins 14 tennis Grand Slam events; on the men's side, Pete Sampras captures 12 titles.

16) The fastest coast-to-coast flight, from Los Angeles to Virginia, is piloted by two US Air Force officers: 68 minutes and 17 seconds. *Quicker than driving from New York City to John F. Kennedy International Airport.*

17) The Leaning Tower of Pisa is closed to the public because of fears that it is falling over. *It is repaired and now called the Not Leaning Anymore Tower of Pisa.*

1991

1) South Africa officially repeals the unjust policy of apartheid. Nelson Mandela celebrates.

2) Leningrad's name is changed to St. Petersburg. *Old Russian stationery has to be burned.*

3) After a bitter US Senate fight, African American Clarence Thomas becomes a US Supreme Court justice.

4) Exxon spends billions of dollars in cleaning up the *Exxon Valdez* oil spill in Alaska.

5) Led by Michael Jordan, the Chicago Bulls win the first of six NBA championships. *Coach Phil Jackson sports 11 NBA championship rings. He has to wear two rings on one finger.*

6) Operation Solomon, a covert airlift, brings 14,000 Ethiopian Jews to Israel. *Pass the Manischewitz.* On one flight, a Boeing 747, there were 1,088 passengers. *Bathrooms were busy!*

7) The Warsaw Pact ends because the Soviet Union no longer exists as the big cheese.

8) America's emergency number, 911, is introduced.

9) Basketball superstar Magic Johnson reveals that he has HIV and announces his retirement from the NBA.

10) A man buys a painting for $4 at a flea market in Pennsylvania. Inside the frame is the first printing of the Declaration of Independence. *He soon sells it for $2.4 million! Nice.*

1992

1) Queen Elizabeth II will pay income tax this year. *But she has no income except for when she sells postcards at the gift shop in Buckingham Palace.*

2) After 30 years, Johnny Carson retires from *The Tonight Show*. *He quipped, "Any time four New Yorkers get into a cab together without arguing, a bank robbery has just taken place."*

3) Mafia boss John Gotti is sentenced to life in prison. *Nothing would stick to the Teflon Don except this imprisonment.*

4) Six days of rioting occur in Los Angeles after four police officers are acquitted of beating Rodney King during a traffic stop. The riots leave 63 dead, 2,300 injured, and $1 billion in financial losses.

5) A 29-pound meteorite plummets to Earth near Peekskill, New York, and crushes a Chevy Malibu. *No dinosaurs are involved.*

6) At the Summer Olympics in Barcelona, the United States wins the gold medal in basketball. The Dream Team, the greatest team ever assembled, led by Michael Jordan, Charles Barkley, and Magic Johnson, are unstoppable.

7) The FDA urges women to stop getting breast implants. *Men are very upset.*

8) Euro Disney opens in France. *Bonjour, Monsieur Mickey.*

9) A shipping container filled with 28,000 rubber ducks is lost at sea. *The ducks are floating and quacking around the world.*

10) Troy State beats DeVry Institute, 258–141, in the highest-scoring college basketball game in history. *Great defense!*

11) The low point of the year occurs in Tokyo at a state dinner when President George H.W. Bush **vomits** all over the Japanese

Prime Minister Kiichi Miyazawa on international TV. *Guess he didn't like the sushi.*

1993

1) Israeli Prime Minister Yitzhak Rabin and PLO Chairman Yasser Arafat shake hands in Washington, DC, after signing the Oslo Accords. *Mr. Rabin then counts his fingers.*

2) Czechoslovakia dissolves, becoming the Czech Republic and Slovakia. *Was spelling the reason for the Velvet Divorce?*

3) A ferryboat in Haiti sinks, killing 1,000. An earthquake in India kills 10,000.

4) South Africans Nelson Mandela and F.W. de Klerk share the Nobel Peace Prize. Originally, both had totally different views about apartheid.

5) No. 1-ranked tennis player Monica Seles is stabbed during a match in Germany. *No, not by her opponent, but by a fan who did not like her tennis outfit.*

6) Police begin a child abuse investigation regarding singing legend Michael Jackson, who said, "Before I would hurt a child, I would slit my wrists."

7) The Mississippi River and Missouri River overflow and cause $15 billion in damages in the Great Flood of '93.

8) Kim Campbell becomes the first female prime minister of Canada as NAFTA becomes law.

9) A 71-year-old man sets a record by consecutively making 2,750 free throws over a 12-hour period. *The streak ends when the janitor closes the gym. The New York Knicks are unsuccessful in signing him.*

10) Federal agents raid the Branch Davidian compound in Waco, Texas, as 76 cult members die.

11) Carol Moseley Braun of Illinois is elected as the first female Black US senator.

12) In the NFL, the Dallas Cowboys win three Super Bowls, while the "Bad Luck" Buffalo Bills lose four straight Super Bowls.

13) Angry wife Lorena Bobbitt makes front-page news when she cuts off her husband's penis with a kitchen knife. *After surgery, he says that everything is "back to normal."*

1994

1) Jordan and Israel sign a peace treaty ending the state of war that has existed since 1948.

2) Genetically engineered tomatoes are available in stores. *What about lettuce and carrots?*

3) After 27 years in exile, PLO Chairman Yasser Arafat returns to Palestine. He is awarded the Nobel Peace Prize, along with Yitzhak Rabin and Shimon Peres.

4) The Northridge earthquake in Los Angeles kills 57 and injures 8,000.

5) Former President Ronald Reagan announces to the country that he has Alzheimer's disease. So sad.

6) MLB players go on strike. There is no World Series this year, for first time since 1904.

7) We are entertained by Oprah Winfrey, Michael Douglas, Céline Dion, Julia Roberts, Tom Hanks, Adam Sandler, John Travolta, and *Woody Allen, who jokingly said, "When I was kidnapped, my parents snapped into action. They rented out my room."*

8) In the first multiracial election in South Africa after the end of apartheid, Nelson Mandela is elected president. He wisely said, "Unlike some politicians, I can admit to a mistake."

9) O.J. Simpson's ex-wife, Nicole Brown Simpson, and her friend Ronald Goldman are found murdered in Los Angeles. After a wild car chase seen on national TV, football legend Simpson is arrested.

10) The United States invades Haiti to restore democracy. The occupation lasts six months, and democracy reappears.

11) The Chunnel, the 31-mile English Channel Tunnel connecting England and France, opens.

12) North Korean leader Kim Jong-il in his biography regarding

golf, says that he shot a 38 under par, with 11 holes in one. *He wants to give Tiger Woods lessons.*

1995

1) O.J. Simpson is found not guilty in the Trial of the Century that lasts 11 months. Attorney Johnnie Cochran famously said regarding the gloves found at the crime scene, *"If it doesn't fit, you must acquit."*

2) An oppressive summer heat wave targets the Midwest, killing 3,000. In Chicago alone, 739 people die.

3) A right-wing Israeli fanatic assassinates Israeli Prime Minister Yitzhak Rabin. He is succeeded by Shimon Peres.

4) A network of caves in France is discovered, with paintings on the walls estimated to be 20,000 years old. *Can the caves be moved to the Louvre?*

5) *While visiting Washington, DC, Russian President Boris Yeltsin is found drunk, wearing only his underwear, and trying to hail a cab. Unless his undies had pockets, how would he pay for the ride?*

6) Barings Bank, the oldest bank in the United Kingdom, collapses. A rogue broker by himself manages to lose $1.4 billion. *He then applies for a job at Barclays but is rejected.*

7) After five years, the *Galileo* spacecraft reaches the planet Jupiter, almost 3 billion miles away. Loads of information is transmitted.

8) Québec City decides to remain part of Canada rather than becoming an independent country. No more "Long live free Quebec."

9) Finally, after 130 years, the state of Mississippi ratifies the 13th Amendment, abolishing slavery. *They thought the Civil War was still being fought.*

10) Cal Ripken Jr. of the Baltimore Orioles breaks Lou Gehrig's record of 2,130 consecutive games played. Three years later, he sets the new record of 2,632 games. Quite a feat!

11) A Chicago stockbroker flies a balloon solo across the Pacific Ocean. In four days, he covers almost 6,000 miles, traveling from Seoul,

South Korea, to Saskatchewan, Canada. *When he lands, the stockbroker asks, "Was the market up today?"*

1996

1) As an April Fools' Day joke, Taco Bell announces that they are buying the Liberty Bell in Philadelphia and *renaming it the Taco Liberty Bell.*

2) Mother Teresa receives honorary US citizenship. Did you know that she was Albanian and not Indian?

3) An IBM computer, Deep Blue, defeats world chess champion Garry Kasparov in a game of chess. *With great confidence, the computer now wishes to play champion Pete Sampras in a tennis match.*

4) The militant Taliban capture the capital city of Kabul in Afghanistan and declare the country a fundamentalist Islamic State.

5) Federal Reserve Chairman Alan Greenspan uses the phrase "irrational exuberance" in describing the dot-com bubble. It takes a couple of years, *but the bubble does pop.*

6) Charles and Diana, the Prince and Princess of Wales, divorce. *Immediately, both go on Match.com.*

7) A bombing at the Summer Olympics in Atlanta injures over 100 people.

8) In the United Kingdom, mad cow disease results in the mass slaughter of British cows. *Why are these cows so angry?*

9) Fox News Channel starts broadcasting, and General Motors introduces the first electric car.

10) In the music world, hip-hop is really hopping. Big stars in music include Whitney Houston, Mariah Carey, Garth Brooks, and Billy Joel.

11) In Scotland, the first cloned mammal, Dolly the sheep, is introduced to the world. *"Well hello Dolly, you're looking swell Dolly."*

1997

1) The largest merger in history takes place as telecommunication

company WorldCom merges with MCI. After five years, an accounting scandal causes the new company to go bankrupt.

2) Kofi Annan of Ghana becomes the seventh secretary general of the United Nations.

3) Weight-loss drug Fen-Phen is taken off the market because it may cause heart problems.

4) Madeleine Albright becomes the first female US secretary of state. At age 59, she discovers that both her parents were secretly Jewish. *Now she loves kosher salami.*

5) In a world heavyweight championship boxing match, title defender Mike Tyson bites off Evander Holyfield's ear and is disqualified. *He says later that he was very hungry.*

6) A very sad day in London Town and all over the world as everyone's favorite, Princess Diana of Wales, dies in a horrific car crash in Paris.

7) China is given control of Hong Kong, as promised by the United Kingdom, while over 1 million chickens are killed in Hong Kong to stamp out the bird flu.

8) Italian fashion designer Gianni Versace is shot to death in Miami Beach by a spree killer.

9) What was on TV this decade? Big shows include *Friends, Twin Peaks, The Sopranos, Sex and the City, Mad About You,* and *Ally McBeal.*

10) The Hale-Bopp Comet, called the Great Comet of 1997, is the brightest comet in the sky and very visible to the naked eye. *If you stick around, it will return in the year 4385.*

11) Old Ironsides, the USS *Constitution,* celebrates its 200th birthday and sets sail for the first time in 116 years. *The original crew is happy to be reunited.*

12) In Iowa, Bobbi McCaughey gives birth to septuplets. *That's seven children. Pampers never had it so good.*

1998

1) Many mergers and buyouts this year: Citicorp and Travelers Group merge. Exxon buys Mobil. Deutsche Bank A.G. buys Bankers Trust Corporation. BMW buys Rolls-Royce.

2) Simultaneous terrorist bombings of US Embassies in Tanzania and Kenya kills 224, injures 4500. In retaliation for terrorist bombings, the United States launches missile attacks on Sudan and Afghanistan.

3) At age 77, US Senator John Glenn becomes the oldest person to go into outer space. In 1962, he was the first American in space. *He can't wait to land and have dinner at 4:00 p.m.*

4) Professional wrestler Jesse Ventura is elected governor of Minnesota. *His opponent gives up when Ventura throws him out of the ring.*

5) For the first time in years, the United States has a budget surplus. At the same time, the banking system in Russia collapses.

6) A convicted South American serial killer, who murdered 400 people over 11 years, is released from prison because of good behavior. *Supposedly, he is arrested again for jaywalking.*

7 Three billion people watch a TV concert by the Three Tenors: Luciano Pavarotti, Plácido Domingo, and who else? No. 3 was José Carreras.

8) A new aircraft carrier, the USS *Harry S. Truman,* is put into service. Question: What is President Truman's middle name? If you said, "Stephen," "Sam," or "Sinbad," you are wrong. *He does not have a middle name, just the letter S.*

9) Google is founded. Its original spelling was *G-o-o-g-o-l.* Apple introduces the first iMac computer.

10) Some of Broadway's biggest shows this decade are *Miss Saigon, Mamma Mia!, The Lion King, Rent,* and *Smokey Joe's Café.*

11) The four largest US tobacco companies agree to a master settlement with 46 states, paying out in excess of $200 billion over a long period of time. Advertising and marketing of tobacco products will be curtailed.

12) A giant asteroid just misses colliding with Earth—by 4 million miles. A headline in the *New York Post* reads: **"Kiss Your Asteroid Goodbye!"**

13) 1998 is the year of the home run. *Some say the ball is juiced; some say the players are juiced!* Mark McGwire hits 70 homers, while Sammy Sosa hits 66.

14) *A cat named Blackie inherits $12.5 million when its owner dies. Plenty of marriage proposals follow.*

15) The FDA approves Viagra, a new drug by Pfizer. *Senior men forget about the early-bird special and line up for the drug.*

1999

1) John F. Kennedy Jr., son of the late US president, crashes after piloting his own plane, killing himself; his wife, Carolyn Bessette Kennedy; and her sister, Lauren Bessette.

2) Lance Armstrong wins his first Tour de France event. He wins the next six annual races consecutively, but all seven titles are later stripped from him because of a doping scandal *and use of training wheels.*

3) The last Checker Cab is retired in New York and sold at auction for $135,000. *The wealthy new owner becomes a taxi driver.*

4) The United States turns over the Panama Canal to the Panamanian government. *With all the locks in the canal, who supplies the bagels? Ha ha.*

5) **"Y2K"** is the magic word this year. It is predicted that the computer bug may cause worldwide disruption on January 1, 2000, but it never happens.

6) The euro is introduced in 11 European countries.

7) The most important authors this decade are John Grisham, Tom Clancy, Danielle Steel, and again Stephen King, who said, "I am the literary equivalent of a Big Mac and fries."

8) People born this year have a better chance of being alive in three different centuries than any other group of humans in history.

9) Former Yugoslavian leader Slobodan Milošević is indicted for war crimes and crimes against humanity. He dies in prison seven years later.

10) The Barbie doll celebrates her 40th birthday. *SpongeBob SquarePants* makes his debut.

11) There are many great Hollywood movies this decade, such as *The Silence of the Lambs, A Few Good Men, Forrest Gump, Fargo, Schindler's List, Malcolm X, Ghost,* and *Dances with Wolves.*

12) **Bluetooth** is introduced to the world. *Toothpaste companies are confused and now experiment with blue toothpaste to combat blue teeth.*

Deaths This Decade of Notable People

- Frank Sinatra, 82. The Chairman of the Board; America's favorite personality.
- Richard Nixon, 81. Thirty-seventh US president. 1969-1974
- Princess Diana of Wales, 36. International icon; mother of Prince William and Prince Harry.
- Mother Teresa, 87. Honored by the Catholic Church as Saint Teresa of Calcutta.
- Jacqueline Kennedy Onassis, 64. Former First Lady and international fashion icon.
- Burt Lancaster, 80. A movie star's movie star.
- Audrey Hepburn, 63. English actress who really was *My Fair Lady.*
- Leonard Bernstein, 72. American composer and conductor whose best known work was *West Side Story.*
- Miles Davis, 65. Master of the trumpet helped create modern jazz.
- Sarah Vaughan, 66. A wonderful jazz and popular singer for 40 years.

- Mickey Mantle, 63. New York Yankee All-Star who won the MLB Triple Crown and was MVP three times.
- Joe DiMaggio, 84. Joltin' Joe, aka **the Yankee Clipper**, won nine World Series championships during his 13-year career.
- Dr. Jonas Salk, 80. American virologist who developed the first successful polio vaccine.
- Dr. Seuss, 87. American children's author who published 60 books, including *Green Eggs and Ham.*
- Sam Walton, 74. American businessman and entrepreneur founded Walmart.
- Dr. Benjamin Spock, 94. Pediatrician wrote *Dr. Spock's Baby and Child Care*, a huge best seller.
- Keith Haring, 31. American pop artist and social activist who popularized graffiti.
- Greta Garbo, 84. Beautiful Swedish actress known for the quote "I want to be alone."

Advances in Science This Decade

Genetically modified food – UV index – Web browser – Black holes confirmed – Text message – Polio-free Western Hemisphere – Jupiter's moon and liquid ocean – Lyme disease vaccine – Ozone layer depletion

Important Innovations of the 1990s

DVD – Plasma TV – Netflix – E-commerce website – Hybrid cars – Spamming – Amazon sells books – Smartphone – Yahoo – HGTV – Emoji – BlackBerry – Photoshop – Sony PlayStation – Tickle Me Elmo – Pentium processor – Segway – JavaScript – Discman – PalmPilot – Floppy disk – Reebok Pump sneakers – Crystal Pepsi – Blockbuster videos – AOL – Napster – Streaming media – 24-hour news cycle –

Portable CD players – Game Boy – Video telephone – Bagless vacuum cleaner – Beanie Babies – Big Bertha golf club

---

In 1990, the population of the world was 5.3 billion people. The United States's population was 249 million people. The average life expectancy of Americans was 75 years.

Did you know that the year 2000 was **a century leap year**, meaning February had 29 days? But the years 1800 and 1900 **did not** have 29 days that month, and **neither will** 2100 and 2200. *Sorry, way too complicated to explain.*

The peaceful 10-year period of the 1990s, **the good decade**, was over. So was the **not so peaceful** 20th century. Clinton wisely said, "The light may be fading on the 20th century, but the sun is still rising on America." In retrospect, the country and the world have experienced "the best and the worst of times" this century, as Mr. Dickens famously wrote a long time ago. Let us hope that the 21st century will provide a maximum of good times and a minimum of bad times. Amen.

11

CENTURY 21

Those were the threats of the 20th century. Briefly, what were the threats to our nation that appeared in the first 20 years of the 21st century?

Oh, nothing much, only:

The biggest one that has occurred so far in century 21 was perhaps the largest negative event in the history of the country. Paraphrasing President Franklin D. Roosevelt, September 11, 2001, was "a date which will live in infamy." Nineteen al-Qaeda terrorists simultaneously hijacked four passenger airlines. Two of the planes crashed into the Twin Towers in New York City, and the buildings eventually collapsed. One plane crashed into the Pentagon in Virginia, and the fourth, headed for Washington, DC, crashed into a field in Pennsylvania. The country was in shock, as almost 3,000 people were killed and 25,000 were injured.

Just days into 2021, a despicable event occurred when hundreds of violent Americans, occupied, vandalized, and looted the Capitol Building of the United States of America. This insurrection was an absolute disgrace! FBI Director Christopher Wray called the action "Domestic Terrorism." The rioters were allegedly supporters of President Donald Trump, who believed that the 2020 election had been rigged and stolen from him, even though he had lost by 7 million votes. Trump was impeached for his action of inciting these followers. In the eyes of the world and our nation, it was truly a terrible day for this country.

In two presidential elections, 2000 and 2016, the candidate with **the most popular votes** was found to be **the loser**. George W. Bush—president No. 43 and the son of George H.W. Bush, president No. 41—was declared the winner of the very close 2000 election over Vice President Al Gore. Florida was the key state, and in a recount, Bush won it buy a mere 500 votes.

In 2016, businessman, TV star, and nonpolitician Trump became president No. 45 in a very close election over Hillary Clinton, a former US senator, secretary of state, and First Lady. Trump had 3 million less popular votes, but because of the Electoral College, he was declared the winner. His legacy includes the fact that he was only the third American president to be impeached—and he was impeached **twice**.

A mysterious and highly contagious coronavirus, COVID-19, broke out in China and traveled quickly throughout the world. The deadly pandemic of 2020 threatened millions of people around the globe, killing many hundreds of thousands. Fortunately, vaccines were developed quickly, which helped abate the disease, but it was too little, too late for those who had died.

Terrorism, a continuous, huge threat both internationally and domestically, kept rearing its ugly head. Attacks in the United States, Europe, Asia, and Africa killed and injured thousands. A sad aspect was the mass shootings of innocent children in their US schools and of people practicing their religion in houses of worship.

The 21st century has been anything but peaceful. There have been at least 140 international wars and skirmishes during its first 20 years. The United States has been affiliated with wars in Asia and Africa, as well as being directly involved in the war in Afghanistan, the war in Iraq, the war against ISIS, and, as President George W. Bush declared, the War on Terror. He used the phrase **"the Axis of Evil"** in 2002 to identify three countries that threatened the United States by sponsoring terrorism and seeking weapons of mass destruction: North Korea, Iran, and Iraq. North Korea, the Rogue State under the leadership of Kim Jong Un, has a nuclear arsenal and long-range missiles capable of reaching America. Iran's main goal is to be the most powerful country in the Middle East. They thrive on hating the United States, Israel, and Saudi Arabia. When and if they do get nuclear weapons, they will be the existentialist threat to the Middle East. Iraq's dictator, Saddam Hussein, was captured after an invasion by coalition forces and executed in 2006. After being almost taken over by ISIS, Iraq remains a country in turmoil.

The Arab Spring, starting in 2010, was a series of anti-government uprisings across the Arab world. Starting in Tunisia, it spread to Libya, Egypt, Syria, and many other Arab countries. The movement's main goals were democracy, human rights, and regime change. New leadership was established in Yemen, Egypt, and Libya. As a result, ISIS arose, civil wars began, and insurgencies were widespread. These events are now called **the Arab Winter**.

Russia, under the leadership of Vladimir Putin, remains a great threat. Although they have been in an economic downward spiral, they still have a huge nuclear arsenal. Putin loved the old Soviet Union and wants Russia to revert back to their old ways. There have been strong rumors that Russia hacked or try to hack the last two US elections. Also, what exactly is the relationship between Mr. Putin and Mr. Trump?

China, long the sleeping giant, really awoke from its hibernation in the opening years of the 21st century. Many experts now regard it as the biggest threat to the United States. China has the second-largest economy in the world (second only to America), as well as the world's largest population and the largest military force (with a growing nuclear arsenal), plus their technology ranks at the top, their space program is expanding, and they have flexed their muscles in the South China Sea area. For sure, they are a force to be reckoned with.

Back home, Bernard Madoff, a fraudulent financier bilked his

investors to the tune of $64 billion. This snowballed into a huge
economic crisis that created a global recession. The cost of this crisis
was estimated to be **$2.8 trillion**. Several major US companies were
forced to file for bankruptcy, and many just disappeared. The culprit
was given 150 years in federal prison and died in jail.

Yet again, racism is hurting our country. The 21st century has seen
many instances of White policemen shooting and killing Black
suspects, which has often sparked violent protests, riots, and looting.
Radical White supremacists, aided by social media, create a major
threat to our tranquility.

Unfortunately, many natural disasters have occurred in the early
years of the century. A massive earthquake in Haiti killed 250,000
people in 2010. An earthquake and subsequent tsunami in Southeast
Asia killed 200,000 people in 2004. In 2005, Hurricane Katrina, the
most costly US storm, ravaged New Orleans, killing thousands. A
drought in East Africa in 2011 affected millions of Africans. A cyclone
in 2008 in Sri Lanka killed 150,000 people. Massive wildfires in California killed hundreds and destroyed so many homes. There were also
floods, landslides, heat waves, and volcanic eruptions. Here's to hoping
the new century will be calmer.

Sadly, the world lost so many influential people in the opening
years of the 21st century. It would take forever to list the passing of all
of those whose lives had a significant impact on the world, be it positive
or negative. In my humble estimation—and not in order of importance
—here are the top 100:

US Supreme Court justice Ruth Bader Ginsburg – Philip Roth –
Larry King – UK Prime Minister Margaret Thatcher – Arnold Palmer
– Fidel Castro – Sean Connery – Maya Angelou – Ray Charles – US
Senator Ted Kennedy – Rosa Parks – Steve Jobs – George Harrison –
Marlon Brando – Tom Seaver – President Ronald Reagan – Nancy
Reagan – Idi Amin – Kirk Douglas – Chuck Berry – Mike Wallace –
US Senator John McCain – Russian President Boris Yeltsin – Mike
Nichols – Gregory Peck – President Gerald Ford – Betty Ford – Ted
Williams – Venezuelan President Hugo Chávez – Dick Clark – Billy

235

Graham – Julia Childs – Roger Ailes – Tom Wolfe – First Lady Lady
Bird Johnson – Hank Aaron – US Supreme Court justice Antonin
Scalia – Yasser Arafat – Muhammad Ali – Les Paul – August Wilson –
Jack Lemmon – Kofi Annan – Toni Morrison – Princess Margaret,
Countess of Snowdon – Joe Paterno – Shimon Peres – US Rep. John
Lewis – Bob Hope – President George H.W. Bush – First Lady
Barbara Bush – J.D. Salinger – Aretha Franklin – Mr. Rogers –
Sheldon Adelson – Neil Armstrong – David Rockefeller – Stephen
Hawking – Chuck Yeager – Yogi Berra – John le Carré – Neil Simon –
Elizabeth Taylor – King Fahd – Arthur Miller – George Steinbrenner
– Michael Jackson – US Senator George McGovern – Walter Matthau
– Kim Jong-Il – Queen Elizabeth the Queen Mother – Johnny Unitas –
Dave Brubeck – Nelson Mandela – Ross Perot – Fats Domino – Don
Rickles – Walter Cronkite – Osama bin Laden – Paul Newman – Elie
Wiesel – Leonard Cohen – Milton Berle – Charlton Heston –
Muammar Gaddafi – Geraldine Ferraro – Mary Tyler Moore – US
Senator John Glenn – Luciano Pavarotti – Katherine Hepburn –
Robert McNamara – Whitney Houston – Jerry Lewis – Peter O'Toole
– Johnny Carson – Sir Edmund Hillary – Sir Alec Guinness – Nora
Ephron – Kobe Bryant.

On the positive side in century 21, there have been two historic
firsts. America elected Barack Obama, an African American US senator, as president (No. 44) in 2008. Twelve years later, in 2020, a
female, Black, Asian senator, Kamala Harris, was elected vice president, along with former Vice President Joe Biden, who became president No. 46.

Social networking and the internet became a gigantic part of American life. Facebook, Twitter, YouTube, and Instagram became everyday
names. Electric cars, replacing the need for gasoline, were in great
demand, and the country waited for driverless cars. The smartphone
was introduced and seemed to do everything but drive your car.

Many states and countries approved same-sex marriage, and many
countries have passed laws in support of LGBT rights.

For the first time in history, the Catholic Church had two popes, as

Pope Benedict resigned and was replaced by Pope Francis. Cryptocurrency was introduced to the world, the United States and North Korea held a summit conference, and Barry Bonds shattered home-run records, although his records were tainted by steroid use.

Some presidential quotes:

George W. Bush: "Freedom itself was attacked this morning by a faceless coward, and freedom will be defended."

Obama: "Now as a nation, we don't promise equal outcomes, but we were founded on the idea everybody should have an equal opportunity to succeed. Where you start should not determine where you end up."

Trump: "We will make America strong again. We will make America proud again. We will make America safe again. And we will make America great again."

Biden: "We didn't crumble after 9/11. We didn't falter after the Boston Marathon. But we're America. Americans will never ever stand down. We endure. We overcome. We own the finish line."

EPILOGUE

Well, by reading my book, you are now an expert on the subject of threats to the United States of America during the 20th century.

You have learned about all the major wars—World War I, World War II, Korea, Vietnam, the Cold War—as well as the minor ones. You have read about the assassinations of important American people, such as President John F. Kennedy, Senator Robert F. Kennedy, Dr. Martin Luther King Jr., and President William McKinley.

The book examined the threats of the villains of the 20th century: Adolf Hitler, Joseph Stalin, Hitler, the KKK, Hitler, Father Charles Coughlin, Hitler, Mao Tse-tung, and, of course, Hitler. Disasters were discussed—hurricanes, earthquakes, pandemics, airplane crashes, AIDS.

Economic threats have been reviewed, such as the 1929 Wall Street crash, the Great Depression, and soaring interest rates and inflation.

Monumental events have been explored: the atomic bomb, Pearl Harbor, the Holocaust, race riots, terrorism, and the political threats of Watergate and impeachment.

Bottom line, this has been an unbelievably threatening century—but nonetheless, we have survived!

Besides all the bad things that we witnessed, so many good things happened as well. We made giant steps in the fields of science, such as vaccines for curing dreaded diseases and new treatments for cancer and heart problems.

The United States won the space race when Neil Armstrong walked on the moon. We made great strides in civil rights, although maybe not enough. Jackie Robinson integrated baseball, opening the door for thousands of Black athletes.

From out of nowhere, technology became a driving force in the economy. The computer, the cell phone, the internet, GPS, and email all revolutionized the field of communication.

You have been apprised of many interesting facts that you can impress your friends with. Now you know about the Great Molasses Flood of 1919 in Boston. You learned what a strobogrammatic number is. You have read about the unique things that former Presidents Andrew Johnson and William Howard Taft did when they left the White House. And you learned of the two unbelievable feats that Deion Sanders accomplished in one week in 1989.

The country and the world have grown in many other respects. In 1900, the population of the world was 1.6 billion people, while the population of the United States was 76 million. Life expectancy for Americans in 1900 was 48. In the year 2000, the population of the world had grown to 6.1 billion; the population of the United States had increased to 282 million. American life expectancy in 2000 was 76 years.

There is an old proverb—"Fool me once, shame on you. Fool me twice, shame on me." The country was fooled often and made lots of mistakes in the 20th century, but anybody can make a mistake. As George Bernard Shaw once put it, "Success does not consist in never making mistakes but in never making the same one a second time."

Hopefully, the United States of America and the rest of planet Earth will learn from the 20th century and will put that knowledge to its best use in the 21st century. Fighting climate change and global warming must be a top priority.

Here's hoping that our new Century will be the best, the smartest, the most caring and most philanthropic—and most important—the most peaceful Century yet.

Amen!